# CiTY·SMART™

## GUIDEBOOK

# Charlotte

by Leigh Pressley

John Muir Publications
Santa Fe, New Mexico

John Muir Publications, P.O. Box 613, Santa Fe, New Mexico 87504

Printed in the United States of America.
First edition.  First printing March 1999.

ISBN 1-56261-415-0
ISSN 1098-299X

Editors: Jill Metzler, Krista Lyons-Gould, Nancy Gillan
Graphics Editor: Heather Pool
Production: Janine Lehmann
Design: Janine Lehmann
Cover Design: Suzanne Rush
Typesetter: Kathleen Sparkes, White Hart Design
Maps: Julie Felton
Printer: Edwards Brothers
Front Cover Photo: © Robb Helfrick—Clock Tower, Queens College, Charlotte, NC
Back Cover Photo: Charlotte Motor Speedway—Start of the 1997 UAW GM Quality 500

Distributed to the book trade by
Publishers Group West
Berkeley, California

# CONTENTS

**How to Use this Book**     v

## 1 Welcome to Charlotte     1
Getting to Know Charlotte 1 • Charlotte History 4 • The People of Charlotte 8 •
Weather 9 • Dressing in Charlotte 10 • When to Visit 10 • Calendar of Events
11 • Business and Economy 14 • Housing 16 • Schools 17

## 2 Getting Around Charlotte     19
City Layout 20 • Public Transportation 22 • Driving in Charlotte 24 • Biking in
Charlotte 26 • Air Travel 26 • Train Service 28 • Interstate and Regional Bus
Service 29

## 3 Where to Stay     30
Uptown Charlotte 31 • North Charlotte 35 • South Charlotte 41 • Central
Charlotte 44 • East Charlotte 49 • West Charlotte 49

## 4 Where to Eat     57
Uptown Charlotte 59 • North Charlotte 63 • South Charlotte 65 • Central
Charlotte 72 • East Charlotte 85 • West Charlotte 87

## 5 Sights and Attractions     88
Uptown Charlotte 90 • North Charlotte 95 • South Charlotte 100 • Central
Charlotte 102 • East Charlotte 108 • West Charlotte 110

## 6 Kids' Stuff     116
Animals and the Great Outdoors 116 • Arts and Crafts 117 • Fun and
Educational 120 • Culture for Kids 122 • Stores Kids Love 122 • Theme
Parks 123 • Places to Play 123

## 7 Museums and Art Galleries     129
Art Museums 130 • Science and History Museums 131 • Specialty
Museums 134 • Art Galleries 137

## 8 Parks, Gardens, and Recreation Areas     142
Parks 143 • Gardens 148 • Recreation Areas 151

## 9 Shopping     156
Shopping Districts 156 • Notable Bookstores and Newsstands 171 •
Markets, Gourmet Groceries, and Health Food Stores 171 • Major Department
Stores 172 • Major Shopping Malls 173 • Factory Outlets 175

## 10 Sports and Recreation     176
Professional Sports 176 • Recreation 180

## 11 Performing Arts     193
Multi-Arts Facilities 194 • Theater 195 • Music and Opera 198 •
Dance 200 • Concert Venues 201 • Buying Tickets 202 • Arts Education 202

## 12 Nightlife                                                      203
Dance Clubs 203 • Music Clubs 205 • Pubs and Bars 207 • Sports Bars 209 •
Comedy Clubs 210 • Movie Houses of Note 210 • Concert Venues 211

## 13 Day Trips from Charlotte                                        213
Blowing Rock 213 • Chapel Hill 216 • Asheville 218 • Winston-Salem 220 •
Hiddenite 222

### Appendix: City•Smart Basics                                      224

### Index                                                            228

# MAP CONTENTS

**Greater Charlotte Zones**     vi

### 3 Where to Stay
Uptown Charlotte               32
Greater Charlotte              36
Central Charlotte              46

### 4 Where to Eat
Uptown Charlotte               60
Greater Charlotte              66
Central Charlotte              74

### 5 Sights and Attractions
Uptown Charlotte               89
Greater Charlotte              96
Central Charlotte             104

### 12 Nightlife
Uptown Entertainment
District                      206

### 13 Day Trips
Charlotte Region              215

# See Charlotte the CiTY·SMaRT™ Way

## The Guide for Charlotte Natives, New Residents, and Visitors

In *City•Smart Guidebook: Charlotte,* local author Leigh Pressley tells it like it is. Residents will learn things they never knew about their city, new residents will get an insider's view of their new hometown, and visitors will be guided to the very best Charlotte has to offer—whether they're on a weekend getaway or staying a week or more.

## Opinionated Recommendations Save You Time and Money

From shopping to nightlife to museums, the author is opinionated about what she likes and dislikes. You'll learn the great and the not-so-great things about Charlotte's sights, restaurants, and accommodations. So you can decide what's worth your time and what's not; which hotel is worth the splurge and which is the best choice for budget travelers.

## Easy-to-Use Format Makes Planning Your Trip a Cinch

*City•Smart Guidebook: Charlotte* is user-friendly—you'll quickly find exactly what you're looking for. Chapters are organized by travelers' interests or needs from Where to Stay and Where to Eat, to Sights and Attractions, Kids' Stuff, Sports and Recreation, and even Day Trips from Charlotte.

## Includes Maps and Quick Location-Finding Features

Every listing in this book is accompanied by a geographic zone designation (see the following pages for zone details) that helps you immediately identify its general location. Staying near UNC Charlotte and wondering about nearby sights and restaurants? Look for the "North Charlotte" label in the listings and you'll know that statue or café is not far away. Or maybe you're looking for Ericsson Stadium, home of the Carolina Panthers. Along with its address, you'll see an "Uptown" label, so you'll know just where to find it.

## All That and Fun to Read, Too!

Every City•Smart chapter includes fun-to-read (and fun-to-use) tips to help you get more out of Charlotte, city trivia (did you know that Charlotte boasts the highest per capita consumption of ketchup in the world?), and illuminating sidebars (for the lowdown on what Charlotteans consider a proper six-course meal, see page 70). And well-known local residents provide their personal "Top Ten" lists, guiding readers to the city's best restaurants, best places to take the kids, best tree-lined streets, and more.

# GREATER CHARLOTTE ZONES

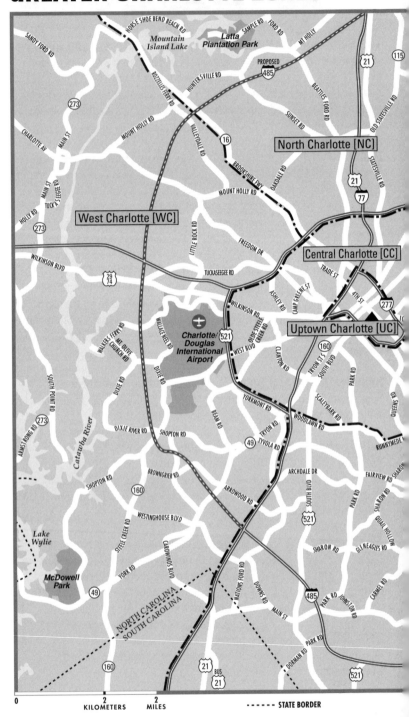

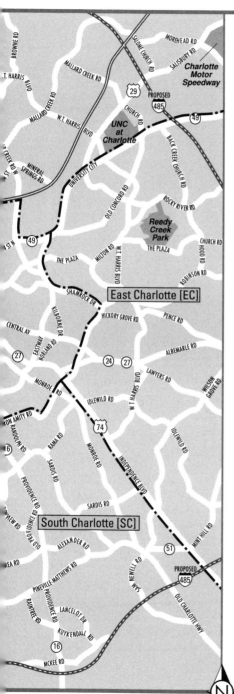

## CHARLOTTE ZONES

**Uptown Charlotte**
Enclosed by Interstates 77 and 277 and NC 16 (Brookshire Freeway).

**North Charlotte**
Covers north of Interstate 85 between North Tryon Street (NC 49) to Interstate 85 North and from Brookshire Freeway (NC 16) to the Lincoln County line.

**South Charlotte**
Covers south of Woodlawn Road between Interstate 77 and Independence Boulevard (U.S. Highway 74).

**Central Charlotte**
Covers a radius of Uptown Charlotte extending three to five miles.

**East Charlotte**
Covers east of Sharon Amity Road, Shamrock Drive, between Independence Boulevard (U.S. Highway 74) and North Tryon Street (NC 49).

**West Charlotte**
Covers west of Billy Graham Parkway between Brookshire Freeway (NC 16) and Interstate 77.

Charlotte Convention & Visitors Bureau

# 1

# WELCOME TO CHARLOTTE

Traditional, yet progressive. Easygoing, but full of energy. A place so friendly that some residents have installed water fountains in their front yards for parched joggers and walkers who need a cool drink.

This is Charlotte, a city that is just beginning to identify itself while enjoying its journey of growth. Smaller than some of its Southern sisters—and happily so—the Queen City offers much of what its larger counterparts can give without as much congestion and crime. Business thrives here, along with a can-do community spirit. There's plenty of old money in Charlotte, but who you are isn't nearly as important as what you can do.

Folks are friendly in this city where race fans, conservative "suits," loft-living yuppies, cutting-edge artists, and minivan-driving moms all get along. From sports fanatics to shopping addicts and history buffs to half-pints looking for kid-size fun, the city offers something for everyone.

Welcome to Charlotte, the South's new crowning jewel.

## Getting to Know Charlotte

If you want to learn the city, start uptown. Newcomers and visitors hear frequent and vocal debate about the "Uptown" versus "Downtown" name. Some folks and several road signs refer to the area as downtown, but most locals say Uptown because of its location on the top of a small hill.

Uptown serves as the central hub of banking and business in Charlotte and increasingly attracts young and old to cultural events, restaurants, pubs, and nightclubs. The heartbeat of the hub, so to speak, is the intersection of Trade and Tryon Streets, nicknamed The Square. Look for tall bronze statues on each corner, and you're there.

Most buildings on the skyline are easy to identify. The 60-story Bank of America Corporate Center stretches the highest and appears to have a white crown on top. The First Union building features a Wurlitzer jukebox shape on the top and is lined in neon green. Wachovia opts for simple and straightforward—its tower is bathed in white light and has the company name on the side. In contrast, Duke Energy spends some energy on its Uptown building: at night, a huge panel shows what look like changing neon pick-up-sticks dancing in the dark. Within Uptown, high-rise housing is

# The Queen City

*Beauties abound here in the Queen City, but a different kind of queen gave Charlotte its name long ago.*

*In 1768, the town incorporated and honored Charlotte Sophia, wife of reigning English monarch King George III. Mecklenburg County takes its name from Queen Charlotte's German homeland of Mecklenburg-Strelitz.*

*The crown insignia that dots everything from street signs to curbside garbage cans here is an adaptation of St. Edward's crown, which was conferred on Charlotte Sophia.*

*Controversy has lingered for years over various statues and depictions of Queen Charlotte, who in some portraits has African rather than European features. Local debate resurged a few years ago when a Queen Charlotte statue with more white features was unveiled at the Charlotte International Trade Center and when the* Charlotte Observer *ran an artist's illustration of the queen with European facial features.*

*Art historians say the truth is murky because 50 images of the queen depict 50 different looks. In those days, artists commonly changed their paintings—especially of royalty—to reflect whatever image the subject wanted.*

*Queen Charlotte's family tree, genealogists say, traces back to Margarita de Castro y Sousa, a black branch of the Portuguese Royal House.*

available in expensive condominiums or in the restored Victorian community of Fourth Ward.

Just across the inner beltline from Uptown is Dilworth, Charlotte's first suburb. East Boulevard bisects the neighborhood and is lined with quirky shops and neighborhood restaurants. Run-down and considered dangerous only 15 years ago, Dilworth today is full of professionals and young families who've refurbished cottages on the pretty, tree-lined streets.

South End, which lines South Boulevard adjacent to Dilworth, continues to offer new eateries, shops, and alternative homes such as lofts, townhouses, and combined living/working spaces.

*Alan Ramsay's* Queen Charlotte, *ca. 1762*

David H. Ramsey—Mint Museum of Art

Myers Park, another historic suburb, has a more elegant, refined, old-money feel. Its homes are some of the city's most expensive because they're near Uptown and, for the most part, on large lots.

SouthPark, home of the Carolinas' largest business community outside of Uptown Charlotte, also features some of the Queen City's nicest homes. Most are middle class, but a few subdivisions such as Morrocroft are so exclusive the curious (and envious) can't get past the private gate.

For more historic flavor similar to Dilworth, try Elizabeth, Plaza-Midwood, and Eastover, off Uptown in a more eastern direction. Look for restored "front porch" communities and interesting shops.

True bohemians bolt to NoDa these days, the arts community on North Davidson Street at 35th and 36th. Galleries, watering holes, and contemporary stores abound in this former mill village.

In North Charlotte, the University City area on W.T. Harris Boulevard is a strip of office parks, new neighborhoods, and apartment complexes. It's congested but full of chain stores and restaurants that accommodate the suburban area's growing population.

The area north of Charlotte outside the city limits includes Huntersville, Cornelius, and Davidson around Lake Norman. The Peninsula, a country club and golf-course community in Cornelius, is home to NASCAR driver Jeff Gordon, former NFL coach Joe Gibbs, and many of the city's rich and famous. Not gated, it's great for bike rides and walks.

South Charlotte offers several country-club communities on Carmel and Providence Roads, as well as more middle-class neighborhoods. Homes as well as office parks are being built in ritzy areas such as

**TIP**

If you drive through the residential areas of Dilworth, Plaza-Midwood, and Elizabeth, look for the neon house numbers glowing in hues of red, purple, pink, blue, and white. The trend began about a decade ago and has stuck in several of Charlotte's more open-minded communities.

Captain Neon at 1533 Central Ave. in Plaza-Midwood and Custom Neon at 824 E. Morehead St. in Dilworth create the neon numbers for around $250.

Ballantyne, with a scaled-down SouthPark feel. For a small-town atmosphere within a large city, try Matthews in the southeast and Pineville due south.

East Charlotte's main drag is Independence Boulevard, which leads from Uptown to Matthews and all the way to Wilmington on the coast. Except for Matthews, it's a land of strip-mall shopping centers, car dealerships, and huge chain stores. Mint Hill, to the east, features large lots and a rural environment.

In West Charlotte, visitors find the airport, high-rise and extended-stay hotels, corporate parks, and heavy industry. Take Billy Graham Parkway to the Charlotte Coliseum and airport or as a route to other areas of the city. Run-down Wilkinson Boulevard also leads to the airport and to Gaston County.

# Charlotte History

Business. What influenced this area in ancient times and what spurred settlements and growth when pioneers arrived 250 years ago remains the city's driving force today.

Generations ago, Native American tribes, including the Cherokees, Catawbas, and Waxhaws, gathered in what is now Charlotte at the intersection of two old trading routes. Today's Trade Street was a dusty path running east–west, while the modern main artery of Tryon Street ran north–south.

The Great Wagon Road from Philadelphia brought scores of

*Gold miners near Charlotte, ca 1880*

Carolina Room, Public Library of Charlotte and Mecklenburg County

# Famous Folks Connected to Charlotte

Fallen televangelists Jim and Tammy Faye Baker
Artist Romare Bearden
Professional wrestler Ric Flair
Evangelist Billy Graham
Seventh U.S. President Andrew Jackson (Waxhaw)
Journalist and broadcaster Charles Kuralt
Author Carson McCullers
Eleventh U.S. President James K. Polk (Pineville)
Western movie star Randolph Scott
Golfer Charles Sifford

Scot-Irish settlers to the Charlotte area in the mid-1700s. North Carolina's Piedmont region formed lush meadows, flowing streams, and hilly terrain, with plenty of trees for log-cabin lumber.

Settlers came here from overseas and from the northern states of Pennsylvania, Maryland, and Delaware to make new homes. Native Americans befriended the few white families that moved in among them, but for the most part the pioneers kept to themselves, cutting down trees, building cabins, preparing the land for crops, and creating a settlement (with a meeting house *and* a still).

In the early 1750s, trade routes to the South Carolina port town of Charleston were established by following Indian trails. Settlers also traded with Cherokees who had access to French and Spanish goods, and worked with Catawba Indian Chief Hagler to build peaceful trade relations with his tribe.

In 1762, the legislature declared the settlement Mecklenburg County. Four years later, a log courthouse was built in the center of the community to begin the development of what is today Uptown. Pioneers built a sawmill and gristmill in 1767, and leaders bought 360 acres for the site of the town they named Charlotte. The town incorporated soon after, and by 1774 the 200-citizen area of Charlotte became the county seat.

Despite naming their town and county after the King of England's German wife, Charlotte, patriots, it is said, later defied King George in May 1775 by signing the Mecklenburg Declaration of Independence.

The Revolutionary War took local patriots north to battles and to a long winter in Valley Forge. But in 1780 at the Battle of Charlotte, British General Lord Cornwallis occupied the town. Patriots soon defeated British and Tory troops at the Battle of Kings Mountain. Less than a month after his arrival, Cornwallis left Charlotte, referring to the town and its people as "a damned hornets' nest."

A 17-pound gold nugget discovered nearby in 1799 regenerated

# CHARLOTTE TIMELINE

**1748** The first Scot-Irish settlers and overseas immigrants arrive in Charlotte, on a site where generations of Native Americans traded goods.

**1766** Uptown development begins with a log courthouse built in the center of the pioneer settlement. A year later, 360 acres are purchased as the Charlotte townsite.

**1775** Mecklenburg Declaration of Independence is reportedly signed.

**1780** Lord Cornwallis occupies town after Battle of Charlotte. He leaves less than a month later, calling Charlotte and its people "a damned hornets' nest."

**1799** Discovery of gold leads to creation of mines and influx of prospectors.

**1837** First branch of the U.S. Mint opens in Charlotte.

**1852** First passenger train arrives in Charlotte to crowd of 20,000. First telegraph office opens.

**1861** North Carolina secedes from the Union. Local men join the Army of the Confederacy.

**1867** Biddle University for Blacks, now Johnson C. Smith University, opens.

**1869** First daily issue of the *Charlotte Observer* hits the streets.

**1873** Charlotte organizes a grade school, the first in the state.

**1887** Electric lights are installed; horsecars appear.

**1909** Independence Building, North Carolina's first skyscraper, opens in Charlotte.

**1919** Five people killed, 25 wounded in streetcar strike riot.

**1921** WBT, first commercial radio station in the South, debuts.

**1936** American Legion Memorial Stadium, airport, and Mint Museum of Art open.

**1947** Television introduced to Charlotte. First Carolinas' Carousel Ball and Parade held.

**1955** Auditorium and coliseum completed for arts and entertainment events.

**1965** First convocation for the University of North Carolina at Charlotte.

**1977** More than 150 new businesses announce openings.

**1987** Charlotte wins NBA franchise.

| | |
|---|---|
| Charlotte named 35th largest U.S. city; receives All-America City Award. | **1990** |
| NationsBank, now known as Bank of America, occupies 60-story corporate tower, the tallest in the Carolinas. | **1992** |
| New 850,000 square-foot Convention Center opens uptown. | **1994** |
| Charlotte becomes second-largest banking center in the United States. | **1995** |
| Ericsson Stadium opens at cost of $180 million. | **1996** |
| Mint Museum of Craft + Design opens uptown; George Seifert hired as second head coach of Carolina Panthers | **1999** |

commerce in Charlotte. The first major gold-producing area in the United States, Charlotte soon had between 75 and 100 gold mines within a 20-mile radius. To handle the prospectors' finds, the U.S. Congress chose Charlotte as the site of the first branch of the Philadelphia Mint. The Federal-style building opened on West Trade Street between what are now Mint and Graham Streets uptown in 1837. More than $5 million in half-eagles, quarter-eagles, and one-dollar gold pieces were coined at the Mint.

Opportunists who came to Charlotte with strike-it-rich dreams later trekked to California's Gold Rush, leaving the Queen City with a gold boom and bust. But Charlotte continued to plan for trading and interstate commerce. In 1849, workers graded a railroad right-of-way from Charlotte to Columbia, South Carolina. Three years later, the first passenger train arrived in Charlotte to an estimated crowd of 20,000. Other technologies also appeared in the Queen City. Steam power reached the area at a flour mill, telegraph lines went up, and the first gaslights illuminated the town.

For several years the Civil War interrupted the city's growth, as men volunteered to fight and the Mint became Confederate Headquarters and a hospital. But soon after the war it was back to business with new industries in cotton and textiles, followed by even more growth with the introduction of streetcars carrying Charlotteans throughout town.

Introduced by Edward Dilworth Latta in 1891, electric streetcars were essential to Charlotte's development in the late 19th and early 20th centuries. At its peak, the streetcar system covered 20 miles of track with 38 cars. Without the streetcars, the city would have been virtually powerless to industrialize the region.

Automobiles arrived in Charlotte in 1904 and the city continued to grow. Hospitals, libraries, theaters, colleges, businesses, and arts groups thrived as the population topped 46,000 in 1920. In 1936, Charlotte's new stadium, airport, and the Mint Museum of Art opened. Buses retired streetcars, and by 1940 the population had reached more than 100,000. But the Queen City's growth didn't stop there.

By 1968, population reached 263,000 for the city and 341,000 county-wide. Charlotte celebrated its bicentennial and won the All-America City designation. Economy, education, health, culture, and births were on the upswing. Skyscrapers grew uptown, interstates opened, banks expanded, and new businesses were born.

In the 1980s, Charlotte earned a National Basketball Association franchise and built a new 25,000-seat coliseum for their Hornets. The team ended its first season with 36 sellout games.

One First Union Center was completed uptown, followed by the 60-story Bank of America Corporate Center in the early '90s. Charlotte won a National Football League franchise soon after, and helped revive nightlife in Uptown with the $180 million Ericsson Stadium.

*Charlotte—a growing city*

© Robb Helfrick

Today growth is strong here, particularly to the north, to the south, and within central suburban areas. Several skyscrapers are under construction uptown, and talk is still ongoing concerning development of an upscale mall and entertainment complex in the old civic center.

As the 21st century approaches, Charlotteans are excited about the direction their city is headed and about its current state as a thriving metropolitan city with Southern charm.

## The People of Charlotte

The South is known for its gracious hospitality, and the people of Charlotte live up to that reputation. It's a place where strangers speak, neighbors wave, and everyone gets acquainted over a glass of sweet iced tea on the front porch.

Charlotte's population will total a projected 507,500 in 1998, while Mecklenburg County will include 628,000 this year. Some 1.3 million people live in the Charlotte area.

Caucasians make up the bulk of the population in Charlotte (70.7 percent), and African Americans still form the largest minority (26.7 percent). But other ethnic groups, including Hispanic, Vietnamese, Korean, Greek, Chinese, German, and Cambodian, are moving here and making their voices heard.

International House serves foreign-born newcomers to Charlotte.

## Charlotte Weather

| | Ave. High Temps (°F) | Ave. Low Temps (°F) | Ave. Inches Rain |
|---|---|---|---|
| January | 49.3 | 29.8 | 3.71 |
| February | 53.4 | 32.2 | 3.84 |
| March | 62.7 | 39.9 | 4.43 |
| April | 71.7 | 48.1 | 2.67 |
| May | 78.8 | 56.9 | 3.82 |
| June | 85.1 | 65.1 | 3.39 |
| July | 88.2 | 69.1 | 3.92 |
| August | 87.1 | 68.4 | 3.73 |
| September | 81.4 | 62.2 | 3.50 |
| October | 71.6 | 49.8 | 3.36 |
| November | 62.2 | 40.8 | 3.23 |
| December | 52.6 | 33.2 | 3.48 |

Source: Climate Office of North Carolina at North Carolina State University

Several special-interest publications, including the *Charlotte Post*, *La Noticia*, and the *Asian Herald*, are published locally.

The city also features an active gay, lesbian, bisexual, and transgender community, with several service organizations and a gay publication that appears every other week.

## Weather

In a word, weather in Charlotte is unpredictable. January can bring nearly 70-degree days one week and snow the next. March may tease locals with a spring-like warm spell, then hammer a final arctic blast. Indian summers aren't uncommon, yet white Christmases are rare.

In terms of numbers, January is the coldest month: its average temperature is 39.3 degrees. Late summers can feel scorching, but the record books say July averages 79.3 degrees. Average annual precipitation is 43 inches.

About the only thing Charlotteans can count on in terms of weather is that the summer months will be hot, humid, and peppered with afternoon thunderstorms. That, and the fact that people young and old, rich and poor, and from every area of the city will be talking about the weather.

Writers, reporters, and authors of nationwide studies have given Charlotte the nod for its business-friendly atmosphere, affordable lifestyle, and bright job market. Here's who's talking about the Queen City—and what they're saying.

- Named nation's #1 pro-business attitude by *Fortune* magazine.
- Chosen nation's most livable city at U.S. Conference of Mayors, 1995.
- Named in *30 Great Cities To Start Out In*, a 1997 book by Sandra Gurvis.
- Ranked as one of the hottest and most affordable housing markets by *U.S. News & World Report*.
- Named No. 5 among Best Large Cities to Start and Run a Small Business by *Entrepreneur* magazine and Dun & Bradstreet.
- Chosen as nation's number-one public library in 1995.

## Dressing in Charlotte

What you wear when visiting Charlotte depends on what brought you to the city. Banking and business are big here, so you're likely to see Brooks Brothers suits and professional, conservative looks Uptown. Once the whistle blows, look for rolled-up sleeves and loosened ties on those oxford shirts or, in many cases, a quick change into a comfortable pair of Levi's.

For evenings of dinner and a show at the theater or symphony, locals in the know dress up. Charlotte's Southern roots and banking background make it especially conservative in this area.

When catching a movie, relaxing with a beer, or checking out a gallery crawl, go casual. Khakis and a nice T-shirt or polo shirt for guys, and casual clothes for women, will suit fine.

One quirk: Coeds who dressed in their Sunday best to attend college football games have carried that tradition over to Panthers and Hornets games. Folks on these hot-ticket dates like to dress up: nice pants and a shirt or sweater for men; and pantsuits, long skirts, or linen shorts with a light sweater for women.

## When to Visit

Four distinct seasons mean there is no bad time to visit Charlotte, although many visitors find the weather more pleasant in the balmy spring and crisp fall. Summers, especially July and August, deliver hot and humid conditions that drive Charlotteans to nearby lakes, area swimming pools, or indoors to the air conditioning.

Pleasant temperatures crop up year-round, but nice days seem to arrive more consistently by mid- to late-March and early April, when chilly mornings give way to warm days.

Spring also brings Charlotte into full bloom. Bradford pears lining the roadways look like cotton-candy trees, while dogwoods, azaleas, daffodils, tulips, and crocuses add layers of color. The smell of freshly cut grass drifts through the air, and blankets of lilac-colored wisteria hang in masses from trees.

Tree-lined street in Myers Park

In early autumn, daytime temperatures generally stay on the warm side as the evenings slowly cool down. In October, bright Carolina-blue skies and white billowy clouds make a striking contrast with maples, oaks, and the many other tree varieties lining Charlotte's streets.

Charlotteans continue to brave the outdoors in November and December and, for the most part, winters are fairly mild. The Queen City really sparkles during the holiday season, and with so many cultural activities and shows on the schedule, it's a great time to visit. Uptown comes to life with illuminated trees, incredible decorations in skyscraper lobbies, and an upbeat, festive spirit.

## Calendar of Events

### JANUARY
Martin Luther King Parade & Celebration, Grady Cole Center

### FEBRUARY
Mid-Atlantic Boat Show, Convention Center
Carolina Golf Show, Merchandise Mart
Southern Spring Show, Merchandise Mart

### MARCH
Charlotte Regional Farmers Market, March–December, 1801 Yorkmont Road
St. Patrick's Day Parade & Festival, Uptown
Paramount's Carowinds Theme Park, March–October, Charlotte

## APRIL

*Charlotte Observer* Marathon, 10-K & Fitness Expo, Convention Center
Charlotte Festival/New Plays in America Series,
    Blumenthal Performing Arts Center
Charlotte Knights Baseball, April–September, Knight's Stadium
Southern Ideal Home Show, Merchandise Mart
Loch Norman Highland Games, Davidson
Mint Museum Home & Garden Tour, Charlotte
Charlotte Steeplechase Races, Union County
YWCA Juniors/Seniors National Swim Competition,
    Mecklenburg Aquatic Center
Center CityFest, Uptown
Festival of India, First Union Atrium, Uptown
Fun Fair, Founders Hall, Uptown

## MAY

Derby Daze, Mint Museum of Art
Lake Norman Festival, Mooresville
Senior PGA Home Depot Invitational, Tournament Players Club at Piper Glen
Charlotte Film & Video Festival
Race Week, Charlotte 300, and Coca-Cola 600, Charlotte Motor Speedway
NASCAR Parade & Speed Street Festival, Uptown
Carolina Legends Folk Music Festival, Andrew Jackson State Park,
    Lancaster, South Carolina

## JUNE

Legends Summer Shootout Auto Racing Series, Charlotte Motor Speedway
Folk Music Festival, Historic Latta Plantation
UltraSwim, Mecklenburg Aquatic Center

---

**TRIVIA**

## Want to lose the Southern twang— or learn to speak as locals do?

One of the most popular college courses in the city is a speech and grammar class taught by Queens College professor Charles Hadley. A Davidson College graduate and Fulbright Scholar, Hadley was first recruited to teach the Southern drawl to none other than Vivien Leigh as she prepared for her role in *Gone With the Wind*. Hadley also helped Charlton Heston, Faye Dunaway, Nick Nolte, and Robert Duvall acquire the drawl.

These days, students and professionals sign up to improve their speaking and possibly their chances in a competitive job market.

Whether you're in town as a temporary tourist or you're a new resident of the Queen City, discover what Charlotte has to offer at INFO! Charlotte, a visitor information center and gift shop at 330 South Tryon Street. Brochures on local attractions, restaurant menus, reports on Charlotte's economy, and even videotapes about Charlotte are available, many for free. For more information, call 704/331-2700 or 800/231-4636.

## JULY

Independence Day fireworks, Uptown and on regional lakes

## AUGUST

Dilworth Jubilee, Latta Park

## SEPTEMBER

NFL Carolina Panthers, September–January, Ericsson Stadium
Matthews Alive Festival, downtown Matthews
Yiasou Greek Festival, Holy Trinity Greek Orthodox Cathedral
Festival in the Park, Freedom Park
Southern Women's Show, Merchandise Mart
International Festival, UNCC
National Balloon Rally, Statesville
Southeastern Origami Festival (biannual), Charlotte

## OCTOBER

Race Week and UAW-GM Quality 500, Charlotte Motor Speedway
Legends Nationals race, Charlotte Motor Speedway
Remodel Charlotte, Merchandise Mart
Great American Antique & Collectible Spectacular, Metrolina Expo Center
Carolina Renaissance Festival, October–November, Huntersville
Charlotte Checkers hockey, October–March, Independence Arena
Southern Ideal Home Show, Merchandise Mart
HomeArama Tour of Homes, various locations
Public Library NOVELLO Festival of Reading, various locations
Christmas Made in the South Craft Show, Convention Center
Waxhaw Scottish Games, Waxhaw
Das OktoberFest, Merchandise Mart
Charlotte International Auto Show, Convention Center
OutCharlotte, citywide
Merge Festival, Marshall Park in Uptown Charlotte

## NOVEMBER

NBA Charlotte Hornets, November–April, Charlotte Coliseum
Holiday House Home Tour, various locations

Southern Christmas Show, Merchandise Mart
Folklife Festival, Historic Latta Plantation
Carolinas' Carousel Parade, Uptown
Holiday Tree Lighting, SouthPark Mall
Festival of Trees, Convention Center
Turkey Trot road race, SouthPark

**DECEMBER**
Christmas Town U.S.A., McAdenville
Fourth Ward Christmas Tour, Fourth Ward, Uptown
College Basketball Tournament of Champions, Charlotte Coliseum
Holiday Skylights Treelighting & Christmas Celebration, Uptown
Reindeer Romp road race, Uptown
The Singing Christmas Tree, Ovens Auditorium
Revolutionary War Christmas, Hezekiah Alexander Homesite
American Craft Council Craft Show, Convention Center
Backcountry Christmas, Historic Latta Plantation
*The Nutcracker* by North Carolina Dance Theatre, Uptown
Shrine Bowl of the Carolinas, Memorial Stadium

# Business and Economy

Charlotteans haven't changed much from the Native Americans who swapped wares at Trade and Tryon, or from the pioneers who settled here for opportunity. Business still drives the community, from major banks in towering skyscrapers to clusters of office parks in the suburbs. Businesses large and small, as well as individuals, are drawn here not only by the fact that economic and commercial activity make the Queen City one of the fastest-growing metropolitan areas in the nation, but also by the pro-business spirit and support that thrive here.

The nation's second-largest banking center behind New York, Charlotte is home to two giants—Bank of America and First Union—with Wachovia a strong third presence. Overall, 17 banks with more than 200 branches, as well as a Federal Reserve Branch, serve Charlotteans.

Textiles, transportation, and distribution also flourish in Charlotte's economy. Manufacturing employs more than 330,000 workers at over 3,800 companies focusing on everything from furniture to electronics.

Many major national and international companies use Charlotte as subsidiary headquarters. Over the past decade, more than 6,000 new firms have invested more than $3.5 billion in new facilities here. In addition, more than 340 foreign-owned companies have facilities in Charlotte, totaling half of all the foreign companies in the state.

North Carolina ranks 33rd-lowest nationally in per capita state and local tax collections. State residents pay a maximum individual income tax rate of 7.75 percent.

Mecklenburg County and the city of Charlotte operate one tax

# Ten Largest Employers in Charlotte-Mecklenburg

1. Carolinas HealthCare System
2. Charlotte-Mecklenburg Schools
3. First Union
4. Bank of America
5. Duke Energy
6. USAirways
7. Presbyterian Healthcare System
8. State of North Carolina
9. City of Charlotte
10. Mecklenburg County

Source: Charlotte Chamber of Commerce

department, which means taxpayers get only one bill. With the exception of Uptown Municipal Service Districts, there are none of the special taxing districts (such as schools or water) that are common in other areas.

A 4 percent state sales tax plus a 2 percent local tax make up the 6 percent Mecklenburg County sales tax. A 3 percent highway tax is tacked on when you buy a motor vehicle. An additional 1 percent tax is collected on prepared-food purchases.

*U.S. News & World Report* ranked Charlotte as one of the hottest and most affordable housing markets in the country in 1996, and Charlotte ranks ninth-lowest nationally in a cost-of-living index for cities of 300,000 to 600,000 people.

In terms of everyday items, here's a guideline of what you can expect to pay in Charlotte:

| | |
|---|---|
| Cost of a five-mile taxi ride: | $8.75 |
| Cost of an average dinner: | $20 |
| Cost of a daily newspaper: | 50¢ Monday through Saturday; $1.50 Sunday |
| Cost of hotel double room: | $75; more Uptown |
| Cost of movie admission: | $6.50, with matinees and special shows ranging from $1.50 to $4.25 |
| Cost of a beer at local pub: | $2.50 to $3.25 |
| Gallon of gas: | About $1.05 |
| Gallon of milk: | $2.50 |
| Loaf of bread: | $1.80 |

# TRIVIA

## Weird and Wacky Facts about Charlotte

1. Charlotte consumes more Beanie Weenies than anywhere else in the world.
2. The Charlotte Crop Walk is the most lucrative in the nation.
3. Charlotte's Habitat for Humanity has built more houses than any other affiliate. The group was also the first to construct a house in 24 hours and the first to have a house raised entirely by women.
4. Charlotte boasts the highest per capita consumption of Spam.
5. According to U.S. Customs, the Charlotte Hornets logo is the single most-seized counterfeit sports logo in the world and the seventh most-seized counterfeit logo of any kind (behind Rolex, Cartier, and Louis Vuitton).
6. WBT-AM is the second-oldest radio station in the country.
7. Charlotte was the first American city to have more people see a show than live in the city. In 1975, more than 400,000 people watched *The Sound of Music* during its 79-week run at the Carolina Theater.
8. Charlotte's Reginald "Moon" Huffstetler holds the world record for treading water (100 hours).
9. Charlotte has the highest per capita consumption of ketchup in the world.
10. In 1799, Reed Gold Mine was the site of the first documented discovery of gold in the United States.

Source: *Charlotte* magazine

## Housing

According to the Multiple Listing Service of the Charlotte Association of Realtors, the average sales price for an existing home through June 1998 was $165,470. In new home construction, the average sales price through June 1998 was $221,275.

Charlotte features all kinds of housing possibilities, including urban living Uptown, New York–style lofts in trendy South End and Elizabeth, renovated cottages in historic districts, spacious homes in old-money areas, and family-friendly neighborhoods in the suburbs.

What newcomers and relocating Charlotteans actually pay hinges on which area of town they choose. For instance, the average sales price of a home in the area encompassing Dilworth, Myers Park, and Matthews in 1997 was $283,752. In the Lake Norman area, single-family homes average $420,381.

Strange things happen in real estate, and Charlotte is no exception. In well-established city neighborhoods, for example, wealthy home buyers have been known to buy a home just for its lot. Instead of living in the quaint cottage, they mow it down and build a gargantuan mansion. In-fill housing (where developers build brick townhouses or condos on a spare plot of land) is also a popular trend these days.

In the rental market, apartment complexes are going increasingly upscale, catering to relocating businesspeople and to consultants on long-term assignments. Monthly rentals range from $300 for a one-bedroom up to $2,400 for a three-bedroom apartment. More than 100,000 apartments and condominium units are up for grabs so rentals are fairly easy to find, except in some popular in-town neighborhoods.

*Independence Building, the first skyscraper in North Carolina*

Household operating costs in Charlotte are considered moderate. Utility costs are competitive with other parts of the nation, and the mild climate helps keep heating and air-conditioning costs down.

## Schools

Serving nearly 96,000 students, the Charlotte-Mecklenburg School System (CMS) is the largest in the Carolinas and ranks 26th in the nation.

A total of 137 schools are included in CMS, and employees number more than 11,500. Average class size is 23 students in kindergarten, 26 students in grades 1 through 9, and 28.5 in high school. CMS transports 62,000 students every day. Ethnic distribution is 50.9 percent Caucasian, 41.4 percent African American, 4 percent Asian American, 2.9 percent Latin American, and 0.5 percent Native American.

Those are the numbers, but the real story is that the CMS struggles to keep up with the city's growth. Hot spots in north Charlotte, the University area, and southeast Charlotte have experienced housing booms and with that, packed schools. Two new high schools recently welcomed students, and another six schools are scheduled to open in the 1998–1999 school year.

Magnet schools, special-interest schools that focus on a specific interest such as math or communications, are a new addition to the traditional curriculum. Campus security officers now patrol and monitor security in middle and high schools. The school system also recently introduced a preschool for disadvantaged four-year-olds.

In 1996, *Money* magazine named Charlotte-Mecklenburg to its list of "Top 100 School Systems in Towns You Can Afford." Even so, controversy lingers. In the 1970s Charlotte successfully integrated its schools through busing, one of the first major cities to do so. But in 1992 the school board worked to reduce crosstown busing by emphasizing magnet schools, schools in areas that draw an ethnic mix, and naturally integrated schools.

A 1996 high-school reassignment plan caused much community uproar from parents who want to retain neighborhood schools. CMS continues to work on student assignment proposals.

Outside of CMS, approximately 12 percent of the children in Mecklenburg County attend private, parochial, or at-home schools.

The Charlotte area also features an outstanding higher-education system, with 17 colleges and universities serving more than 70,000 students.

Leigh Pressley

# 2

## GETTING AROUND CHARLOTTE

As the largest city in the Carolinas, Charlotte has earned a regional reputation for bad drivers and terrible traffic. Of course, some of our habits warrant it. For four consecutive years, Mecklenburg County has been named the most dangerous driving city in the state by AAA Carolinas. Mecklenburg has 7.7 percent of the state's traffic, but 11 percent of the accidents. It's not uncommon to hear reports of "road rage", and the local newspaper runs a weekly column about commuting and driving in the city.

Traffic reporters in Charlotte have an easier job than a San Diego weather forecaster. Tune in nearly every weekday morning, and you'll hear about the same traffic hot spots: I-77 from north to Uptown and farther south at its merge with I-485; W.T. Harris Boulevard in north Charlotte's University area; Pineville-Matthews Road (Highway 51) stretching through south Charlotte; Independence Boulevard from east to Uptown; and Providence Road from south to Uptown.

What's the key word? Uptown. Skyscrapers hold a lot of workers, who in turn drive a lot of cars. Unfortunately, most Charlotteans head to and from work at the same time and often take the same major routes. Commuters from surrounding towns and counties also flood the roads, which tend to be outgrown before they're even completed.

Public transportation is available, but Charlotteans love their cars and the independence that comes with them. In March 1998, Charlotte-Mecklenburg began a year-long study and public discussion on mass transit and options such as special lanes for buses only, light rail, and commuter trains.

Everyone admits it's time to do something about traffic in Charlotte, but no locals want to fund it, have it interrupt their lives, or change the character of the city they call home. So until we get it all figured out, be prepared for white knuckles, stop-and-go driving, and a sea of red brake-lights.

## City Layout

Charlotte is notorious for its impossible system of roads. For instance, a single street may change names as many as five or six times. First you're on Billy Graham, then Woodlawn, next Runnymede, then Sharon Lane, Sharon Amity, and finally Harris—and it's all the same street. Or how about Tyvola, which becomes Fairview, Sardis, Rama, and Idlewild? One road, many names.

On the flip side, other Charlotte streets have the same name for intersecting streets. Take a right off Queens and hey, you're still on Queens. Turn left off Providence and yep, it's still Providence. And how about a double whammy—those two quirks happen in the same Myers Park intersection.

The system baffles visitors and newcomers, but once folks have learned to drive by landmarks instead of street signs, the confusion becomes part of Charlotte's charm.

Here's an overview.

Uptown Charlotte, bordered by Interstates 77 and 277 (John Belk Freeway) and the Brookshire Freeway, uses a true grid system. Trade and Tryon, the ancient paths that brought Native Americans to swap wares and that pioneer settlers followed, are the main arteries uptown. Their intersection is known as The Square; look for the four bronze statues, one on each corner.

Streets that run east–west are numbered in Uptown, with Stonewall

*One of Charlotte's first electric trolleys, ca 1890*

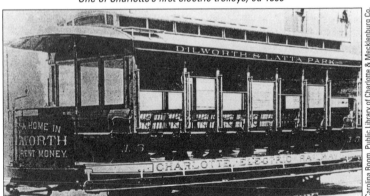

Carolina Room, Public Library of Charlotte & Mecklenburg Co.

substituted for First and Trade stuck between Fourth and Fifth. (That's Charlotte for you.) North of Tryon are Church, Poplar, Mint, and Graham Streets; south of Tryon are College, Brevard, Caldwell, Davidson, and McDowell Streets.

Uptown Charlotte acts as the hub of a wheel and, for the most part, its spokes are pretty straight. South Boulevard extends from Uptown, winding through South End and eventually down to Pineville. A bit to the west, I-77 also runs south down to Fort Mill, South Carolina. To the east, other south-bound routes are Providence Road (Highway 16), Park Road, and Monroe Road.

Independence Boulevard (Highway 74) stretches from Uptown Charlotte southeast to Matthews, on through Monroe and Wingate, and across the state all the way to Wilmington on the coast. Albemarle Road, Central Avenue, and The Plaza take East Charlotteans in and out of Uptown.

Tryon Street (Highway 29/49) extends from Uptown through northeast Charlotte and on to the University area. Interstate 77 heads due north and is a straight shot to the Lake Norman towns of Huntersville, Cornelius, and Davidson. Brookshire Boulevard (Highway 16) snakes northwest to Mountain Island Lake.

West of Uptown, Wilkinson Boulevard (Highway 74) leads past the Charlotte/Douglas International Airport and into Belmont and Gastonia. Interstate 85 runs parallel with Wilkinson, but is not immediately accessible from Uptown.

One of the most common complaints about Charlotte's roads is that the spokes of its "wheels" have few cross streets. There is no inner belt, and the city's outer belt, I-485, will be under construction until the year 2008.

# Public Transportation

The hub of public transportation in the Queen City is Uptown's Charlotte Transportation Center. A covered, drive-through facility at 310 East Trade Street, the CTC is the only completely covered, retail-oriented transit facility in the nation.

Passengers can reach nearly all of Charlotte's bus routes from the CTC, buy weekly bus passes, get schedule information, retrieve lost articles, obtain a transit photo ID, do their banking, grab lunch, seek medical care, and buy sundries and souvenirs under one roof. Shops and services line the inside of the transportation barn, and buses stop at stations in the middle.

Charlotte Transit buses move about 43,000 folks a day over 43 routes. Fare is $1 for local and $1.40 for express; drivers do not make change.

Buses marked "Local" operate from 5 a.m. to midnight Monday through Saturday and from 5:30 a.m. to midnight Sunday. "Express" buses operate during peak hours, from 6 to 9 a.m. and from 3 to 6 p.m. weekdays. To reduce travel time, Express buses run nonstop from designated points to Uptown.

"Special" buses take four crosstown routes: West Boulevard to Beatties Ford Road, Uptown to UNCC, SouthPark to UNCC, and SouthPark to West Boulevard.

When waiting for an approaching bus, look for the destination sign above the windshield to confirm it's the bus you need. The bus route number and final destination are on the sign; Express buses say "Express" or use an X.

Bus stop signs are blue, green, and white with the Charlotte Transit logo and phone number, and are placed along routes where buses make scheduled stops. Park 'N' Ride signs are white, blue, and green, and are posted at parking lots that offer free parking and a place to board the bus.

## TRIVIA

Average travel times in minutes to Uptown Charlotte during the morning rush:

| | |
|---|---|
| From Belmont: | 25 |
| Cornelius: | 27 |
| Davidson: | 29 |
| Huntersville: | 22 |
| Matthews: | 33 |
| Mint Hill: | 5 |
| Pineville: | 27 |

Source: Charlotte Chamber of Commerce

Monthly and weekly passes feature unlimited rides anytime, anywhere. Bus passes are available at Charlotte-Mecklenburg Government Center, the Charlotte Transportation Center, Harris-Teeter grocery stores, as well as at Wayne's Supermarkets.

Residents and visitors with special transportation needs for the elderly or disabled can call 704/336-2637 for information.

The Charlotte Department of Transportation also offers a computerized carpooling program to help people form carpools and vanpools. To find out more, call 704/336-2275 or 704/336-3897.

Charlotte Transit publishes a "Welcome to Charlotte" brochure listing suggested city attractions and the corresponding bus numbers to take. The pamphlet includes entries for art, shopping, science, family amusement, and history. Each booklet is printed in English with translations in Spanish, French, German, Arabic, and Russian. For information, call Charlotte Transit at 704/336-RIDE.

## Charlotte Trolley

Some Charlotteans believe the future of the city's transportation lies in its past.

In the 1930s, Uptown Charlotte bustled with streetcar trolleys transporting residents to work and around town for errands. What are now the history-filled neighborhoods of Dilworth, Myers Park, Elizabeth, and Plaza-Midwood thrived with the help of the trolley that ensured residents in these suburbs a way into the city.

Buses replaced the trolley streetcars in the 1950s, but preservationists rallied to restore the old No. 85 streetcar and put it back in service. Today, the Charlotte Trolley runs from the South End trolley barn at 2104 South Boulevard at Atherton Mill to the edge of Uptown at Stonewall and College.

More than just a way into town, the enclosed trolley with gleaming wood and brass rails features uniformed conductors and motormen who point out historical landmarks along the 30-minute ride. Now trolley supporters hope to extend the tracks through Uptown and eventually to other parts of the city.

Trolley hours are 10 a.m. to 9 p.m. Friday and Saturday and 10 to 6 Sunday on the hour and half-hour. Round-trip tokens are $2. For more information, call 704/375-0850.

Several private companies such as EZ Rider, Uni-Park, 49er Shuttle, CommuteRide, and Carowinds Connection operate along commuter routes throughout the city. Carpool and vanpool services are also available. Call the individual transportation companies listed in the Yellow Pages for details.

## Uptown Circuit

A consortium of businesses have teamed with the Charlotte Department of Transportation to support Uptown Circuit, a fleet of free electric buses that serve as an Uptown shuttle. The electric buses travel McDowell, Fourth, College, Sixth, Church, Stonewall, Third, Davidson, and Second Streets. Service runs from 7:30 a.m. to 6 p.m. weekdays. For information, call 704/376-1164.

## Driving in Charlotte

Everyone talks about Charlotte's rotten drivers, but no one thinks that label applies to him. Motorists speed through city streets, run red lights, pull out in front of other cars, refuse to let merging drivers in, and ignore the fact that they block traffic by inching out into intersections in bumper-to-bumper lines. Their philosophy seems to be, "If I don't look other drivers in the eye, there's no obligation to let them into stopped traffic."

Overall, the polite, courteous drivers outnumber the bad eggs, but there are always a few who make other motorists honk the horn or give the international single-digit salute.

Remember these tips when driving in Charlotte: Stay alert for others who are not. Count to five before you proceed through a new green light and ignore the honking that may erupt behind you. Never assume that

---

## Driving Queen Charlotte

*When Police Chief Dennis Nowicki arrived in Charlotte in 1994, he quickly learned—and tired—of Charlotte drivers' bad habits. Nowicki established a special traffic unit, and doubled it to 12 officers a few years later. At some Charlotte intersections, cameras now record stoplight violations.*

*Large, portable, digital signs that remind drivers of the speed limit and display the speed they are currently driving are also used in Charlotte to slow folks down. Other city officials are recruiting companies to donate billboards with safe-driving messages and distributing bumper stickers that read, "Speed Shatters Lives."*

*The Charlotte Department of Transportation has tried several methods of slowing drivers. Speed humps, which are 22 feet wide and four inches tall in the middle, slow traffic by 10 mph and aren't destructive to cars. Traffic circles use planted trees and shrubs in the middle of an intersection to make drivers go around the circle to turn. Speed tables, boldly painted as large pedestrian crosswalks, are extra-thick layers of asphalt in intersections to raise the road level to that of the curb. Chicanes incorporate several landscaped islands placed in a zigzag pattern on a street to block one lane and slow traffic.*

---

# Park Pay & Post

*Many streets in Uptown Charlotte use parking meters, but the city has also installed Park Pay & Post vending machines in the 200 and 400 blocks of North Tryon Street. Drivers insert coins or bills into the machine, which produces a receipt drivers place face up on top of the dash. Parking spaces with the Park Pay & Post machines, like meters, cost $1 an hour.*

*Designed to reduce sidewalk clutter while retaining on-street parking, the machines are about the size of a newspaper rack and can do the work of 15 parking meters. Europeans frequently use Park Pay & Post vending machines, but only a few U.S. cities have them, including Aspen, Fort Lauderdale, and San Diego.*

*If you opt not to insert money into the machine, don't be surprised to find a $25 citation.*

an oncoming driver will turn just because his blinker is on, and vice versa. Many of Charlotte's thoroughfares don't have center turn lanes, and people often just go for it. Don't try parallel parking for the first time in Uptown Charlotte; bite the bullet and pay for a space in the deck. Never react if another driver beeps, gestures, or curses; road rage does happen.

## Highways

Several major interstates and highways serve the Charlotte area. Interstate 77 runs north to Lake Norman and Iredell County, and south to Fort Mill and eventually to Columbia, South Carolina. Many of the rush-hour headaches revolve around I-77 because it's only two lanes to the north and under heavy congestion and ongoing widening to the south.

Interstate 77 connects with I-85 north of Uptown. Drivers headed southwest to Gaston County or northeast to Concord and Kannapolis can bypass much of Charlotte's center city traffic using I-85.

U.S. Highway 74 is also known as Independence Boulevard east of Uptown and Wilkinson Boulevard to the west. Both are well-traveled routes, although Independence has a reputation for stop-and-go traffic due to its numerous stoplights outside of central Charlotte.

NC 49, called Tryon Street in town, leads to Lake Wylie, South Carolina, in the southwestern part of the county and to the Harrisburg/Concord area on the northeast.

## Parking Tips

An abundance of parking decks in Uptown Charlotte prevent drivers from roaming the streets in search of a space. For best results, know your route before you go and ask for the location of the nearest deck.

Plan to pay around $3 for two hours' time, or more by the day. Always take the parking deck ticket to your destination; many validate for their customers and clients.

If you see a sign warning of tickets or towing, believe it. When Carolina Panthers games are played Uptown, tow trucks are busier than on a snowy January night.

# Biking in Charlotte

When it comes to biking as a means of transportation, Charlotte is just getting its training wheels. Bikes must battle cars and other vehicles for space on already squeezed roads; designated bike paths are hard to find. Charlotte has only nine miles of bike paths, compared with Raleigh's 48 paved miles.

In 1998, Charlotte-Mecklenburg officials selected a citizens advisory committee and set aside $100,000 for a consultant to prepare a bicycle master plan. The Mecklenburg County Park and Recreation Department has also hired a consultant to study its greenways and plans for building hiking and bike trails along creeks. Bicycle enthusiasts hope the move signals an effort to build new roads with enough space to incorporate bike lanes, to design off-road bike paths within new subdivisions, and to build short bike paths where cars cannot go.

# Air Travel

For a place full of people either coming or going, Charlotte/Douglas International Airport sure wants a lot of them to stay. The three-level, 1-million-square-foot terminal has adopted a Southern approach to hospitality that seems to say, "Slow down, sit a spell, relax for a bit."

For instance, white wooden rocking chairs sit next to the people-movers that run travelers to and from various concourses. In the atrium, added in 1994, is a piano that passengers often play while others wait for flights or grab a bite to eat. Restaurants, snack shops, mall-quality stores, and specialty boutiques are scattered throughout the airport's main level.

Outside, a 17th-century baroque-style sculpture and fountain portrays Queen Charlotte with flowing skirts, tendriled hair, and a crown on her fingertips as she extends a welcome to all. Benches, trees, and beds of beautiful blooms complete the look. Passengers polled in a recent national survey voted Charlotte/Douglas International Airport the third most

*Charlotte/Douglas International Airport*

popular in the United States, behind the Tampa, Fla., and Pittsburgh, Pa., airports.

Still, the airport averaged 500 daily flights and carried 22.8 million passengers in 1997, making it the country's 20th-busiest airport. Charlotte/Douglas is also home to one of USAirways' two largest hubs nationwide.

From central Charlotte, the airport's location west of Uptown makes it easily accessible from several routes. Those in north, south, and east Charlotte will face more traffic getting into central Charlotte than they will around the terminal itself.

About a 20-minute drive from Uptown, the airport is easily reached via Billy Graham Parkway or Wilkinson Boulevard. From Uptown, take South Tryon Street to Billy Graham Parkway and follow the signs; or take I-277 to Wilkinson Boulevard (Highway 74/29) and follow the terminal markers.

North Charlotteans take I-85 South to avoid city traffic, then exit onto Billy Graham Parkway. Those in east Charlotte take Independence Boulevard, which becomes Wilkinson. With the I-485 outer loop as yet unfinished, south Charlotteans are stuck with first getting to town, then making their way west to the airport. The easiest route is on I-77 North to Billy Graham Parkway. Airport exits are clearly marked.

Carolina Transportation Airport Express (704/359-9600) is the airport's designated shuttle offering service to Uptown Charlotte, major hotels, and most business districts. Look for the shuttle service's burgundy signs outside Zone C on the Baggage Claim Level. Other shuttles can be caught at the outside curb on the Baggage Claim Level.

Taxi service is readily available on the outside curb of the Baggage

## Major Airlines Serving Charlotte/Douglas

*Air Canada, Concourse A, 800/776-3000*

*American, American Eagle, Concourse A, 800/433-7300*

*British Airways, Concourse D, 800/247-8217*

*Continental Airlines, Concourse A, 800/523-3273*

*Delta/ASA/Comair, Concourse A, 800/221-1212*

*Northwest Airlines, Concourse A, 800/225-2525*

*Transworld Airlines, Concourse A, 800/221-2000*

*United, United Express, Concourse A, 800/241-6522*

*USAirways, USAirways Express, Concourses A–D, 800/428-4322*

Claim Level. There is a set fee between the airport and designated zones, including Uptown. For more rate information, see the curbside attendant.

Courtesy vehicles from select hotels and motels are also available. Information on those offering pick-up service can be obtained through the Welcome Center on the Baggage Claim Level. For information, call 704/359-4027.

## Train Service

Charlotte's Amtrak station offers daily trains to Raleigh, Atlanta, New York, and New Orleans, providing access to all routes.

North Carolina destinations, including Kannapolis, Salisbury, High Point, Greensboro, Burlington, Durham, Cary, Raleigh, Selma, Wilson, and Rocky Mount, can be reached via daily service on Amtrak's Carolinian trains. The Carolinian also proceeds to Richmond, Virginia; Washington, D.C.; Philadelphia; and New York.

The Carolinian trains feature meals, snacks, and beverages in the food service car; access for elderly citizens and people with disabilities; Railfone service; and Carolina Club

*Queen Charlotte statue outside C/DIA*

Leigh Pressley

Service with pillows, complimentary beverages, newspapers, and video and audio programming.

Popular routes from Charlotte include the 8 a.m. train to Raleigh arriving at 11:49 a.m. One-way tickets range from $19 to $30. Charlotte to Washington, D.C., is another top seller; one-way tickets range from $52 to $95.

Amtrak's Charlotte station is at 1914 North Tryon Street, directly across from WSOC-TV just outside of Uptown. Call the 24-hour Charlotte station at 704/376-4416. For ticket, schedule, and route information, call Amtrak at 800/872-7245.

## Interstate and Regional Bus Service

Carolina Trailways and Greyhound bus lines serve Charlotte with routes throughout the region and country. The two major bus services share terminals at 601 West Trade Street in Uptown Charlotte. For fare and schedule information, call 704/372-0456 or 800/231-2222.

In addition, many local bus lines specialize in charters and tours to destinations across the United States and Canada for school, church, civic, and corporate groups.

The Park Hotel

# 3

## WHERE TO STAY

As Charlotte becomes one of the Southeast's most thriving metropolitan cities, its accommodations follow. Currently, the Queen City boasts some 15,000 rooms, including four-star, four-diamond hotels; quaint bed-and-breakfasts; charming Southern inns; extended-stay facilities; economy motels; family-friendly campgrounds; and corporate apartments.

Who visits Charlotte?

As the second-largest banking center in the country and the home of several major companies, Charlotte attracts corporate travelers, some of whom arrive for conferences at the uptown Charlotte Convention Center.

Sports bring fans to Carolina Panthers and Charlotte Hornets games. Major NASCAR races each May and October at Charlotte Motor Speedway light up "No Vacancy" signs like a summer swarm of lightning bugs.

Generally, visitors find high-rise luxury hotels uptown, while full-service and extended-stay hotels are concentrated in the University City area in North Charlotte, the Executive Park area in West Charlotte, and the SouthPark area in Central/South Charlotte.

Smaller, charming inns and bed-and-breakfasts set up shop throughout the city, but most are found in historic neighborhoods such as Dilworth, Myers Park, and Elizabeth, just outside Uptown.

In addition to the lodgings listed here, many national hotel chains are represented in various areas of Charlotte.

*Price rating symbols:*
| | |
|---|---|
| **$** | **Under $50** |
| **$$** | **$50 to $75** |
| **$$$** | **$75 to $125** |
| **$$$$** | **$125 and up** |

# UPTOWN CHARLOTTE

## Hotels

### ADAM'S MARK HOTEL
555 S. McDowell St.
Charlotte, NC 28204
704/372-4100
$$$–$$$$
Charlotte's largest hotel features two separate towers, 613 guest rooms, two restaurants, a nightclub, and 52,000 square feet of meeting space on the edge of Uptown. Convention-goers walk four blocks to the Charlotte Convention Center; but most of Uptown's restaurants, nightspots, and cultural sites are a longer haul. Inside, look for a spacious central lobby in green and taupe with fresh flowers, brass, and Asian-inspired accents. Uniformed staff are friendly and helpful. Business travelers enjoy the amenities: shoe-shine stand, gift shop, concierge, and in-room hair dryers and iron/ironing board. After work, wind down in the indoor/outdoor pool, health club, racquetball court, sauna, Jacuzzi, or fine Northern Italian restaurant (with singing servers). & (Uptown)

### CHARLOTTE MARRIOTT CITY CENTER
100 W. Trade St.
Charlotte, NC 28202
704/333-9000
$$$–$$$$
Overlooking the intersection of Trade and Tryon Streets in what's known as The Square, you can't get any closer to the heart of Uptown. The Charlotte Marriott City Center, with 334 rooms, stretches 19 stories and offers spectacular views. Walk through the skylight atrium of the adjoining office building to the lobby of marble and dark wood, where valets in long, red, double-breasted coats and plumed

helmets await. Enjoy the breakfast buffet, sandwiches at the bar and grill, and dinner plus a cigar bar on-site. A complete room renovation in early 1998 updated the decor, and the luxury-hotel amenities are here: indoor pool, whirlpool, health club, ballrooms, meeting space, concierge, and gift shop. Splurgers, try the $450 presidential suite with oversized rooms, brass fixtures, and 53-inch TVs. & (Uptown)

### DOUBLETREE HOTEL
895 W. Trade St.
Charlotte, NC 28202
704/347-0070
$$$
You've got to love a hotel that gives you warm chocolate-chip cookies upon check-in. But even without the friendly bribe, the DoubleTree would attract business and leisure travelers looking for something unique. Located eight blocks from central Uptown, this is the closest hotel to Ericsson Stadium and a favorite of football fans in town for the game. Off the recently renovated marble-and-rich-wood lobby are several sitting areas that feel like your own living room. One looks like a library, another like a sunken den; all are private and quiet. The eight-story, 187-room hotel offers a restaurant, lounge, health club, spa, outdoor pool, free parking, and plenty of those cookies to take home. & (Uptown)

### THE DUNHILL HOTEL
237 N. Tryon St.
Charlotte, NC 28202
704/332-4141; 800/252-4666
$$$–$$$$
Charlotte's only Historic Landmark Hotel, The Dunhill offers quiet elegance and exemplary service on a smaller, 60-room scale. Opened in 1929 as the Mayfair Manor, the hotel

# UPTOWN CHARLOTTE

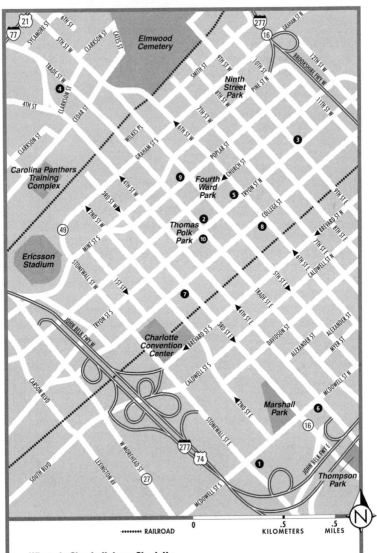

✦✦✦✦✦✦ RAILROAD

0      .5      .5
KILOMETERS   MILES

## Where to Stay in Uptown Charlotte

1 Adam's Mark Hotel
2 Charlotte Marriott City Center
3 Days Inn Uptown
4 DoubleTree Hotel
5 The Dunhill Hotel
6 Four Points Hotel
7 The Hilton Charlotte & Towers
8 Holiday Inn Center City
9 The Inn Uptown
10 Radisson Plaza Hotel

set tongues wagging with its un-heard-of 10 stories and private baths, telephones, and radios. After the Depression and several mismanaging owners, the hotel closed in 1981. Preservationists who returned the hotel to its original elegance in 1988 did such a good job that they went bankrupt. But others stepped in, and The Dunhill continues to thrive. Arts patrons walk to Spirit Square, and kids love Discovery Place next door. Details include turn-down service, valet parking, limousine, complimentary continental breakfast, period furnishings, and original art. Casual pub fare is available or enjoy more formal dining with three meals daily. Meeting space; health club privileges. &. (Uptown)

## FOUR POINTS HOTEL
**201 S. McDowell St.**
**Charlotte, NC 28204**
**704/372-7550**
**$$$$**
Sheraton recently took over this 193-room hotel on South McDowell Street on the edge of Uptown Charlotte. It's an easy walk to the Charlotte Convention Center, but a short drive may be necessary at night to reach the heart of Uptown's shops, restaurants, and cultural attractions. Business and leisure travelers enjoy amenities including 10,000 square feet of meeting space on one floor, convenient parking, a restaurant and sports tavern, oversized executive rooms with access to the Club Lounge, an outdoor pool with sundeck, on-site exercise room, and admission to the nearby Mecklenburg Aquatic Center. &. (Uptown)

## HILTON CHARLOTTE AND TOWERS
**222 E. Third St.**
**Charlotte, NC 28202**
**704/377-1500**
**$$$$**
The Hilton is the only Uptown hotel and one of just two in the Queen City to earn AAA's Four Diamond Award. The ritziest hotel uptown and the choice of many executives and celebrities, the Hilton's 22 floors begin with an impressive marble-and-richwood lobby with vaulted ceiling and grand staircase. Built in 1990 in the heart of the business district, this is Charlotte's newest, major Uptown hotel. Just four years later, new owners spent $5 million refurbishing its 407 rooms. Amenities include a bistro and bar, meeting space, concierge, USAirways ticket office, shops, and access to the overstreet walkway that links Uptown attractions. Guests may use the 50,000-square-foot well-appointed YMCA, along with a state-of-the-art business center. A grand choice for receptions and meetings; ballrooms and conference suites include massive chandeliers and elegant furnishings. Going to the Convention Center? Take a few steps under a covered breezeway and you're there. &. (Uptown)

## HOLIDAY INN CENTER CITY
**230 N. College St.**
**Charlotte, NC 28202**
**704/335-5400**
**$$$**
Guest rooms and corridors have new carpet and wallpaper, and a full-service business center debuted in early 1998 at this 10-year-old hotel at the corner of College and 6th Streets. Located four blocks from the Convention Center among abundant nightlife, the 300-room, 30-suite hotel features many of the same amenities as luxury hotels at a reduced cost. A 1950s-themed restaurant serves three meals daily, while the

The Dunhill Hotel in Uptown Charlotte is the city's only Historic Landmark Hotel. Originally opened in 1929 as the Mayfair Manor, the hotel was designed by renowned Charlotte architect Louis Asbury, Sr., who introduced the elegance of the era with private baths, telephones, and radios. At the hotel's opening, the *Charlotte Observer* called the 10-story Mayfair "an impressive addition to Charlotte's skyline." Today, it is dwarfed by skyscrapers galore.

pub draws the after-work crowd. There's also a gift shop, room service, pool, fitness center, ballrooms, meeting space, and additional eateries in an adjacent office tower. The best feature? Its 16th-story rooftop terrace—it's the only Uptown hotel that has one (others put a terrace on lower floors). Jog on the half-mile track or simply relax and check out the skyline. ₺ (Uptown)

### RADISSON PLAZA HOTEL
101 S. Tryon St.
Charlotte, NC 28280
704/377-0400; 800/333-3333
$$$–$$$$
If location is key, the Radisson is the place. Overlooking The Square, Charlotte's first luxury hotel is a mirrored, sharp-angled, 15-story building. The second-level, marble-floored lobby looks down on a changing art exhibit, and connects to an overstreet walkway linking hotels, performing-arts spaces, and attractions. A top-to-bottom 1994 renovation still looks fresh in the 366-room hotel. Amenities include a business center, free parking, 24-hour security, meeting rooms, ballrooms, fitness center, rooftop pool, two restaurants, lounge, adjacent boutiques, Panthers packages, and access to the private, well-equipped Tower Club athletic center.

Ask for rooms in the building's point—they have odd-shaped dimensions, vaulted ceilings, and incredible views. ₺ (Uptown)

### Motels

### DAYS INN UPTOWN
601 N. Tryon St.
Charlotte, NC 28202
704/333-4733; 800/325-2525
$$
Budget travelers choose this two-story, 129-room motel for its competitive price and central location within walking distance of Discovery Place, the Convention Center, Ericsson Stadium, and the heart of Uptown Charlotte. Most units are your standard motel rooms, but some include king-sized beds, small refrigerators, microwaves, coffeemakers, and iron/ironing board. Continental breakfast with juice, doughnuts, and bagels is included. Free parking, outdoor pool, security doors, fax service, and cable with free HBO. No frills, but an adequate alternative for the frugal. ₺ (Uptown)

### Bed-and-Breakfasts

### THE INN UPTOWN
129 N. Poplar St.
Charlotte, NC 28202

704/342-2800; 800/959-1990
$$$–$$$$

Business guests choose this 1890 home, Uptown's only bed-and-breakfast, for its proximity to Charlotte's corporate mecca, for its well-appointed rooms, and for amenities including in-room TVs, gas-log fireplaces, and local innkeepers with advice on little-known eateries and hangouts. Pleasure travelers will enjoy the short walk to restaurants, cultural activities, and Ericsson Stadium. Couples should ask for the Tower Suite with its mauve-and-black decor and a spiral staircase leading to a black-tiled Jacuzzi and a stained-glass window looking out on the city's skyline. A welcome, comfortable alternative to the anonymity of Uptown's bigger hotels. Full breakfast included. Corporate rates available. No pets; no children under 7. (Uptown)

# NORTH CHARLOTTE

## Hotels

**CHARLOTTE HILTON AT UNIVERSITY PLACE**
**8629 J.M. Keynes Dr.**
**Charlotte, NC 28262**
**704/547-7444**
**$$$–$$$$**

Just off busy Harris Boulevard in growing northeast Charlotte, this 12-story, 243-room brick hotel is minutes from UNCC, University Research Park, Blockbuster Pavilion, and Charlotte Motor Speedway. Despite the area's congestion, the Hilton provides a calming oasis with a peaceful lake and half-mile fitness trail behind the property. Plenty of ballroom and meeting space accommodates business travelers, with a health club, outdoor pool, restaurant, and three-tier beach club for after hours. Other

## Movin' on Up

Uptown, plans are underway to build what will be the city's largest hotel, a 30-story Westin Hotel with 800 rooms and a 1,750-car parking deck. Located at College and Stonewall, the new Westin will be a four-star hotel with two ballrooms, tennis courts, bars, restaurants, and meeting rooms. City officials, who agreed to chip in $16 million of the $134 million price tag, believe it will benefit the Charlotte Convention Center, which reportedly loses meetings every year because of the lack of hotel rooms in Uptown. The Westin could open by 2001.

On the other end of Uptown at South Mint and West Second streets, an 11-story, 150-suite Residence Inn is planned for a location across from Ericsson Stadium. The only Uptown extended-stay hotel, the Residence Inn will feature a full-service kitchen in each suite, catering to guests staying a week or longer.

# GREATER CHARLOTTE

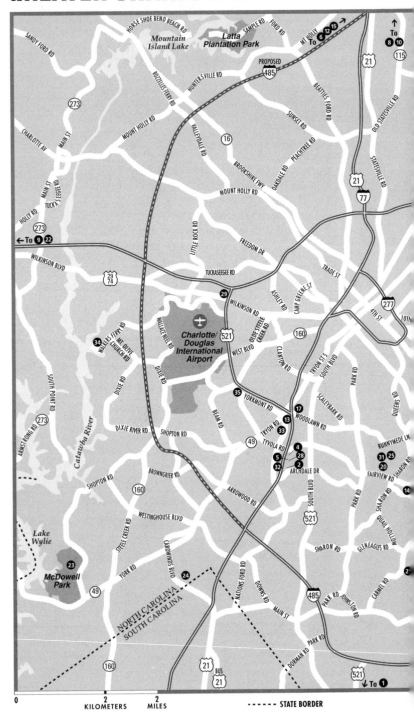

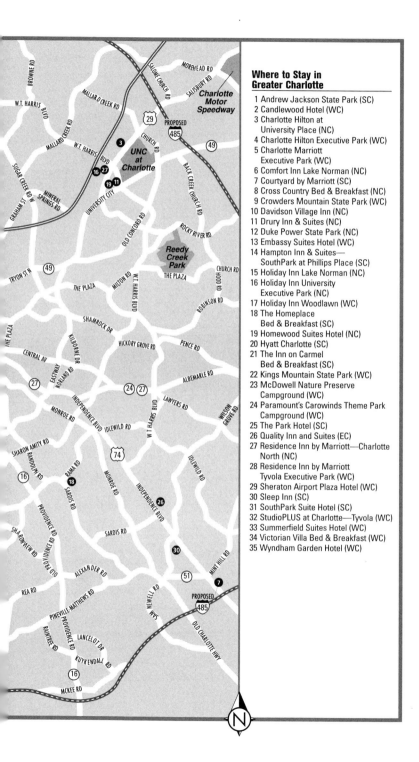

## Where to Stay in Greater Charlotte

1 Andrew Jackson State Park (SC)
2 Candlewood Hotel (WC)
3 Charlotte Hilton at University Place (NC)
4 Charlotte Hilton Executive Park (WC)
5 Charlotte Marriott Executive Park (WC)
6 Comfort Inn Lake Norman (NC)
7 Courtyard by Marriott (SC)
8 Cross Country Bed & Breakfast (NC)
9 Crowders Mountain State Park (WC)
10 Davidson Village Inn (NC)
11 Drury Inn & Suites (NC)
12 Duke Power State Park (NC)
13 Embassy Suites Hotel (WC)
14 Hampton Inn & Suites— SouthPark at Phillips Place (SC)
15 Holiday Inn Lake Norman (NC)
16 Holiday Inn University Executive Park (NC)
17 Holiday Inn Woodlawn (WC)
18 The Homeplace Bed & Breakfast (SC)
19 Homewood Suites Hotel (NC)
20 Hyatt Charlotte (SC)
21 The Inn on Carmel Bed & Breakfast (SC)
22 Kings Mountain State Park (WC)
23 McDowell Nature Preserve Campground (WC)
24 Paramount's Carowinds Theme Park Campground (WC)
25 The Park Hotel (SC)
26 Quality Inn and Suites (EC)
27 Residence Inn by Marriott—Charlotte North (NC)
28 Residence Inn by Marriott Tyvola Executive Park (WC)
29 Sheraton Airport Plaza Hotel (WC)
30 Sleep Inn (SC)
31 SouthPark Suite Hotel (SC)
32 StudioPLUS at Charlotte—Tyvola (WC)
33 Summerfield Suites Hotel (WC)
34 Victorian Villa Bed & Breakfast (WC)
35 Wyndham Garden Hotel (WC)

amenities include a gift shop, USAirways ticket office, shuttle service, access to nearby Gold's Gym, and a bridge that links the hotel to a shopping center, movie theater, and lakeside restaurants. A new addition opening in 1999 will boost the hotel to 393 rooms. ৬ (North)

## DRURY INN & SUITES
**415 W. W.T. Harris Blvd.**
**Charlotte, NC 28262**
**704/593-0700**
**$$–$$$**

A good value for cost-conscious travelers who don't want to give up amenities, Drury opened in January 1998 with 144 rooms including several suites with small refrigerators, microwaves, coffeemakers, and pull-out sofa beds. Business-class king rooms also offer recliner, spacious work area, and dataport telephone. No matter what size the room, Drury guests receive popcorn and soda snack service daily, free breakfast buffet, and a complimentary manager's cocktail each weeknight. Despite the lower price, you won't have to give up an indoor/outdoor pool with sundeck, Jacuzzi, exercise room, meeting rooms, on-site laundry, and business services. Near UNCC, Blockbuster Pavilion, major office parks, and Charlotte Motor Speedway. Extended-stay visitors welcome. Children 18 and under stay free in parents' room. ৬ (North)

## HOLIDAY INN UNIVERSITY EXECUTIVE PARK
**8520 University Executive Park Dr.**
**Charlotte, NC 28262**
**704/547-0999**
**$$$**

Like other North Charlotte hotels, the Holiday Inn University Executive Park draws business travelers in town for work at nearby corporate parks and pleasure-seekers taking in races at Charlotte Motor Speedway or events at Blockbuster Pavilion and UNCC. This Holiday Inn offers the standard amenities and clean, affordable rooms, but not much to set it apart from other hotels. The 175-room, seven-story hotel has some suites with microwaves and small refrigerators. There's an outdoor pool, health club, whirlpool, sauna, and a casual, American-style restaurant with bar and lounge. Business people will like voicemail capability in their rooms, but will have to use the front desk to send and receive faxes. The upside is the complimentary hot breakfast buffet. ৬ (North)

## Motels

## COMFORT INN LAKE NORMAN
**20740 Torrence Chapel Rd.**
**(I-77 at Exit 28)**
**Cornelius, NC 28031**
**704/892-3500**
**$$–$$$**

The details make the difference at this award-winning, three-story brick Comfort Inn convenient to Lake Norman, Davidson College, and North Charlotte attractions. Window boxes planted with colorful pansies greet visitors outside their rooms. In the parquet-floored lobby, an old-style popcorn machine, fresh fruit, and brewing coffee are always available for snack-seekers. The complimentary breakfast includes pastries, muffins, bagels, hot and cold cereals, fresh fruit, and beverages. Lodging at the 90-room motel, which is 25 minutes from Uptown Charlotte, includes six suites with living room areas and six standard rooms with Jacuzzis. For those in need of relaxation, an outdoor pool and rocking chairs provide a great escape. ৬ (North)

## HOLIDAY INN LAKE NORMAN
**I-77 North, Exit 28 at Highway 73**
**Cornelius, NC 28031**
**704/892-9120**
**$$$**

The only full-service motel on this busy Lake Norman exit, the Holiday Inn features 119 guest rooms, some with Jacuzzis, refrigerators, and microwaves. Hospitality rooms are available, along with meeting space and banquet or reception accommodations for up to 150 people. The on-site restaurant serves three meals a day, and guests enjoy nightly lounge entertainment including free shag dancing lessons on Monday ("shag" is a popular beach-music dance), karaoke Wednesday, and Friday beach music nights. All guest rooms at this two-story motel come with coffeemaker and iron/ironing board. A large outdoor pool is surrounded by a garden courtyard. ᶜ (North)

## *Bed-and-Breakfasts*

## CROSS COUNTRY BED & BREAKFAST
**13530 McCord Rd.**
**Huntersville, NC 28078**
**704/948-0688**
**$$$**

The birds chirp, the cows moo, and the breeze blows quietly in this serene country setting 25 minutes north of Uptown Charlotte. Three rooms await in the one-story B&B; one with a private bath and two that share facilities. Corporate travelers with business north of Charlotte, snowbirds driving through, and locals with relatives in town are the typical guests. Look for a country theme with antiques, quilts, wicker accents, and a heaping helping of Southern hospitality. The full breakfast includes fresh fruit, innkeeper Suzanne Crawford's personally homemade breads, jams, and jellies. In warm weather, relax on the back porch or take in the flowers, vegetable garden, and pond. (North)

## DAVIDSON VILLAGE INN
**117 Depot St.**
**Davidson, NC 28036**
**704/892-8044**
**$$$**

If you're looking for a small, college-town atmosphere just 30 minutes north of Charlotte, try the quaint yet contemporary Davidson Village Inn. The 18-room, European-style inn blends the amenities of a luxury hotel with the intimacy of a bed-and-breakfast. Davidson College's cafeteria once stood on this spot across from campus, and the property was later a

If you're planning a trip to Charlotte around Memorial Day (May) or in early October, start your engines early. Charlotte Motor Speedway hosts NASCAR events such as the Coca-Cola 600 each May and the UAW-GM Quality 500 each October.

Hotels, motels, inns, bed-and-breakfasts, campgrounds, and every hit-the-hay hangout from boardinghouses to doghouses rev up their prices and jack up their required stays to three-night minimums.

Plan early—and be prepared to pay at least $50 more per room than usual.

Retreat to *The Homeplace Bed & Breakfast*, p. 43

boardinghouse and post office. Laid-back innkeepers in khakis and Birkenstocks built the three-story brick building four years ago. The decor is neutral creams and tans with a splash of black and red in the lobby, which features a marble floor, curved glass-block wall, and comfortable places to sit and snack by the fire. Continental breakfast included, with room service provided by next-door neighbor Jasper's Restaurant. Nice details include custom-bottled toiletries, terry robes, fitness center access, and suites with small kitchens. Children welcome. ♿ (North)

## Extended-Stay

### HOMEWOOD SUITES HOTEL
8340 N. Tryon St.
Charlotte, NC 28262
704/549-8800
$$$

Feel at home on the road at the residential-style Homewood Suites Hotel near UNCC, office parks, and Charlotte Motor Speedway. The 112-unit hotel includes suites ranging from 490 to 575 square feet with separate living room and sleeping areas. Kitchens include full-size refrigerator with ice-maker, microwave, stove, toaster oven, dishwasher, coffee-maker, and utensils. Full-size sofa beds in each room provide out-of-sight sleeping space if needed. Each suite also features two TVs, VCR, work table, voicemail, large bathroom with separate vanity, and daily news-paper service. Some suites offer wood-burning fireplaces. In the lodge-style lobby, relax by the double-sided gas-log fireplace, enjoy the compli-mentary breakfast and evening dinner reception, or rent movies in the suite shop. There's also a business center, outdoor pool and whirlpool, exercise room and outside sport court, laundry, fishing pond, complimentary grocery shopping service, and same-day dry cleaning. With all that, you may not want to go home! ♿ (North)

### RESIDENCE INN BY MARRIOTT—CHARLOTTE NORTH
8503 N. Tryon St.
Charlotte, NC 28262
704/547-1122
$$$–$$$$

Extended-stay hotels are on every corner in this area, surrounded by office parks and companies including Bank of America, First Union, IBM, Verbatim, Bell South, AT&T, and Philip Morris. But Residence Inn holds its own against the competition, this time with a modern twist on its English Tudor look. The layouts differ from the West Charlotte Residence Inn; these are one- or two-bedroom suites. All have fully equipped kitchens and sep-arate living and sleeping areas; the two-bedroom suites offer two private bedrooms with full baths and an adjoining living space. Whether here for business or for fun at nearby Charlotte Motor Speedway, guests enjoy the outdoor pool, Jacuzzi, exercise room, on-site laundry, daily housekeeping, and VCR rental. Pets are permitted for an extra fee. ♿ (North)

## Campgrounds

### DUKE POWER STATE PARK
**159 Inland Sea Lane**
**Troutman, NC 28166**
**704/528-6350**
**$**
Nearly an hour north of Charlotte, just past Mooresville, Duke Power State Park features a tent-only group camping facility and an area for family tents and trailers. The park covers more than 1,400 acres and includes easy hiking trails, a 33-acre lake with swimming and boat rentals, boat access to Lake Norman, fishing spots, and nature study programs for all ages and interests. In 1999, the park will open an enclosed community building with kitchen facilities for corporate meetings and family reunions. (See also Chapter 8, Parks, Gardens, and Recreation Areas.) Call for hours. Limited wheelchair access. (North)

# SOUTH CHARLOTTE

## Hotels

### COURTYARD BY MARRIOTT
**11425 E. Independence Blvd.**
**Matthews, NC 28105**
**704/846-4466; 800/321-2211**
**$$–$$$**
Business travelers reportedly designed the Courtyard hotels, and it appears they thought of nearly every-

thing at this 121-room location, opened in January 1998. Rooms have balconies, and many feature adjoining suites, vaulted ceilings, and Jacuzzis. For business functions, reserve a separate meeting room or a hospitality suite. Each room includes desk, coffeemaker, hair dryer, iron, and full-size ironing board. During down time, try the outdoor pool, fully equipped exercise room, hot tub, lounge, or breakfast buffet. Not as many frills as Uptown digs, but a better price with many of the same basics. Uptown is a mere five miles away, and there are scores of chain restaurants, movie theaters, stores, and nightspots in the immediate area. ♿ (South)

### HAMPTON INN & SUITES— SOUTHPARK AT PHILLIPS PLACE
**6700 Phillips Place Court**
**Charlotte, NC 28210**
**704/319-5700; 800/HAMPTON**
**$$$–$$$$**
Hampton Inn has gone upscale at this 124-room hotel with 36 suites, a Georgian lobby with hardwood floors and a marble-surrounded cathedral fireplace. Located in the ritzy Phillips Place shopping center, Hampton Inn debuted in March 1998. Rooms vary from standard with double or king beds to two-room suites with full kitchen, fireplaces, entertainment centers, whirlpool bath, and a dressing area. Hot waffles and fresh muffins await at the complimentary breakfast; manager's receptions include hot hors d'oeuvres, beer, and wine. Full fitness center, outdoor pool, Jacuzzi, business center, and convenience store complete the package. Some of Charlotte's top eateries, including Palm and Dean & Deluca, are steps away in Phillips Place, along with upscale stores and a 10-screen stadium-seating theater. ♿ (South)

## HYATT CHARLOTTE AT SOUTHPARK
**5501 Carnegie Blvd.**
**Charlotte, NC 28209**
**704/554-1234**
**$$$–$$$$**

Business travelers choose the 262-room Hyatt for its proximity to South-Park, the second-largest business center in the Carolinas behind Uptown Charlotte, and pleasure travelers like it for its location across from SouthPark Mall. But many visitors want to camp out in the hotel's impressive, three-story atrium with its Mexican-tiled fountain, olive trees, and plenty of sitting areas. The focal point of the seven-story hotel, the atrium is home to a Mediterranean/Northern Italian restaurant serving three meals daily. Built in 1989, the Hyatt renovated its rooms and suites in early 1998. Corporate types are the focus with work desks, enhanced lighting, and two-line speaker phones with dataport. Club chairs, ottomans, crown molding, and artwork make it feel like home. Amenities include a lounge, 24-hour room

*The lobby of the Hyatt Charlotte SouthPark*

Hyatt Charlotte at SouthPark

service, meeting space, ballrooms, fitness center, indoor pool, sundeck, gift shop and shuttle. ♿ (South)

## THE PARK HOTEL
**2200 Rexford Rd.**
**Charlotte, NC 28211**
**704/364-8220**
**$$$$**

Once upon a time, a prom-going teenager ran to his mother in a panic. His tux included a "real" tie-it-yourself bow tie. Neither knew the proper procedure, but they immediately drove to one place in town that would: The Park Hotel. They rushed to the South-Park-area hotel with its uniformed doormen and valets, and walked past the illuminated fountain, into the marbled lobby with its elegant chandeliers, original artwork, and overflowing bouquets of fresh flowers. The full-time concierge gave a quick demonstration, and all lived happily ever after. Guests of the 194-room hotel must feel the same way in oversized rooms that blend 18th-century furnishings with modern conveniences. It's a French-milled-soap, terry-robe, chocolate-on-the-pillow kind of hotel, a member of Preferred Hotels & Resorts Worldwide. Try scrumptious Sunday brunch at Morrocrofts, then work it off in the heated swimming pool or state-of-the-art health club. Then again, lounging on the patio, dancing in the fairy tale of a ballroom, or shopping at the swanky stores just behind the hotel could be more fun. ♿ (South)

## SLEEP INN
**9900 Matthews Park Dr.**
**Matthews, NC 28105**
**704/841-1660**
**$$**

Cheaper doesn't always mean "cheap." At this 80-room hotel, opened

The Park Hotel, which prides itself on being Charlotte's most expensive place to stay, has welcomed such domestic and imported politicians as Ronald Reagan, George Bush, Jimmy Carter, Gerald Ford, John Major, and Mikhail Gorbachev, as well as celebrities including the Rolling Stones, Billy Joel, Whoopi Goldberg, and Elizabeth Taylor.

in November 1997, you get plenty of amenities for a fraction of the price. Located just off Independence Boulevard, it's a straight shot to Uptown Charlotte and the heart of the city. Continental breakfast is included, and rooms are equipped with voicemail, dataport, and free HBO. Meeting space is also available at this four-story, clean, affordable hotel with an outdoor pool and a vaulted-ceiling lobby. Shopping centers with department stores, boutiques, restaurants, and movie theaters await nearby. ᕕ (South)

## SOUTHPARK SUITE HOTEL
6300 Morrison Blvd.
Charlotte, NC 28211
704/364-2400
$$$–$$$$

Stretch out and make yourself at home in 700-square-foot suites with parlor, full kitchen, separate bedroom, and a balcony overlooking the grand terraced garden courtyard and outdoor pool. This all-suite hotel across from SouthPark Mall offers apartment-style amenities in a luxurious setting. Refrigerator, stove, dishwasher, coffeemaker, toaster, iron, and ironing board are provided, along with two TVs. When you're tired of cocooning, try the café for breakfast, lunch, or dinner. There's also a full fitness facility, whirlpool, sauna, and large outdoor pool. The three-story brick hotel features 10 meeting and banquet rooms, along

with a ballroom that holds 300. For a jaw-dropping party, however, go with the open-air courtyard and its illuminated trees, poolside tables, and relaxing atmosphere. ᕕ (South)

## Bed-and-Breakfasts

### THE HOMEPLACE BED & BREAKFAST
5901 Sardis Rd.
Charlotte, NC 28270
704/365-1936
$$$

One of the first B&Bs to open in Charlotte, The Homeplace has offered solitude in city surroundings for the past 14 years. How? Situated on 2.5 acres at Sardis and Rama Roads near the SouthPark area, The Homeplace hides behind trees and sits well off the road. It was built in 1902 as a Presbyterian minister's home. Today, the innkeepers blend country and Victorian themes with quilts, lace curtains, velvet and floral furniture, folk art, and dried hydrangeas. Plan to relax when you visit; there are no phones in the rooms and few TVs. Instead, take in the gardens, porches, and gazebo (all have been photographed for several magazines and B&B guidebooks). Full breakfast; no pets and no children under 10. (South)

### THE INN ON CARMEL BED & BREAKFAST

*The centrally located
Radisson Plaza Hotel, p. 34*

**4633 Carmel Rd.
Charlotte, NC 28226
704/542-9450
$$$**

In the land of South Charlotte's stately homes, country clubs, and well-manicured lawns, The Inn on Carmel is the only B&B around. Business travelers frequent here as do relatives of neighbors. Don't expect a historic home or a Victorian or country decor, but do look for tasteful, traditional furnishings with a twist in this two-story painted-brick home that opened in October 1996. Bright raspberry walls, slate floors, a vaulted ceiling, and a winding staircase greet visitors in the foyer. Guests curl up with a book in the cheery, comfortable Morning Room or watch TV in the Gathering Room. Four bedrooms await, one with a spectacular custom-made, iron four-poster bed and others incorporating

French pine, wicker furniture, and a Laura Ashley feel. The location is suburbia, but it's a quick drive to SouthPark and various interstates allowing easy access to the city. Full breakfast included. No pets; no children under 12. (South)

### Campgrounds

**ANDREW JACKSON STATE PARK
196 Andrew Jackson Park Rd.
Lancaster, SC 29720
803/285-3344
$**

Just 35 minutes south of Charlotte near Lancaster, South Carolina, Andrew Jackson State Park has 25 campsites within its 360-acre park. The United States' seventh president was born and raised here, and there's a bronze statue of the man known as "Old Hickory" and a museum focusing on pioneer life from 1750 to 1850. Nature trails, an 18-acre lake, picnic shelters, and an amphitheater complete the park's amenities. (See also Chapter 8, Parks, Gardens, and Recreation Areas.) Call for hours. Fee for camping and activities. Limited wheelchair access. (South)

## CENTRAL CHARLOTTE

### Hotels

**BEST WESTERN
MERCHANDISE MART
3024 E. Independence Blvd.
Charlotte, NC 28205
704/358-3755
$$**

If you're set on staying next to the Charlotte Merchandise Mart, Ovens Auditorium, or Independence Arena, try this seven-story hotel on busy East Independence. No scenery whatso-

# TRIVIA

The Park Hotel is the only Charlotte establishment to earn both AAA's Four Diamond Award and Mobil's Four-Star Award. The Hilton Charlotte and Towers in Uptown nabbed the city's second Four Diamond distinction when it was previously owned by Westin.

ever, but the location is prime if you're visiting for conventions or shows at these facilities. The Best Western attempts to spice up its surroundings with a baby grand piano and flower arrangements in the lobby, but overall, the property seems dated. The price, however, beats Uptown and farther down Independence towards Matthews. Amenities include meeting rooms, restaurant, on-the-house cocktails each night in the lounge, complimentary continental breakfast, and free parking. Look for the Best Western logo and digital clock on the top corner of the building. & (Central)

## HOLIDAY INN INDEPENDENCE
**3501 E. Independence Blvd.**
**Charlotte, NC 28205**
**704/537-1010**
**$$**

Just a few minutes outside Uptown, this Holiday Inn is located less than one-half mile from the Charlotte Merchandise Mart, Independence Arena, and Ovens Auditorium. Because of traffic on this major thoroughfare, however, walking is out of the question. This 176-room hotel, built in 1968 as a Ramada Inn, now drips with overdone Southern charm. A grand staircase, white columns, wrought-iron detail, chaises, and gilded mirrors remind visitors of Tara. Inviting pool and courtyard are behind the hotel. Restaurant serves three meals daily; bar open evenings. Five banquet rooms are also available. A bit outdated, but clean and

a good bargain compared to Uptown prices. & (Central)

## Bed-and-Breakfasts

### ELIZABETH BED & BREAKFAST
**2145 E. 5th St.**
**Charlotte, NC 28204**
**704/358-1368**
**$$$**

Elizabeth, Charlotte's second oldest suburb, is just minutes from Uptown and features many restaurants and shops that draw locals-in-the-know to their color and character. The Elizabeth B&B welcomes business and pleasure travelers to the Craftsman-style home built in 1923 and used as a rooming house for many years. You'll find simple lines, hints of Frank Lloyd Wright, and bold colors, including black, white, and red in the living room and a lavender finish outside. Three rooms with private baths and one two-room suite are available. Many B&Bs try to make guests feel at home; the Elizabeth succeeds with a collection of antique beaded handbags on the walls and old black-and-white photographs of the innkeeper's relatives. Full breakfast included. No pets; no children under 12. (Central)

### THE MOREHEAD INN
**1122 E. Morehead St.**
**Charlotte, NC 28204**
**704/376-3357; 800/MOREHEAD**
**$$$$**

Recommended by the *New York Times*,

# CENTRAL CHARLOTTE

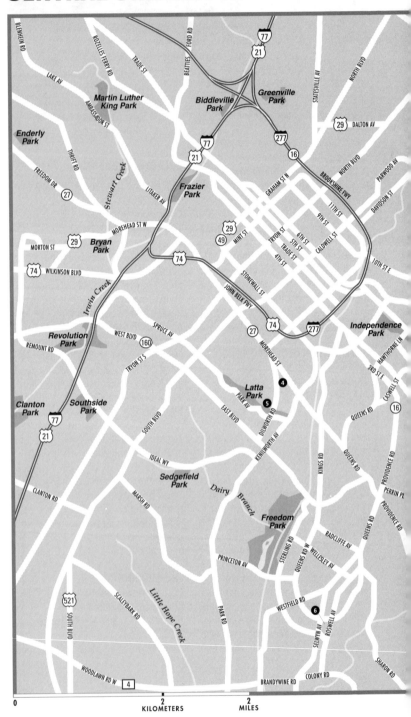

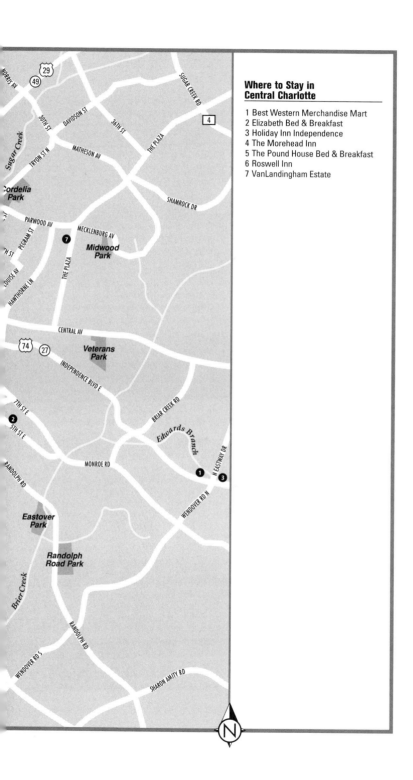

## Where to Stay in Central Charlotte

1 Best Western Merchandise Mart
2 Elizabeth Bed & Breakfast
3 Holiday Inn Independence
4 The Morehead Inn
5 The Pound House Bed & Breakfast
6 Roswell Inn
7 VanLandingham Estate

this elegant Southern estate sits minutes from Uptown Charlotte among Dilworth's tree-lined streets and sprawling historic homes. Originally built in 1917 and renovated in 1995, the Main House's first floor includes the expansive Great Room, library, dining room, and tearoom, as well as The Solarium, a beautifully furnished suite with sitting room, sunken whirlpool bath, adjoining bedroom, and private entrance. The central reading parlor, meeting room, and seven guest suites with private baths make up the second floor. Across a courtyard is the Coddington Apartment, a two-story, two-bedroom dwelling with living room, fireplace, dining room, and kitchen; as well as The Carriage House, with two additional guest suites. This luxurious boutique inn offers down comforters, terry robes, Caswell-Massey soaps, complimentary snacks, and full breakfast— a real treat. ♿ (Central)

## THE POUND HOUSE BED & BREAKFAST

**1529 Dilworth Rd.**
**Charlotte, NC 28203**
**704/343-0834**
**$$$**

A canopy of trees shades Dilworth, known for its grand, historic homes and the charm that makes Charlotte's first suburb the perfect bed-and-breakfast location. Adjacent to Uptown, Dilworth features some of the city's top restaurants, boutiques, and scenery. The Pound House, in the heart of Dilworth overlooking Latta Park, was built between 1924 and 1925 for the Pound family, and remained under their ownership until 1991. An English country–style home, the B&B was renovated in the early 1990s to a clean, simple, Arts and Crafts style with antique furniture, pottery, textiles, glass, metal, and artwork from the period. A featured stop on the Dilworth Home Tour, the B&B has two rooms with private baths and the entire bottom floor open to guests. In back, be sure to see the Japanese meditation garden with

*Experience quiet elegance at The Dunhill Hotel, p. 31.*

Hensley Fontana—The Dunhill Hotel

waterfall and koi pond. Full breakfast included. No pets; no children under 12. (Central)

**ROSWELL INN**
**2320 Roswell Ave.**
**Charlotte, NC 28207**
**704/332-4915**
**$$**

Like going home to grandma's house, this 70-year-old yellow clapboard colonial in the heart of historic Myers Park sits amid a neighborhood canopied by trees and adorned with elegant homes. Innkeeper Lea Harrison raised four children here and now rents out three of the rooms to business and pleasure travelers, wedding parties, and Charlotteans' visiting relatives. Rooms and parlors are light and airy, with hardwood floors, Oriental rugs, fireplaces, silver service, crystal vases, fresh flowers, and porcelain figurines. In spring, enjoy a patio and gardens featuring prize-winning irises, day lilies, and other blooms. Breakfast includes homemade rolls and biscuits, Harrison's favorite coffee-cake recipe, fresh fruit, orange juice, and coffee. No pets; no smoking. (Central)

### Other

**VANLANDINGHAM ESTATE**
**2010 The Plaza**
**Charlotte, NC 28205**
**704/334-8909**
**$$$$**

Built for a wealthy cotton broker and his wife in 1913, the VanLandingham Estate is an impressive, elegant inn only three miles from uptown Charlotte in the historic Plaza-Midwood neighborhood. Previous owners opened the estate to seminars, receptions and meetings; a new group who bought the VanLandingham in January 1998 has welcomed overnight guests as

well. The estate offers four guest rooms in the main house and two in the carriage house among the property's four acres of herb, evergreen, water, rock and flower gardens. Renting the entire property for a gala is also an option; catering is done in-house. ♿ (Central)

## EAST CHARLOTTE

### Hotels

**QUALITY INN AND SUITES**
**2501 Sardis Road North**
**Charlotte, NC 28227**
**704/845-2810**
**$$–$$$**

A fine choice for business and pleasure travelers looking for lodging close to Matthews and East Charlotte corporate parks. Several nice touches grace this three-story brick hotel, including landscaped areas with planted flowers and marble floors in the small lobby. The property's 100 rooms and mini-suites are newly decorated, and include coffeemaker, dataport phones, and iron and ironing board. Amenities include a hearty continental breakfast, complimentary *USA Today* newspaper and access to a fully equipped fitness center. If you tire of the hotel restaurant, Chili's Bar & Grill, Blue Marlin Seafood Kitchen, Carolina Country Barbecue, and Scoreboard Sports Restaurant are just across Sardis Road. ♿ (East)

## WEST CHARLOTTE

### Hotels

**CHARLOTTE HILTON**
**EXECUTIVE PARK**
**5624 Westpark Dr.**

# The Morehead Inn

*Now one of Charlotte's best-known and respected properties, The Morehead Inn has a long and interesting history in the Queen City. The first private home in Charlotte to have electricity, gas, and air conditioning, it was built in 1917 for Marjorie and Charles Campbell Coddington, who made a fortune as the exclusive Buick dealer in the Carolinas.*

*London architect William Peeps, who built many of the stately homes in Dilworth, designed the Coddington's home to reflect their entertaining lifestyle. The couple became social and civic players in the Charlotte community, but their lives ended tragically when both drowned in separate accidents, three years apart.*

*Known to locals as the Old Coddington House for years, the home remained a private residence until 1980. After several owners, it was converted into an urban country inn in 1984.*

*Today, the two-story white clapboard home with its green tile roof and ivy climbing the double chimneys hosts wedding recep- tions, small conferences, black-tie galas, and anyone looking for a lovely place to stay the night.*

Charlotte, NC 28217
704/527-8000
$$$–$$$$

Surrounded by office parks, this Hilton accommodates mainly corporate clients in both business and after-hours leisure. Each of the 178 rooms includes a desk, and telephones come with dataports and voicemail. In the hotel's 34 suites you'll find a separate living room with dining area, wet bar, refrigerator, coffeemaker, and two TVs. When the day is done, wind down in the lobby lounge, café, fitness center, heated swimming pool, or Jacuzzi. Dark wood, dim lighting, heavy furniture, and neutral colors give the lobby a masculine, study at- mosphere. For receptions, inquire about the courtyard with its three-tiered fountain in the center. During cold weather the courtyard is en- closed and heated. No charge for children of any age when they occupy their parents' room. ♿ (West)

**CHARLOTTE MARRIOTT EXECUTIVE PARK**
5700 Westpark Dr.
Charlotte, NC 28217
704/527-9650
$$$–$$$$

Whether you're traveling for busi- ness, pleasure, or a combination of the two, this place includes all the amenities you'll need. The 297-room hotel is a cream-colored high-rise overlooking I-77. The view isn't much, but the site does offer easy access to major thoroughfares that will zip you to various parts of the city. The marble-floored lobby leads to a bar and grill, which serves American cuisine including seafood, pasta, and steaks in addition to lunch and dinner. The Marriott also offers an indoor/outdoor pool, health club, TV lounge, ballrooms, meeting rooms, shoe-shine station, gift shop, and airport shuttle. Nonsmoking rooms are available. & (West)

### EMBASSY SUITES HOTEL
4800 S. Tryon St.
Charlotte, NC 28217
704/527-8400
$$$–$$$$

If you've ever been a guest at an Embassy Suites hotel, you most likely haven't forgotten the experience. The open atrium and plant-filled courtyard allow visitors to look from the first to the top floor. The atmosphere is calming and relaxing—despite the fact that with 274 rooms, the Embassy Suites is one of Charlotte's largest hotels. Each room is actually two: a living room and bedroom with wet bar, microwave, refrigerator, coffeemaker, two telephones, and two TVs with cable and in-room movies. Newspapers appear at your doorstep each morning, and when you arrive for the huge (and free) breakfast buffet, a chef prepares omelets, waffles, and other goodies to your liking. A complimentary manager's reception is held each evening. Amenities include room service, indoor pool, whirlpool, sauna, steam room, fitness center, free parking, and complimentary transportation to the airport and

within three miles of the hotel. & (West)

### HOLIDAY INN WOODLAWN
212 Woodlawn Rd.
Charlotte, NC 28217
704/525-8350
$$$

The third-largest hotel in Charlotte, this Holiday Inn features 425 guest rooms and meeting facilities for groups from 10 to 1,000. Scenery here is lacking, but the location is great, with easy access to I-77, Billy Graham Parkway, I-85, the airport, and both Uptown and central Charlotte. Plus, it's tucked back in a shopping center with a Krispy Kreme doughnut shop, a favorite treat of Southerners. A long list of amenities includes a full-service restaurant, lounge, gift shop, USAirways ticket office, complimentary airport transportation, secretarial and fax service, shoe-shine stand, fitness center, outdoor pool, and more than 17,000 square feet of meeting and conference space. & (West)

### SHERATON AIRPORT PLAZA HOTEL
3315 S. I-85 at Billy Graham Pkwy.
Charlotte, NC 28208
704/392-1200
$$$–$$$$

One of the only upscale, full-service hotels at the airport, the Sheraton caters to business travelers and many of the folks who arrive on some 500 flights per day. Overlooking I-85 at Billy Graham Parkway, the Sheraton is near Uptown, Ericsson Stadium, and the Charlotte Coliseum. There's not much scenery (except a blur of cars), but the Sheraton can take you away from the rat race with an indoor/outdoor pool, Jacuzzi, sauna, fitness center, Oscar's restaurant, and several ballrooms and meeting rooms. All of the 222 rooms

# Grand VanLandingham

*One of Charlotte's unique lodging sites, the VanLandingham Estate is the only intact parcel that remains from an exclusive country community known as Chatham Estates.*

*Charlotte, a farming town long ago, was approaching a crossroads with the arrival of a transportation and textile boom. Automobiles were just becoming available as an alternative to streetcars. Chatham Estates, now Plaza-Midwood, sat three miles from Uptown and offered five-acre plots to the wealthy.*

*Cotton broker Ralph VanLandingham and his socialite wife, Susie, were among the first to build in Chatham Estates upon moving here from the mountains of Linville, North Carolina, in 1913. Susie, who grew up in Atlanta, had tired of city life and insisted on country living, albeit rich country living. So Ralph used Linville limestone in the California bungalow–style home, and transplanted rhododendron, camellias, hickories, redwoods, and cedars from the mountains to Charlotte.*

*The estate was eventually willed to UNCC, which created the VanLandingham Glen using rhododendrons and other trees and plants from the grounds.*

*The stock market crash and Depression forced many of the neighborhood's wealthy homeowners to sell off parcels of land. But the VanLandingham Estate stayed intact, and remains the only surviving five-acre plot from the days of Chatham Estates.*

feature voicemail, dataports, and coffeemakers. Club-level rooms include a lounge with complimentary continental breakfast and hors d'oeuvres. ♿ (West)

**WYNDHAM GARDEN HOTEL**
**2600 Yorkmont Rd.**
**Charlotte, NC 28208**
**704/357-9100; 800/WYNDHAM**

**$$$**
Five minutes from the airport and just down the street from the Charlotte Coliseum, the Wyndham focuses mainly on corporate clients in this area peppered with business parks. The U-shaped hotel spreads its 173 rooms and suites over three floors that look out over a spacious courtyard with landscaped garden

and pool. Meeting space and board rooms aren't as palatial as the bigger hotels, but the Wyndham offers a more intimate atmosphere. After work, enjoy the indoor whirlpool, exercise room, and lounge. The café serves breakfast, lunch, and dinner; morning coffee and evening room service are also available. Complimentary airport transportation. ♿ (West)

## Bed-and-Breakfasts

### VICTORIAN VILLA
### BED & BREAKFAST INN
**10925 Windy Grove Rd.**
**Charlotte, NC 28208**
**$$$–$$$$**
Innkeepers Chan and Nancy Thompson moved a worn ranch-style home built in the early 1920s from nearby Wilkinson Boulevard to their property on Lake Wylie, then began refurbishing the home into a blue-and-white, gingerbread-trimmed Victorian. Slate and rooftop ornaments came from Charlotte churches, and much of the design was modeled after the well-known Victorians in Uptown's Fourth Ward. Three rooms and three suites are available; ask for one over the garage with slanted ceilings and a high deck overlooking the lake. Suites come with refrigerators, wet bars, stereos, and VCRs. Guests will also enjoy the outdoor pool, fishing dock, and a full breakfast in a room with a wall of windows facing the water. Other details are a gazebo, glassed-in meeting room, and period antiques. Two-night minimums on weekends. No children under 12. (West)

## Extended-Stay

### CANDLEWOOD HOTEL
**5840 Westpark Dr.**
**Charlotte, NC 28217**
**800/946-6200**
**$$–$$$**
Business travelers often choose extended-stay facilities such as Charlotte's new Candlewood Hotel. The 81-suite Westpark Drive location opened in 1997; a 122-suite University area Candlewood debuts in 1998. Westpark Drive isn't big on scenery—I-77, office parks, and a strip of hotels surrounded by one of Charlotte's most congested traffic areas. If you're looking for more of an apartment than a hotel room, Candlewood will suit your needs with fully equipped kitchens (microwave, dishwasher, stove, coffeemaker, and full-size refrigerator with ice-maker), compact disc players, 25-inch TVs with VCR, laundry facilities, fitness center, oversized desks, recliners, personalized voicemail, two-line phones, and conference capabilities. ♿ (West)

### RESIDENCE INN BY MARRIOTT
### TYVOLA EXECUTIVE PARK
**5800 Westpark Dr.**
**Charlotte, NC 28217**
**704/527-8110; 800/331-3131**
**$$$–$$$$**
Another extended-stay hotel, but in an English-Tudor cottage design with outdoor entrances offering easy access. The Executive Park location features 80 units, including 20 two-story penthouse suites. An under-construction addition will add another 30 units in a hotel-like design. Rooms have full-size kitchens, work space, multiple phone jacks, and daily housekeeping. Amenities include outdoor pool and hot tub, laundry facilities, and athletic court. The nearby full-service Marriott Hotel also offers a pool, Jacuzzi, restaurant, lounge, and weekday valet service for Residence Inn guests. Pets are welcome for an added fee. ♿ (West)

Victorian Villa Bed & Breakfast Inn

*Victorian Villa Bed & Breakfast Inn, p. 53*

**STUDIOPLUS AT CHARLOTTE—TYVOLA**
**5830 Westpark Dr.**
**Charlotte, NC 28217**
**704/527-1960**
**$$**

Business travelers abound in this area, dubbed Executive Park, and StudioPLUS is one of several hotels specializing in long-term stays. One- and two-nighters are also welcome, but you'll find most of the amenities are geared to the "suits": fully equipped kitchens with full-size refrigerators (but no dishwashers), direct-line telephones with personalized voicemail and dataport, expanded cable, work desks, weekly housekeeping, free local calls, on-site laundry, one-day dry cleaning, fitness center, outdoor pool. Some of the 71 units have large living rooms with full-size sleeper sofas. You can't bring Bowser, however; furry friends aren't welcome. ♿ (West)

**SUMMERFIELD SUITES HOTEL**
**4920 S. Tryon St.**
**Charlotte, NC 28217**
**704/525-2600**
**$$$–$$$$**

From a few nights to a few months, stays of all lengths are welcome at this extended-stay, all-suite hotel at Billy Graham Parkway near I-77 and I-85, the airport, and the Charlotte Coliseum. One- and two-bedroom suites are available, all with spacious living rooms, two TVs, VCRs, fully equipped kitchens, and separate phone lines with voicemail. Enjoy complimentary breakfast buffet daily in the den-like lobby with working fireplaces and comfortable sitting areas. Weekday social hours are also free for guests. Additional amenities include a 24-hour on-site convenience store, guest laundry, outdoor pool, sport court, heated whirlpool spa, and exercise room. Courtesy airport transportation. ♿ (West)

### *Campgrounds*

**CROWDERS MOUNTAIN STATE PARK**
**522 Park Office Lane**

**Kings Mountain, NC 28086**
**704/853-5375**
**$**

Serious, experienced campers head to Crowders Mountain State Park 35 minutes west of Charlotte for its primitive, pack-in camping. Recreation at the nearly 3,000-acre park includes rock climbing, hiking two large peaks, 15 miles of trails connecting the two outcrops, fishing, canoeing, and a wide range of nature programs. (See also Chapter 8, Parks, Gardens, and Recreation Areas.) Call for hours. Fees for shelters, canoes, and camping. Limited wheelchair access. (West)

**KINGS MOUNTAIN STATE PARK**
**1277 Park Rd.**
**Blacksburg, SC 29702**
**803/222-3209**
**$**

Just over the South Carolina state line, 45 minutes west of Charlotte, this site includes 119 campsites with electric and water hookups and two dump stations. A trading post sells provisions at the 6,832-acre park, and recreation includes swimming, fishing, boat rentals, miniature golf, a 17-mile hiking trail, scenic drive, picnic shelter, and Living History Farm. (See also Chapter 8, Parks, Gardens, and Recreation Areas.) Call for hours. Admission: Memorial Day–Labor Day, $2 per vehicle; other times free. Fee for activities. (West)

**MCDOWELL NATURE PRESERVE CAMPGROUND**
**15222 York Rd.**
**Charlotte, NC 28217**
**803/831-2285**
**$**

Mecklenburg County Park & Recreation and Crowders Creek Outdoors operate this park on Lake Wylie, which borders North and South Carolina to the west of Charlotte. With more than 900 acres of rolling woods, the park is still just 15 minutes from the city and a favorite retreat of nature-lovers. Overnight camping is available in 88 campsites, including rented 12-by-12

# Ten Largest Hotels in the Charlotte Area

1. Adam's Mark, 613 rooms
2. Charlotte Marriott City Center, 434 rooms
3. Holiday Inn Woodlawn, 425 rooms
4. The Hilton Charlotte and Towers, 407 rooms
5. Charlotte Hilton at University Place, 393 rooms
6. Radisson Plaza Hotel Charlotte, 366 rooms
7. Holiday Inn Center City, 300 rooms
8. Charlotte Marriott Executive Park, 297 rooms
9. Embassy Suites Hotel, 274 rooms
10. Hyatt Charlotte, 262 rooms

Source: Charlotte Convention & Visitors Bureau

platform tents, RV parking spots, and tent camping in a drive-up gravel site or primitive walk-in site. Amenities include rest rooms, showers, dump site, and public phone. Activities are planned, and there is a playground, horseshoes, boating, fishing, hiking, and a nature center. Paramount's Carowinds Theme Park and baseball at Knights Stadium are nearby. (See also Chapter 8, Parks, Gardens, and Recreation Areas.) Open for camping daily Mar 1–Nov 30; weekends only Dec–Feb. & (West)

## PARAMOUNT'S CAROWINDS THEME PARK CAMPGROUND
**I-77, Exit 90 at Carowinds Boulevard**
**Charlotte, NC 28241**
**704/588-2600; 704/587-9116**
**$**

Planning to spend your dough on the carnival games and junk food at Paramount's Carowinds? The theme park's campground is the ticket. Located in Southwest Charlotte at the border of North and South Carolina, the campground features 207 wooded sites for tents, campers, and RVs. Parents love it for the price; kids love it for the adjacent 100-acre theme and water park with wild roller coasters, shows, restaurants, water slides, and an area built just for half-pints. The campground includes water, sewer, and electricity hookups; grills; restrooms with showers; and a coin-operated laundry. The Trading Post Lodge, swimming pool, and miniature golf course are open on a limited basis. Open year-round, although water is not available at campsites in cold-weather months. Discount tickets and free transportation to park. & (West)

Cosmos Café

# 4

# WHERE TO EAT

The South is known for its slow-cooked vegetables, sugar-water tea, and stick-to-the-ribs meats and potatoes, and Charlotte doesn't disappoint when it comes to down-home cookin'.

But as the largest urban area in the Carolinas, the Queen City is also the crowning jewel of the culinary scene. You'll find dim sum carts and Dover sole, sushi and peel-and-eat shrimp, falling-off-the-platter steaks, and freshly baked focaccia. Barbecue, a longtime North Carolina favorite, comes served on paper plates or topped with cornbread and piled high in a martini glass. Hot dog stands sit near six-course, fine-dining establishments.

Always a trend-setter, Charlotte was one of the first cities to introduce pizza (hard to imagine, huh?), and today it continues to push the envelope. Uptown cafés mix New World cuisine with art galleries, martini bars, sushi stations, and a cigar lounge. We're the first in the Carolinas to have a Morton's of Chicago, Palm, and Sullivan's Steak House.

We'll eat just about anything, and a lot of it.

This chapter begins with a list of restaurants organized by the type of food offered. For details about each restaurant, see the following listings. Restaurants are organized alphabetically by geographical zone.

Price rating symbols indicate how much you can expect to pay for an appetizer, entrée, and dessert for one:

**Price rating symbols:**
| | |
|---|---|
| $ | Under $10 per person |
| $$ | $11 to $20 |
| $$$ | $21 to $30 |
| $$$$ | $31 and up |

## American

Blue Marlin (North, Central, East), p. 63

Carolina Country Barbecue (East, West) p. 85

Cino Grille (South), p. 68

Dikadee's Deli (Central), p. 77

Dilworth Diner at Wad's (Central), p. 77

Fenwick's on Providence (Central), p. 78

Fifth Street Cafe (Uptown), p. 61

Frank Manzetti's Bar & Grill (South), p. 68

Harper's Restaurant (South), p. 68

Mimosa Grill (Uptown), p. 62

Providence Bistro & Bakery (North), p. 64

Providence Café (Central), p. 82

The Roasting Company (South), p. 71

Sonoma on Providence (Central), p. 82

The Village Tavern (South), p. 71

## Asian

Baoding (Uptown, South), p. 59

Cafe Saigon (South), p. 65

Dim Sum (Central), p. 78

P.F. Chang's (South), p. 69

## Brew Pubs

Lake Norman Brewing Company (North), p. 64

Rock Bottom Brewery & Restaurant (Uptown), p. 63

Southend Brewery & Smokehouse (North, Central), p. 83

## Cajun/Creole

Bayou Kitchen (Central), p. 73

Cajun Queen (Central), p. 73

Zydeco (Central), p. 84

## Down Home

Anderson's (Central), p. 73

Gus' Sir Beef (Uptown, Central), p. 61

Price's Chicken Coop (Central), p. 82

Simmons Fourth Ward Restaurant (Uptown), p. 63

## Fine Dining

Campania (South), p. 65

The Epicurian (Central), p. 78

The Lamplighter (Central), p.79

Mangione's (Central), p. 80

McNinch House (Uptown), p. 62

Morrocrofts (South), p. 69

Palm (South), p. 70

Swing 1000 (Central), p. 84

The Townhouse (Central), p. 84

## French

La Bibliotheque (South), p. 69

Marais (Central), p. 81

## International

CiBi (Central), p. 77

Cosmos Café (Uptown), p. 61

The Pewter Rose (Central), p. 81

Porcupine Cafe (Central), p. 82

## Italian

Bertolini's (South), p. 65

Caffe 521 (Uptown), p. 59

Castaldi's Italian Bistro (North, Central), p. 76

Frankie's Italian Grille (Central), p. 79

The Open Kitchen (Central), p. 81

Villa Antonio (South), p. 71

Wolfman Pizza & Pasta (South, Central), p. 72

Zarelli (Central), p. 84

## Local Flavor

Alexander Michael's (Uptown), p. 59

Green's Lunch (Uptown), p. 61

Hotel Charlotte (South), p. 68

Mr. K's (Central), p. 81

Lupie's Cafe (Central), p. 80

Pike's Old Fashioned Soda Shop (East, Central), p. 87

Vinnie's Sardine Grill & Raw Bar (Central), p. 84

Vinnie's Southside Sardine Grill & Raw Bar (South), p. 71

### Mexican
La Paz (Central), p. 79
Ole Ole (Central), p. 81

### Sports Bars/Restaurants
Champps Americana (Central), p. 77
Jocks & Jills Sports Grill
(West), p. 87

### Steaks
Alston's (Central), p. 72
Beef N' Bottle (Central), p. 73
Morton's (Uptown), p. 62
Sullivan's (Central), p. 83

# UPTOWN CHARLOTTE

### ALEXANDER MICHAEL'S
**401 W. Ninth St., Charlotte**
**704/332-6789**
**$$**

The ambitious menu at this Fourth Ward favorite offers a wide range of fresh seafood, pastas, sandwiches, salads, and specials. Housed in a turn-of-the-century building once occupied by the Queen City's general store, the tavern-like restaurant surrounded by historic Victorian homes features wooden tables and booths with memorabilia on the walls. Try the quesadillas pan-fried with crab or Caribbean chicken, the Fourth Ward stroganoff, and the house specialty known as "What It Is." (Psst. It's blackened chicken tenders over rotini with Cajun creme sauce.) Lunch Mon–Sat; dinner nightly. Closed Sunday, Apr. 1–Labor Day. No reservations. Limited wheelchair access. (Uptown)

### BAODING UPTOWN
**227 W. Trade St. in Carillon**
**Building, Charlotte**
**704/370-6699**
**$$**

Voted Best Chinese Cuisine by *Charlotte's Best* magazine three years running, Baoding (pronounced bowding) takes its name from the Chinese town that serves as Charlotte's sister city. Baoding near SouthPark is the main restaurant; a second location operates beside Morton's of Chicago in the Carillon Building Uptown. Far from a stereotypical Chinese restaurant, Baoding features a relaxing atmosphere with sunken dining areas, skylights, high ceilings, bright surroundings, and murals depicting the Great Wall of China. Szechuan chicken, Baoding shrimp, Singaporean rice noodles, and sesame chicken are popular choices for dining in or for takeout. Fresh ingredients are key. Lunch Mon–Fri; dinner Mon–Sat. Closed Sun. Additional location: 4722 Sharon Rd. in Sharon Corners Shopping Center, Charlotte, 704/552-8899. Reservations accepted for six or more. Limited wheelchair access. (Uptown)

### CAFFE 521
**521 N. College St., Charlotte**
**704/377-9100**
**$$-$$$**

The late-night place to hang out in Uptown, a visit to Caffe 521 finds tuxedo-clad theater patrons, orchestra buffs, and the post-show performers and musicians themselves. But with paper and crayons on tables, cranked up jazz tunes, and smoking welcome everywhere, plenty of regulars show up in jeans for a late-night meal, too. The Italian menu emphasizes seafood, thin-crust pizzas, cappuccino, and decadent desserts. Favorites are calamari appetizers and chocolate pecan ecstasy, a dark chocolate cake with caramel, chocolate mousse, and pecans. Lunch

# UPTOWN CHARLOTTE

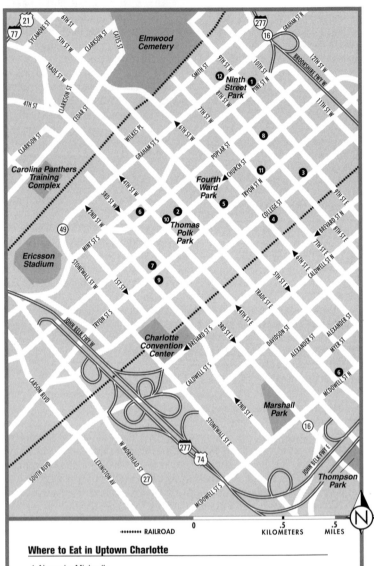

---- RAILROAD

0     .5
KILOMETERS

.5
MILES

## Where to Eat in Uptown Charlotte

1 Alexander Michael's
2 Baoding Uptown
3 Caffe 521
4 Cosmos Café
5 Fifth Street Cafe
6 Green's Lunch
7 Gus' Sir Beef Uptown
8 McNinch House
9 Mimosa Grill
10 Morton's of Chicago
11 Rock Bottom Brewery & Restaurant
12 Simmons Fourth Ward Restaurant

Mon–Fri; dinner Mon– Sun. Dinner served to 2 a.m. Fri–Sat. & (Uptown)

## COSMOS CAFÉ
**300 N. College St., Charlotte**
**704/372-3553**
**$-$$$**

A one-of-a-kind Charlotte restaurant, Cosmos Café mixes new world cuisine with a sushi station, art gallery, and martini/cigar bar. The owners of Mythos, Charlotte's most cutting-edge nightclub, opened the eclectic café next door to their Uptown club in 1997. With a wide selection of mezes and tapas plus wood-fired pizzas and pastas, the culinary influences at Cosmos are mainly Mediterranean, French, Spanish, Greek, and Italian. The Japanese-style sushi bar just makes it more interesting. Try the dim sum with lobster and fresh ginger that's delivered in a four-inch bamboo steamer; the California roll with rice, seaweed, carrots, imitation crab, and avocado; the neptune pizza with grilled shrimp, smoked mozzarella, and fresh basil on an herbed crust; or the bourbon pecan cheesecake with pecan pralines. Upstairs, more than 60 types of martinis and 40 kinds of stogies await. A funky find that draws everyone from bankers in Brooks Brothers to starving artists with pierced noses. Lunch, dinner daily. Reservations accepted for 20 or more. & (Uptown)

## FIFTH STREET CAFE
**118 W. Fifth St., Charlotte**
**704/358-8334**
**$$**

Located in one of the few remaining historic buildings in Uptown Charlotte, this former handkerchief factory packs in the work crowd at lunch and the pre-theater group at dinner with a hearty helping of regulars throughout.

Exposed brick walls and an open atrium are highlighted with local art. The menu offers a bit of everything, from fresh pasta and seafood to beef, chicken, pork, and vegetarian dishes. Try chicken ballantine, a grilled chicken dish sautéed with artichokes and mushrooms in a sun-dried tomato cream sauce, Carolina crab cakes, or grilled pork tenderloin with raspberry merlot sauce. Do not leave the premises without a sliver of the Toll House Pie. Half a block from Spirit Square and the Blumenthal for theater buffs. Lunch, dinner Mon–Sat. Closed Sun. Reservations recommended. & (Uptown)

## GREEN'S LUNCH
**309 W. Fourth St., Charlotte**
**704/332-1786**
**$**

The happening place for hot dogs, Green's Lunch has packed the house for franks smothered with secret-recipe chili since 1936. Burgers, bologna sandwiches, and healthy fare such as grilled chicken are also available, but it's the hot dogs that draw families and Uptown workers for a quick, inexpensive bite to eat. Dieters beware—breakfast includes eggs, bacon, sausage, biscuits, grits, home fries and pancakes for those who aren't cholesterol-conscious. Southern style at its best. Breakfast Mon–Fri; lunch Mon–Sat. Closed Sun. Additional location: 811 E. Trade St., Charlotte, 704/376-8954. No reservations. & (Uptown)

## GUS' SIR BEEF UPTOWN
**324 S. Tryon St., Charlotte**
**704/347-5741**
**$**

For nearly 30 years, Gus' Sir Beef has served up home-grown vegetables, stick-to-the-ribs meats, banana

**TIP**

If you enjoy the tapas, mezes, martinis, sushi, and cigars at Uptown Charlotte's Cosmos Café, step next door to Mythos for late-night dancing and people-watching. The Queen City's most cutting-edge nightclub, Mythos, and Cosmos Café share the same forward-thinking, progressive owners. Both are at the corner of College and Sixth in Uptown's Entertainment District.

pudding, and Southern-style iced tea. The original on Monroe Road still thrives, but business folks head uptown at lunch for the satellite location in Latta Arcade. Everything here is fresh; you won't find cans in the cupboard. The list of 15 available vegetables changes daily, but favorites are fried squash and spinach with rice. For hearty eaters, there's roast beef, beef tips on rice, homemade chicken and dumplings, and fried chicken. Service is fast, and the long-time waitresses are friendly. Like grandma's cooking. Lunch Mon–Fri. Closed Sat, Sun. No credit cards. Additional location: Gus' Sir Beef, 4101 Monroe Rd., Charlotte, 704/377-3210. No reservations. ♿ (Uptown)

**MCNINCH HOUSE**
**511 N. Church St., Charlotte**
**704/332-6159**
**$$$$**
If you can't close the deal here—whether it's a mega-merger or popping the question—the deal isn't workable. One of only two Charlotte restaurants to earn AAA's Four Diamond Award in 1998, the McNinch House specializes in six-course continental meals with antique china, crystal, silver, and linens in the owner's 1892 Fourth Ward Victorian home. Make a reservation (usually 10 days in advance, but up to a year for holidays), then select an entrée from a list with lamb, fowl, seafood, salmon, lobster, veal, venison,

and beef tenderloin. Chef/owner Ellen Davis takes care of the rest. Count on nearly four hours from hors d'oeuvres and wine to dessert, and around $150 per person. Dinner Tues–Sat. Reservations only. Limited wheelchair access. (Uptown)

**MIMOSA GRILL**
**327 N. Tryon St., Charlotte**
**704/343-0700**
**$$-$$$**
Global cuisine with a Southern twist. Mimosa Grill, on the bottom floor of Two First Union Center under the Charlotte Hornets mural, is an upscale casual favorite. A wall of windows overlooks the plaza, while original art, gleaming wood, and columns of rock quarried from North Carolina give the restaurant a rustic yet elegant feel. All fresh and prepared to order, dishes combine unusual elements (an Asian shrimp spring roll with Georgia peanut dipping sauce and papaya slaw) and striking presentation (pulled barbecue pork in a martini glass piled with mustard slaw and buttermilk cornbread). Seafood, chicken, steak, wood-burning pizzas, and salads are popular. Free valet parking after 5:30. Lunch, dinner daily. Sunday brunch. Call-ahead seating lunch; dinner reservations recommended. ♿ (Uptown)

**MORTON'S OF CHICAGO**
**227 W. Trade St., Charlotte**
**704/333-2602**

**$$$$**

Power dining with all the good things in life. Aged prime beef, Maine lobster, single malt scotch, cigars, and decadent desserts. Located on the ground level of the Carillon Building, Morton's creates a masculine atmosphere with high ceilings, chandeliers, crooning Sinatra, and dark, deep mahogany wood. Expect huge portions—the smallest steak is 14 ounces, the largest a whopping, fall-off-the-plate 48 ounces. Lobster, seafood, shrimp, veal, and chicken are also available. Finish (if you can) with the hot Godiva cake made with chocolate cake, Godiva liqueur, a warm gooey center, and vanilla ice cream on the side. Heaven. Free valet parking, cigar friendly, jackets suggested. Dinner nightly. Reservations recommended. ♿ (Uptown)

## ROCK BOTTOM BREWERY & RESTAURANT
**401 N. Tryon St., Charlotte**
**704/334-2739**
**$$-$$$**

Rock Bottom Brewery & Restaurant features classics with a twist on a varied menu with sandwiches and burgers, pasta, pizza, salads, and a range of entrées. Start with a Southern Flyer lager brewed in-house and the nachos, a mountain of multicolored tortilla chips piled high with refried beans, spicy cheese, jalapenos, and red onions. The gourmet grilled cheese features three cheeses, roasted red peppers and fresh vegetables on focaccia bread. Brick-oven pizzas pile on barbecue chicken, oven-roasted corn, and cheddar. Lowcountry shrimp and grits arrives with a tiny bottle of Tabasco. Finish with deep dish apple pie and roll yourself to the car. (See also Chapter 12, Nightlife.) Lunch, dinner daily. Bar

menu until last call. No reservations. ♿ (Uptown)

## SIMMONS FOURTH WARD RESTAURANT
**516 N. Graham St., Charlotte**
**704/334-6640**
**$**

For years, owner Dorothy Simmons cooked down-home meats and vegetables for her husband and son to a constant refrain of, "You can cook! You can cook! Open a restaurant." She did, and now everyone from the power suits to pro athletes chuck the calorie/cholesterol watch for her country-style meals. The menu resembles a Southern feast—meat loaf, barbecue ribs, cube steak, baked or fried chicken, smothered pork chops, and croker fish, plus 11 vegetables, macaroni and cheese, squash casserole, Southern green beans, pinto beans, rice and gravy, steamed cabbage, collards, candied yams, cole slaw, broccoli casserole, and potato salad. Peach cobbler or banana pudding finish it off. Breakfast, lunch, dinner daily. No reservations. ♿ (Uptown)

# NORTH CHARLOTTE

## BLUE MARLIN
**9321 J.W. Clay Blvd.**
**at University Place, Charlotte**
**704/510-2080**
**$$-$$$**

A "seafood kitchen" with three locations in the Queen City, Blue Marlin specializes in Lowcountry, or Charleston area, cuisine. Fried seafood platters are plentiful, but there are plenty of upscale offerings too. Try stoneground grits with creek shrimp, andouille sausage, and tasso gravy; Cajun mahi-mahi, or the Orleans, a mahi filet topped with crab meat and crawfish in a wine-butter sauce. For landlubbers, there's pasta and salad, steak and pork chops. Lunch Mon–Fri; dinner nightly. Additional locations: 1511 East Blvd., Charlotte, 704/334-3838 and 2518 Sardis Road North, 704/847-1212. No reservations. & (North)

## LAKE NORMAN BREWING COMPANY
**19707 Liverpool Parkway, Cornelius**
**704/892-5622**
**$$-$$$**

One of the few independent restaurants among the ho-hum chains at Lake Norman, this microbrewery off of Interstate 77's Exit 28 carries four standard and two dark select beers, plus seasonal brews that rotate regularly. Sandwiches range from the traditional—burgers and grilled chicken—to the more adventurous such as grilled portabello mushroom. Appetizer favorite is drunken shrimp marinated in beer and pizza with chicken and black beans. Rice, vegetables, pesto pasta salad, steak fries, and garlic mashed potatoes are also available. In the entrée section, the Brewing Company steps away from standard bar fare for aged beef, fresh salmon, roasted duck, catch of the day, and lamb chops. Live music and home of Davidson College cheering section. Lunch, dinner daily. Reservations for 25 or more. & (North)

## PROVIDENCE BISTRO & BAKERY
**8708 J.W. Clay Blvd., Charlotte**
**704/549-0050**
**$$-$$$**

Piled-high sandwiches on hearty, fresh-baked focaccia; heaping salads topped with blackened chicken, grilled salmon, and fresh fruit; thin-crust pizzas, sinful creamy pastas and interesting specialties that couple Jamaican jerk pork chops with pineapple cilantro salsa; or grilled tuna with jasmine rice cakes, Asian vegetables, and a soy pineapple vinaigrette. Providence Bistro & Bakery, which overlooks a small lake in the University Place shopping center near UNCC, is

*Swim in the seafood at Blue Marlin, p. 63.*

Photography by Gerin Choiniere

a welcome respite from the standard chains surrounding it. Live jazz Saturday nights; acoustic tunes accompany Sunday brunch on the patio. Central location is in the heart of Myers Park and a favorite among stiff competition. Lunch, dinner daily. Sunday brunch. Dinner to midnight Fri–Sat. Additional location: Providence Café, 110 Perrin Place, Charlotte, 704/376-2008. Reservations accepted for large groups. ♿ (North)

# SOUTH CHARLOTTE

## BAODING
**4722 Sharon Rd., Charlotte**
**704/552-8899**
**$$**
See listing for Baoding under Uptown Charlotte heading.

## BERTOLINI'S
**6902 Phillips Place Ct., Charlotte**
**704/553-1456**
**$$-$$$**
Traditional northern Italian with an emphasis on pasta, Bertolini's is the only Carolinas location for the 10-restaurant chain owned by Morton's of Chicago. You'll find bright colors, murals, many windows, white tablecloths with paper and crayons, and an upbeat, lively atmosphere in what is modeled after an Italian street festival. Start with the calamari appetizer served with a tangy caper and garlic tomato sauce, followed by tagliolini tossed with shrimp, scallops, and lobster. For dessert, spaghetti ice is homemade vanilla gelato sliced like spaghetti noodles, topped with strawberry sauce à la marinara, and sprinkled with white chocolate that resembles parmesan cheese. Lunch, dinner daily. Reservations accepted. ♿ (South)

## CAFE SAIGON
**7629 Pineville-Matthews Rd., Charlotte**
**704/544-7770**
**$-$$**
With English explanations on the menu, delicate flavors, and the option to order dishes mild to wild in spice, Cafe Saigon is a great place for newcomers to Vietnamese food. Owner Hien Le describes the southern Asian cuisine as a cross between Thai and Chinese. Popular dishes include rice vermicelli, thin rice noodles spiced with lettuce, basil, and mint and combined with shrimp, pork, or beef. Spring rolls with shrimp and vegetable rolls with rice paper are favorite appetizers; others opt for seafood, curry entrées, and vegetarian dishes. A cozy, neighborhood restaurant that has thrived through word-of-mouth business. Lunch, dinner daily. Reservations for five or more. ♿ (South)

## CAMPANIA
**6414 Rea Rd., Charlotte**
**704/541-8505**
**$$$$**
Voted Best New Restaurant and Best Italian Restaurant by two local magazines, Campania features authentic, romantic fine dining with a focus on southern Italy. Named for the region around Naples where chef-owner Ciro Marino's family came, the south Charlotte restaurant plays up its Mediterranean roots with tomato-based sauces, garlic, capers, and olives. "Naples was dominated by everyone from the Greeks to the Romans to the Moors and the Spanish," says Marino. "We like to think we've picked up on all the best things about those cuisines, too." Winner of Wine Spectator Award of Excellence. Nearly 80 burning candles and Italian music set the mood, too. Dinner

# GREATER CHARLOTTE

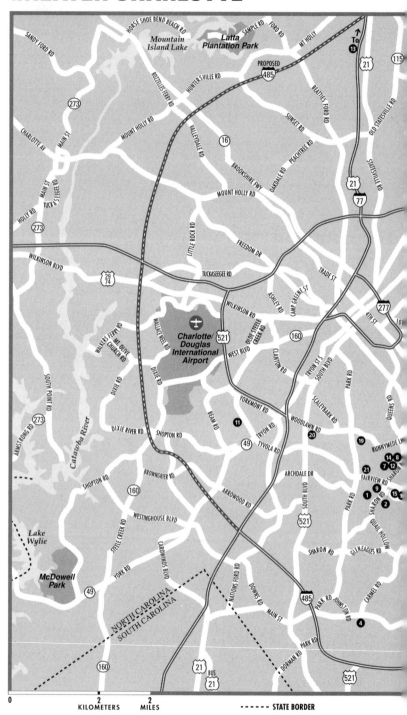

0    2    2
KILOMETERS    MILES    ------ STATE BORDER

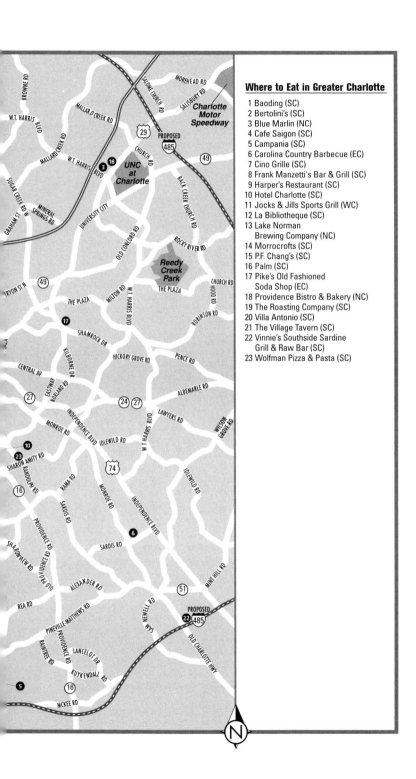

## Where to Eat in Greater Charlotte

1 Baoding (SC)
2 Bertolini's (SC)
3 Blue Marlin (NC)
4 Cafe Saigon (SC)
5 Campania (SC)
6 Carolina Country Barbecue (EC)
7 Cino Grille (SC)
8 Frank Manzetti's Bar & Grill (SC)
9 Harper's Restaurant (SC)
10 Hotel Charlotte (SC)
11 Jocks & Jills Sports Grill (WC)
12 La Bibliotheque (SC)
13 Lake Norman
   Brewing Company (NC)
14 Morrocrofts (SC)
15 P.F. Chang's (SC)
16 Palm (SC)
17 Pike's Old Fashioned
   Soda Shop (EC)
18 Providence Bistro & Bakery (NC)
19 The Roasting Company (SC)
20 Villa Antonio (SC)
21 The Village Tavern (SC)
22 Vinnie's Southside Sardine
   Grill & Raw Bar (SC)
23 Wolfman Pizza & Pasta (SC)

Mon–Sat. Closed Sunday. Reservations recommended. ♿ (South)

## CINO GRILLE
**6401 Morrison Blvd., Charlotte**
**704/365-8226**
**$$-$$$**

Many folks assume Southwestern cuisine means spicy Mexican food, but Cino Grille sets them straight. Dubbed American food just southwest of traditional, popular dishes include pan-seared tuna with smoked chili-papaya relish, avocado egg rolls with tamarind dipping sauce, and black bean and roasted corn ravioli in a red pepper creme sauce with grilled chicken. For dessert, try grilled banana bread with warm caramel, Mexican chocolate, hot banana compote, and homemade ice cream. Relaxed and warm with adobe half walls, original art, white tablecloths, and a patio, Cino Grille turns into a happening hot spot at night with martinis, cigars, and live jazz on weekends. Lunch, dinner daily. Reservations recommended Sun–Thurs. Call-ahead seating Fri–Sat. ♿ (South)

## FRANK MANZETTI'S BAR & GRILL
**6401 Morrison Blvd., Charlotte**
**704/364-9334**
**$$-$$$**

Folks flock to the hearty American fare and Pittsburgh-style steaks at Frank Manzetti's, a longtime Charlotte restaurant across from SouthPark Mall. Appetizers include wings, chili cheese fries, and the popular onion-ring loaf, while six nationalities of nachos sub for the now ubiquitous gourmet thin-crust pizzas. Try South of the Border nachos for traditional style or experiment with nachos topped with Thai chicken, fresh salmon, or creamed spinach. Steaks and chops, baby back ribs, seafood, pasta, chicken dishes, salads, burgers, and sandwiches make up the rest of the meat-focused menu. The all-American theme continues through dessert with apple pie à la mode, milkshakes, and Carnegie deli cheesecake. Lunch, dinner daily. No reservations. Call-ahead seating. ♿ (South)

## HARPER'S RESTAURANT
**6518 Fairview Rd., Charlotte**
**704/366-6688**
**$$**

A sister restaurant to Mimosa Grill Uptown, Harper's is a more casual, traditional option with California-style wood-burning pizzas and grilled items, American sandwiches, and freshly prepared salads, dressings, and desserts. There aren't any big surprises or strange combinations, so it's great for folks who want big portions of simple American food that's fresh and consistently good. Chicken, steaks, pasta, and fish round out the menu. A hot spot for Hornets players and fans after games, Harper's also features cherry wood, stone floors, exposed brick, and low lighting throughout the restaurant and separate bar area. Lunch, dinner daily. Additional location: 301 E. Woodlawn Rd., Charlotte, 704/522-8376. No reservations. Call-ahead seating. Valet parking after 5:30. ♿ (South)

## HOTEL CHARLOTTE
**705 S. Sharon Amity Rd., Charlotte**
**704/364-6955**
**$$**

It's not a hotel, but its furnishings are pieced together from the original Hotel Charlotte that bustled with business Uptown in the Queen City's early days. The bar, 130 years old, came from Atlanta in the 1930s and is lined with beers from around the world. Today,

Hotel Charlotte is a family-friendly eatery with plate glass windows across the front, a speakeasy entrance, and a menu with something for everyone. Creole and Cajun specialties are emphasized; others go for the chicken, vegetables, steak, and sandwiches. Kids menu, too. Lunch Tues–Fri; dinner Tues–Sat. Closed Sun–Mon. No reservations. & (South)

### LA BIBLIOTHEQUE
**1901 Roxborough Rd., Charlotte**
**704/365-5000**
**$$$$**

For years, La Bibliotheque was the only AAA Four Diamond award winner in the Carolinas. A few hotels and another restaurant in Charlotte have since earned the prestigious distinction, but no one locally can rival the French-American restaurant's record of six wins. Dover sole and rack of lamb are popular choices; the menu also includes Norwegian salmon, crab, shrimp, lobster, oysters, escargot, pork tenderloin, filet mignon, steak Diane, swordfish, and rib eye. "The library" in French, La Bibliotheque lives up to its name with 4,367 books dating from the 1800s to 1970s. Ceiling murals, chandeliers, mahogany wood, an old-fashioned copper cappuccino machine, and a crystal meeting room make it an impressive and unique place to dine. Lunch Mon–Fri; dinner Mon–Sat. Closed Sunday. Reservations recommended. & (South)

### MORROCROFTS
**2200 Rexford Rd. in The Park Hotel, Charlotte**
**704/364-8220**
**$$-$$$**

With heavy hitters from Michael Jordan to Mikhail Gorbachev staying at The Park Hotel, in-house restaurant Morrocrofts holds its own in the finely appointed hotel. Dark wood, classical piano, linen, fresh flowers, china, and silver set the mood, but it's not as stuffy as you might think. Servers are attentive, but not overbearing, and the mood is comfortable and relaxing in an elegant atmosphere. The continental cuisine covers seafood, chicken, fowl, steak, pasta and salads; and the lunch buffet at around $12 includes soup, salad, fresh fruit, vegetables, starches, and several entrées. Morrocrofts also boasts the best Sunday brunch in Charlotte with a huge spread, ice sculptures, a dessert table, and a beautifully presented buffet. Breakfast, lunch, dinner daily. Sunday brunch. Dinner, brunch reservations recommended. & (South)

### P.F. CHANG'S
**6809-F Phillips Place Ct., Charlotte**

Planning to subscribe to the Queen City's daily newspaper, the *Charlotte Observer*? Pay a year's subscription in advance and save 25 percent at 200 Charlotte area restaurants and nightclubs.

The "Gusto" card saves diners money at such notable eateries as Alston's, Bayou Kitchen, Pewter Rose, Fifth Street Cafe, The Townhouse, and Zydeco.

# What comes with a six-course meal?

*At the McNinch House in Uptown Charlotte, fine dining patrons begin with wine and hors d'oeuvres as they look around the downstairs of the 1892 Victorian home that chef/owner Ellen Davis spent 10 years meticulously restoring.*

*Only six tables are served each night, and dinner here typically runs between three and a half to four hours. There are no menus; diners pre-select entrées and Davis chooses the rest. Shellfish is the opening course, often times a Carolina favorite, crab cakes with mustard sauce. Soup follows, and the McNinch House makes about 30 varieties such as potato and apple bisque or shiitake mushrooms and wild rice.*

*A Victorian-style, dainty salad with a curry and pear chutney dressing is third, and sorbet to clean the palate is fourth. The main course, the entrées, comes fifth. Rack of lamb with rosemary mustard crust is the house specialty, but other popular choices are fowl, seafood, salmon, lobster, veal, venison, and beef tenderloin. Save room for the sixth course, often white chocolate mousse laced with roasted macadamia nuts and raspberry sauce. And wine? The McNinch House has 60 to 80 bottles in its cellar—also a big part of the special-occasion dinners.*

**704/552-6644**
**$$**

An upscale Chinese bistro in Charlotte's nicest shopping center, P.F. Chang's puts an American twist on culinary creations from the major regions of China. A large mural over the display kitchen is a dramatic recreation of a 12th-century narrative screen painting, while the sculptures at the restaurant's entry represent the 11th century when lions guarded royal mausoleums. Appetizers include a range of dumplings, meats, and spicy vegetables wrapped in lettuce cups. Beef, pork, chicken, and seafood entrées are available, along with salads, basic noodle dishes, and vegetarian plates. Servers are friendly and helpful with first-timers, and diners are encouraged to share with others at the table so that everyone samples a wide variety. With patrons ranging from Dennis Rodman to Jeff Gordon, you never know who you'll see. Lunch, dinner daily. No reservations. Takeout available. ♿ (South)

**PALM**
**6705-B Phillips Place Ct.,**

**Charlotte**
**704/552-7256**
**$$$$**

A coup for the Queen City, Palm adds an exclusive flavor to Charlotte's increasingly high-profile dining scene. As the 15th member of the Manhattan-based chain, the Charlotte Palm is in the smallest of the restaurants' markets but has interesting features of its own, with a cigar bar and private dining room. Known for its caricatures of celebrities, athletes, and businesspeople, Palm blends the cartoon depictions with mahogany, leather, and an attractive bar area. The menu, based in steak and lobster, also includes veal, lamb, fish, and a heavy selection of pasta. Expect huge portions. Lunch Mon–Fri; dinner nightly. Reservations recommended. ♿ (South)

**THE ROASTING COMPANY**
**1601 Montford Dr., Charlotte**
**704/521-8188**
**$**

A Boston chain made it popular, but The Roasting Company did rotisserie chicken before rotisserie chicken was cool. At this casual hangout, Costa Rican marinades spice up chicken, pork, and a wide range of vegetables, plus anything else you can think to slosh it on. Plates are heaping and cheap; the service is friendly and the atmosphere features plain wooden booths, folded paper menus, and a self-serve drink station. Pay when you order, give your first name, and the order is usually ready by the time your wallet's back in place. Lunch, dinner daily. No reservations. No credit cards. ♿ (South)

**VILLA ANTONIO**
**4707 South Blvd., Charlotte**
**704/523-1594**

**$$$**

Fine dining with a heavy dose of fun. You'll find white tablecloths, candles, and fresh flowers, but you won't have to whisper or pay attention to the proper order of forks. Most servers have worked at Villa Antonio for more than a decade and do it for a living, not between college breaks. Regulars benefit from the camaraderie, and the restaurant is known for its high level of service. Food here is northern Italian with some southern Italian dishes thrown in. Popular items are the veal shop, veal shank, and a seafood bouillabaisse with everything that swims in the sea. Desserts—canoli, tiramisu, and more than a dozen cakes and pies—are all homemade. Attire ranges from shorts and sandals to dressy. Lunch Mon–Fri; dinner nightly. Dinner reservations recommended. Dinner available to midnight nightly. ♿ (South)

**THE VILLAGE TAVERN**
**4201 Congress St. in The Rotunda, Charlotte**
**704/553-7842**
**$$-$$$**

There's something for everyone—and someone from every crowd—at this American eatery with fresh fish, steak, chicken, New York style pizza, salads, and sandwiches. Weekdays bring business diners from around SouthPark; singles congregate on Friday nights; Saturdays draw families, and church-goers stop by for Sunday brunch. Signature items include Maryland-style crab cakes, maple-cured pork chops, Caribbean salmon, crab dip, and hot spinach tortilla dip. Desserts range from the "World's Smallest Sundae" (a perfect, one-scoop size) to the double-decker cheesecake big enough for three. One of the best patios in town and a great place for live jazz on Thursday nights May through September. Lunch Mon–Sat; dinner nightly; Sunday brunch. No reservations. Call-ahead seating. & (South)

## VINNIE'S SOUTHSIDE SARDINE GRILL & RAW BAR
**142 E. John St., Matthews**
**704/849-0202**
**$-$$**

A raw bar that makes you feel like there's sand between your toes, Vinnie's attracts long lines with daily dollar-beer specials, live music several nights a week, and roll-up-your-sleeves buckets of oysters, clams, and shrimp. Huge orders of seafood, as well as chicken sandwiches, tuna melts, and homemade soups like shrimp bisque, gumbo, and clam chowder. Tailgate at the South End location before Panthers games, then hitch a ride on the Vinnie's shuttle. Nearly always packed. Lunch, dinner daily. Appetizers available to 11 p.m. Additional location: 1714 South Blvd., Charlotte, 704/332-0006. No reservations. & (South)

## WOLFMAN PIZZA & PASTA
**106 S. Sharon Amity Rd., Charlotte**
**704/366-3666**
**$$**

Voted Best Pizza in Charlotte each year it's been open, Wolfman introduced California-style pizza to the Queen City. Top-quality cheeses and meats plus fresh produce make the difference, along with friendly service and a laid-back atmosphere. Sausage and ground beef are seasoned and cooked in the kitchen; sauces come from original recipes; bacon is real, not bits. Create your own pizza or choose from specialties like the Shrimp & Pesto, Mykonos, New Mexico, or Roasted Veggie. Howlzones, better known as calzones, are also

The inviting Cino Grille, p. 68

available, along with wine and beer. Pasta dishes offered at some locations. Take-out and prepared, bake-at-home pizzas available. Lunch Mon–Sat; dinner nightly. Additional locations: 8318 Pineville-Matthews Rd., Charlotte, 704/543-9653; 10620 Providence Rd., Matthews, 704/845-9888; 3333 Pineville-Matthews Rd., Matthews, 704/341-8551; 2839-A Selwyn Ave., Charlotte, 704/377-4695; Cotswold Mall, 704/366-3666. No reservations. & (South)

## CENTRAL CHARLOTTE

## ALSTON'S
**1812 South Blvd., Charlotte**
**704/342-1088**
**$$$**

An independent prime steak house, Alston's serves the top 1 percent of aged, prime beef. The locally owned, cozy restaurant is modeled after Chicago and New York steakhouses, and offers a quieter, more intimate feel than some of its high-dollar chain competitors. Fresh seafood such as Maine lobster, swordfish,

The Nabatoff Group—Cino Grille

salmon, and tuna are also offered in this white-tablecloth eatery with soft lighting, but steak is the main draw. Other details that set Alston's apart—a display kitchen, original oil paintings, cigars at the bar, and a nod from *Wine Spectator* for its selection of drinks. Dinner Mon–Sat. Closed Sunday. Reservations recommended. ও (Central)

## ANDERSON'S
**1617 Elizabeth Ave., Charlotte**
**704/333-3491**
**$**
You know a restaurant is good when it's been here 52 years and brings folks from other cities. Anderson's packs them in with fresh vegetables, home-cooked meats, and the "world's best" pecan pie. Veal and chicken parmigiana, chicken-and-cheese casserole, fish, spaghetti, pizza, steaks, and fried chicken offer something for everyone, but many folks go for the vegetable plates loaded with string beans, limas, corn, broccoli, carrots, squash, and fried okra. A gallstone's throw away from Presbyterian Hospital, Anderson's is a favorite haunt of doctors and nurses, as well as the rest of Charlotte. Beer and wine, too. Breakfast, lunch Mon–Sat; dinner Mon–Fri. Closed Sun. No reservations. ও (Central)

## BAYOU KITCHEN
**1958 E. Seventh St., Charlotte**
**704/332-2256**
**$$**
An old cowboy once said, "Only a fool argues with a skunk, a mule, or the cook." You won't be complaining at this neon-lit Cajun cowboy and bayou hangout that served the Rolling Stones when they performed in Charlotte. Appetizers include alligator or crawfish boulettes, cheddar-stuffed

fried jalapenos, and catfish fingers. From the heart of Texas, try the house specialty, sliced beef barbecue-smoked over a wood fire for 18 hours. The Bayou section offers fried seafood, gumbo, creole, etouffee, jambalaya, and po' boy sandwiches. Wash it down with a cold beer and you're in business. Lunch, dinner. No reservations. ও (Central)

## BEEF N' BOTTLE
**4538 South Blvd., Charlotte**
**704/523-9977**
**$$-$$$**
Best-selling author Patricia Cornwell, a former *Charlotte Observer* reporter, spilled the beans on this insiders-only steak joint in "The Hornet's Nest." Opened in 1977, it deceives many with its plain exterior but intimate atmosphere inside. Soft lighting, candles, old woodwork, no dress codes, and crooning from the '40s, plus steak that's just as good as Morton's at a fraction of the price. Crackers and delicious cheese are complimentary; follow with a salad tray and a menu that goes beyond aged beef with frog legs, snapper, scampi, lobster, and oysters rockefeller. Don't miss the deep dish apple pie piled high with cinnamon ice cream. Dinner Mon–Sat; closed Sunday. Reservations recommended. Limited wheelchair accessibility. (Central)

## BLUE MARLIN
**1511 East Blvd., Charlotte**
**704/334-3838**
**$$**
See listing for Blue Marlin under North Charlotte heading.

## THE CAJUN QUEEN
**1800 E. Seventh St., Charlotte**
**704/377-9017**
**$$$**

# CENTRAL CHARLOTTE

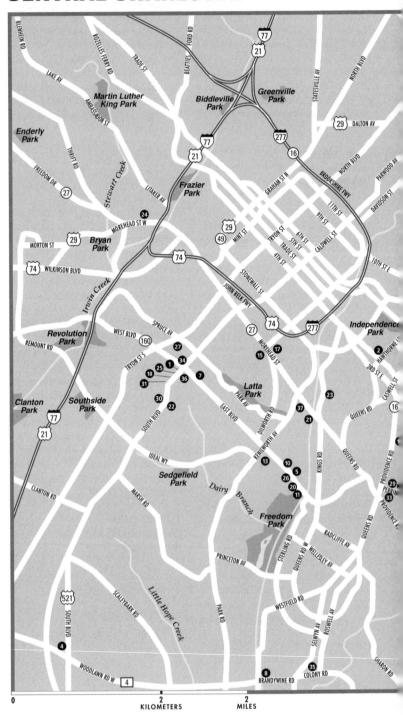

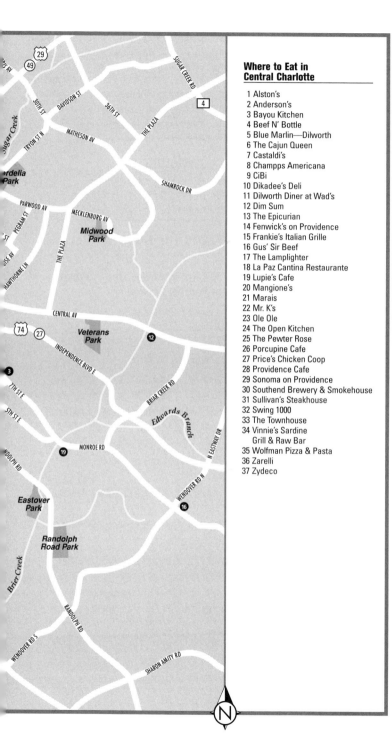

## Where to Eat in Central Charlotte

1 Alston's
2 Anderson's
3 Bayou Kitchen
4 Beef N' Bottle
5 Blue Marlin—Dilworth
6 The Cajun Queen
7 Castaldi's
8 Champps Americana
9 CiBi
10 Dikadee's Deli
11 Dilworth Diner at Wad's
12 Dim Sum
13 The Epicurian
14 Fenwick's on Providence
15 Frankie's Italian Grille
16 Gus' Sir Beef
17 The Lamplighter
18 La Paz Cantina Restaurante
19 Lupie's Cafe
20 Mangione's
21 Marais
22 Mr. K's
23 Ole Ole
24 The Open Kitchen
25 The Pewter Rose
26 Porcupine Cafe
27 Price's Chicken Coop
28 Providence Cafe
29 Sonoma on Providence
30 Southend Brewery & Smokehouse
31 Sullivan's Steakhouse
32 Swing 1000
33 The Townhouse
34 Vinnie's Sardine
   Grill & Raw Bar
35 Wolfman Pizza & Pasta
36 Zarelli
37 Zydeco

A mile from uptown in the history-filled Elizabeth neighborhood, The Cajun Queen is a longtime favorite for Charlotteans celebrating a special occasion. A Dixieland jazz band plays live nightly and sets a festive and fun, yet casual atmosphere throughout the two-story home originally built in the early 1900s. Decor is New Orleans all the way with Mardi Gras beads on tables, walls in purple and mustard yellow, and murals with silhouettes of dancers, musicians, and waiters.

Relax with a glass of wine on the patio, then dine on fresh fish or authentic Cajun dishes such as gumbo, jambalaya, and étouffée. Friendly wait staff is glad to help those uninitiated in Cajun fare. Dinner only. Reservations recommended Sun–Thurs; no reservations Fri–Sat. Limited wheelchair accessibility. (Central)

**CASTALDI'S**
**311 East Blvd., Charlotte**
**704/333-6999**

---

## Top Ten Restaurants for Guys with Big Appetites

**By Sam Mills, former NFL Pro Bowl/Carolina Panthers linebacker and current Panthers coach**

1. Best After-Game Restaurant: Southend Brewery & Smokehouse, 2100 South Blvd., Charlotte (Central).

2. Best Down-Home Cooking: McDonalds Cafeteria, 2810 Beatties Ford Rd., Charlotte (Central)

3. Best Restaurant Off the Beaten Path: Simmons Fourth Ward Restaurant, 516 N. Graham St., Charlotte. (Uptown)

4. Best Restaurant to Take Friends: Providence Cafe, 110 Perrin Place, Charlotte. (Central)

5. Best Neighborhood Hangout: Copeland's of New Orleans, 10215 Park Rd., Charlotte (South) and University Executive Park Dr., Charlotte (North).

6. Best Sunday Brunch: Adam's Mark Hotel, 555 S. McDowell St., Charlotte (Uptown).

7. Best Special Occasion Restaurant: The Lamplighter, 1065 E. Morehead St., Charlotte (Central).

8. Best Sports Restaurant: Jocks & Jills, 4109 South Stream Blvd., Charlotte (West).

9. Best Chinese Restaurant: P.F. Chang's Chinese Bistro, 6809-F Phillips Place Court in the Phillips Place Shopping Center, Charlotte (South).

10. Best Family Restaurant: TGI Fridays, 5371 E. Independence Blvd, Charlotte (East) and 409 W. W.T. Harris Blvd., Charlotte (North).

**$$**

A small rainbow-colored neon sign lights the way to the original Castaldi's on restaurant-lined East Boulevard in central Charlotte's Dilworth. Once a boarding home where Carson Mc-Cullers wrote *The Heart Is a Lonely Hunter*, the historic house built in 1900 is now occupied by two ghosts and a poltergeist who occasionally show up at night. But not to worry, the dining experience at Castaldi's is comfortable and friendly, with huge portions, vividly painted walls, and a beautiful back patio built around 120-year-old trees, grapevines, and a water fountain. Fresh pasta, homemade sauces, bread baked on site, and mozzarella sprinkled on it all. Real-deal Italian. Lunch Mon–Fri; dinner nightly. Sunday brunch. Additional location: 9715 Sam Furr Rd. in Northcross Center, Huntersville, 704/896-0047. Reservations accepted. ఉ (Central)

## CHAMPPS AMERICANA
**1601 E. Woodlawn Rd., Charlotte**
**704/523-1443**
**$$**

Count on taking a good half-hour to read the 130-item menu at this American eatery with sandwiches, steaks, pasta, seafood, burritos, pizzas, and salads. Twenty televisions are spread throughout the three-level restaurant and outdoor patio; a group of 12 televisions forms one of the largest screens in the city. A live DJ spins tunes; and specialty nights get the crowd involved in karaoke, full-court bingo, open mike sessions, and prize giveaways. Don't miss the Messy Sundae with vanilla ice cream and caramel in a long-stem wine glass that is smothered and rolled in hot fudge. Lunch, dinner daily. Sunday brunch. Reservations accepted. ఉ (Central)

## CIBI
**1601 E. Seventh St., Charlotte**
**704/344-0844**
**$$$**

Pronounced "chee-bee," it means foods in Italian. This eclectic restaurant that blends French, Italian, and Asian cuisines is set up in a historic 1910 home in Elizabeth that was saved from the wrecking ball by preservationists. Fresh and seasonal, the menu changes every four to six weeks. Baked mussels and fresh bread are award winners; other favorites are duck, lamb, and lemon pasta with caviar and chives. The spacious old home features large fireplaces, warm colors, original light fixtures, and an Arts and Crafts decor. Dinner Tues–Sun. Closed Monday. Reservations recommended for Fri–Sat. Limited wheelchair accessibilty. (Central)

## DIKADEE'S DELI
**1419 East Blvd., Charlotte**
**704/333-3354**
**$**

A hopping deli on the main drag of Dilworth, Dikadee's is a longtime Charlotte eatery known for its great selection of sandwiches and friendly staff. Grab a table on the large patio overlooking East Boulevard and order from among 28 sandwiches on seven types of bread. Nearly a dozen salads, quiche, and Southern-style sides like potato salad, barbecue beans, and fruit round out the menu. Don't miss the huge dessert case inside with cheesecake, key lime pie, Snickers bar pie, brownies, and cookies. A popular place to play hooky and hang out on warm-weather days. Lunch Mon–Sat. Closed Sun. No reservations. ఉ (Central)

## DILWORTH DINER AT WAD'S
**1608 East Blvd., Charlotte**

**704/333-0137**

**$**

One for the money, two for the show, three to get ready . . . Cool cats who like to step back in time head to this 1950s-style diner for Coke floats, crispy fries, and thick shakes meant for two straws. Slide into a booth created from the back seats of '55 Chevys or hop up on red leather and chrome stools at the counter. Burgers, hot dogs, fried bologna, and Blue Plate specials followed by malts and homemade pies. Bring your dancing shoes; Elvis tunes and other '50s faves pour from the jukebox. Lunch, dinner. No reservations. ﴾ (Central)

## DIM SUM
**2920-B Central Ave., Charlotte**
**704/569-1128 or 704/569-1668**
**$-$$**

In ancient China, the preparation of food was an art form that catapulted chefs to high social standing and wives that couldn't cook well to the lowest rung. Meals often included 50 courses of tiny serving sizes, what is now known as dim sum or literally translated, "heart's delight." The small morsels are steamed, fried, baked, or grilled and contain a range of ingredients from duck to shrimp, pork, or eggplant. At Charlotte's Dim Sum restaurant, carts filled with the bite-sized appetizers are rolled to each table so diners can choose their favorites. Try spring rolls, fried shrimp balls, shrimp dumplings called *har gow*, pork rolls with oyster sauce, and stuffed eggplant or bean curd. Rice dishes and entrées also available. Lunch, dinner daily. Reservations accepted. ﴾ (Central)

## THE EPICURIAN
**1324 East Blvd., Charlotte**
**704/377-4529**

**$$$$**

One of Charlotte's first and longest-running fine dining establishments, The Epicurian opened in 1959 on the corner of East Boulevard and Scott Avenue in Dilworth. In mid 1998, owners began transforming the 1.1-acre property into a 30,000-square-foot, two-level shopping center to be anchored by the restaurant. Plans call for a two-level building and terrace overlooking East Boulevard. The old building will be demolished, but the Greek owners plan to keep serving the Queen City. During the holidays, Charlotteans flock to the restaurant for its incredible biscuits, and The Epicurian won't let them down even if the kitchen is on hiatus. The Epicurian hopes to reopen by fall 1999. (Central)

## FENWICK'S ON PROVIDENCE
**511 Providence Rd., Charlotte**
**704/333-2750**

**$$**

A cozy neighborhood restaurant that's often overlooked in the press,

*The large portions
at Palm, p. 70*

Palm Management Corporation

Fenwick's features steaks, seafood, sandwiches, salads, and a great dessert menu. Tight quarters find teenagers on their first date sitting beside older Myers Park regulars or single people striking up conversations over food at the bar. A simple yet varied American menu offers something for everyone, and many Fenwick customers choose the small eatery for homemade desserts before or after events at the nearby Mint Museum and Manor Theatre. The menu always includes nearly 10 desserts such as pecan cream pie, key lime pie, bread pudding, and apple crisp smothered in Haagen-Dazs. Lunch, dinner Mon–Sat. Closed Sunday. No reservations. Limited wheelchair access. (Central)

## FRANKIE'S ITALIAN GRILLE
**800 E. Morehead St., Charlotte**
**704/358-8004**
**$$-$$$**
Sinatra croons, the lights dim, and the savory smells of sauce-laden pastas float through the air at Frankie's, a large Italian restaurant with an American feel. Fresh-baked bread starts the meal, but don't indulge too much. Entrées at Frankie's are huge; mixing bowls of spaghetti and meatballs, brick-sized hunks of lasagna, and chicken parmigiana with two large breasts. Shrimp and angel hair pasta, plus thin-crust pizzas are other favorites. Plan to take home half so there's room for the equally large desserts made for sharing—try the apple pie covered in ice cream or the à la mode brownie drowning in chocolate sauce. Lunch Mon–Fri; dinner nightly. Lunch reservations for seven or more; dinner reservations any time Sun–Thurs and up to 7 p.m. Fri–Sat. Call-ahead seating Fri–Sat after 7. & (Central)

## GUS' SIR BEEF
**4101 Monroe Rd., Charlotte**
**704/377-3210**
The original with home-cooked meats, a farmer's market worth of Southern vegetables, banana pudding, and tea sweetened the Southern way. See listing for Gus' Sir Beef under Uptown Charlotte heading. Lunch, dinner Mon–Sat. Closed Sun. No credit cards. Reservations for eight or more. & (Central)

## THE LAMPLIGHTER
**1065 E. Morehead St., Charlotte**
**704/372-5343**
**$$$$**
Charlotte's favorite special-occasion restaurant for 18 years, The Lamplighter makes a meal feel like a fabulous dinner party with its romantic atmosphere in a 1923 Spanish stucco Tudor home. Original heavy wood, arched doorways, and fireplaces highlight the elegance of this Dilworth mansion, which is graced with linen tablecloths, fresh flowers, china, crystal, dim lighting, classical music, and tuxedoed servers. The French continental menu includes beef, veal, pork, seafood, and some wild game, but the signature crab cakes are known city-wide. Winner of the *Wine Spectator* Best Of Award of Excellence, The Lamplighter offers 600 varieties of wine. For dessert, try crème brulée or deep dish chocolate walnut pie topped with French vanilla ice cream. Formal but friendly, it's a favorite of prom-goers, too. Dinner nightly; reservations recommended. & (Central)

## LA PAZ CANTINA RESTAURANTE
**1916 South Blvd. in South End**
**Steelyard, Charlotte**
**704/372-4168**
**$$**

A Myers Park mainstay for 18 years, La Paz moved its tasty Tex-Mex and can't-have-just-one margaritas to trendy South End in 1998. You'll find fresh fish, shrimp, vegetarian dishes, and standard Tex-Mex fare such as quesadillas, nachos, tostados, burritos, and tacos served with Mexican rice and refried beans. La Paz uses fresh ingredients and always has a friendly atmosphere. Voted Best Margaritas in Charlotte, it's a hot spot on Margarita Monday. Try the frozen strawberry. Lunch, dinner daily. No reservations. & (Central)

## LUPIE'S CAFE
**2718 Monroe Rd., Charlotte**
**704/374-1232**
**$$**
You don't know Charlotte until you've done Lupie's, a favorite Queen City hangout that draws out-the-door crowds for stomach-rumbling chili, juicy burgers, piled-high nachos, and down-home vegetable plates. Wooden booths and barstools make for a comfortable, laid-back atmosphere highlighted by black-and-white pho-

tos of Lupie's employees past and present, neon bar signs, and quirky details like Gumby in the tip jar. Don't miss mashed potatoes on Monday (industrial size vats vanish in minutes) and chicken-and-dumplings on Thursday. Lunch, dinner Mon–Sat. Closed Sunday. No reservations. No credit cards. & (Central)

## MANGIONE'S
**1524 East Blvd., Charlotte**
**704/334-4417**
**$$$**
Despite the frequent limos parked outside, Mangione's sits somewhere comfortably between fine dining and a casual trattoria. Traditional northern and southern Italian dishes are served with a focus on fresh ingredients, locally grown produce, and homemade everything from mozzarella to desserts. The *penne salmone*, a Norwegian salmon, was voted best entrée by *Charlotte's Best* magazine. White tablecloths, candles, and fresh flowers make it look fancy, but the clientele includes everyone from bankers doing busi-

**TRIVIA**

When Italian immigrants named Pio Bozzi and John Ganzi opened the first Palm in Manhattan 72 years ago, the official issuing business licenses misunderstood their thick accent and wrote down "Palm" instead of "Parma," the region of Italy they came from and the chosen name for their new eatery.

The mistake stuck, and today Palms are in Los Angeles, Dallas, Denver, Manhattan, and other large cities around the United States.

Palm started as a spaghetti house in 1926, and during the Depression, artists from nearby King Features Syndicates drew cartoons on the walls in exchange for lunch. Caricatures of staff and regular customers followed, and now each restaurant displays the likeness of area athletes, businesspeople, and celebrities.

ness to teenagers in prom dresses. A Charlotte favorite since 1976. Lunch Mon–Fri; dinner Mon–Sat. Closed Sun. Lunch reservations for six or more. Dinner reservations recommended. ♿ (Central)

## MARAIS
### 1400 E. Morehead St., Charlotte
### 704/334-8860
### $$$

Chef/owner Ed Steedman earned the Grande Diplome from Le Cordon Bleu in Paris, and it shows. He's passionate about French cuisine and happy to share his love for Paris and its food with newcomers. A sister restaurant to Zydeco, Marais is mirrored after an authentic Parisian bistro and serves classic French meals. There's a cozy, neighborhood feel, but the menu is ambitious with 14 entrées, including pork, filet, veal chop, duck, lobster, sea bass, tuna, and salmon. The 250-bottle wine list is exclusively French, and the kitchen spends up to five minutes per plate on presentation. Textured walls, a mahogany finish, and only 55 seats give it a warm feel. Dinner Mon–Sat. Closed Sun. Reservations recommended. ♿ (Central)

## MR. K'S
### 2107 South Blvd., Charlotte
### 704/375-4318
### $

Restaurants rarely last in Charlotte if they don't measure up, so it says something that the family-owned Mr. K's has served burgers and shakes since 1967. The small restaurant is the perfect place to go after Little League games, before a Saturday night movie, or on the way home from work. Comfort food at its best, Mr. K's is best known for the Big K, its quarter-pounder with cheese grilled before your eyes. Thick-cut, homemade

onion rings, shaved ice sodas and every kind of ice cream from soft serve to sundaes round out the menu. Go once and they'll never forget your name and your favorite meal. Lunch, dinner Mon–Sat. Closed Sunday. No reservations. ♿ (Central)

## OLE OLE
### 709 S. Kings Dr., Charlotte
### 704/358-1102
### $$

A combination of Spanish, Latin American, and Mediterranean cuisine, Ole Ole serves a range of dishes including paella, filet mignon stuffed with sautéed lobster and pasta. Try traditional desserts with a twist, such as Ole Ole's special-recipe flan, a three-milk pound cake that is dipped in condensed milk and cream. White tablecloths, rich wood, and low lights dress things up, but it's a casual place at heart. A neighborhood hangout that encourages folks to stay a while, Ole Ole brings regulars from across Charlotte, not tourists expecting sombreros on the walls. Lunch Mon–Fri; dinner nightly. ♿ (Central)

## THE OPEN KITCHEN
### 1318 W. Morehead St., Charlotte
### 704/375-7449
### $-$$

A 1952 landmark where many Charlotteans discovered pizza, the Open Kitchen serves Italian cuisine in a casual atmosphere. Families appreciate the budget-minded prices and easy-to-clean, slick red gingham tablecloths. Romantics go for the low, amber-colored lighting provided by votive candles. Those in a festive frame of mind aren't disappointed either, as the Open Kitchen manages to be lively, yet laid-back. Food is real-deal Italian with scallopine, parmigiana, cacciatorre, lasagna, spaghetti, and pizza. Lunch Mon–Fri; dinner nightly. Dinner reservations recommended. & (Central)

## THE PEWTER ROSE
**1820 South Blvd., Charlotte**
**704/332-8149**
**$$$**
The Pewter Rose changes its varied ethnic menu quarterly, but you can usually count on the Chesapeake crab cakes, buttermilk trout with lemon crab sauce, duck breast, hummus platter, and smoked salmon plate. Built in an old warehouse in South End, The Pewter Rose believes in visual stimulation. Ceilings stretch 14 feet high, wood beams are exposed, support poles are wrapped in tiny white lights, and tall potted palms bring the outdoors in. A flea market mix of old lamps and wall hangings adds an eclectic element. The Pewter Rose is also known for its *Wine Spectator* award-winning wine list, relaxing patio, and funky cigar bar downstairs. A sister establishment to the cutting-edge club Tutto Mondo. Lunch, dinner daily. Reservations for six or more. (Central)

## PORCUPINE CAFE
**1520 East Blvd., Charlotte**
**704/376-4010**
**$$$**
House-cured salmon on a Yukon gold potato pancake, confit red onions, and lemon caper crème fraîche. Grilled sirloin steak with wild mushroom relish, horseradish mashed potatoes, and watercress salad. North Carolina trout wrapped in grape leaves with black currant almond couscous and a chick pea stew. With interesting combinations, Porcupine Cafe blends American food with Mediterranean influences to create its own innovative style. The

menu changes four to six times a year, but there's always a tomato basil pizza, pasta, fish, meat, and a vegetable dish. Beers and wines are American only, and breads and desserts are baked in-house daily. Try the candy plate of homemade truffles. Dinner Tues–Sat. Closed Sun–Mon. Reservations recommended Fri–Sat. & (Central)

## PRICE'S CHICKEN COOP
**1614 Camden Rd., Charlotte**
**704/333-9866**
**$**
Conductors on the Charlotte Trolley running from South End to the edge of Uptown point out Price's Chicken Coop as the best fried chicken in the city. And they may be right. A 60-year-old institution, the Coop causes lunchtime traffic jams as folks maneuver for a parking place and run inside for the take-out only fare. In the late 1930s, four brothers opened a fresh poultry market; patrons chose their live chicken, and workers returned with it plucked. The frying replaced the do-it-yourself method in 1962. Today, workers box up the fried chicken, shrimp, and fish for folks who eat it in the car and toss the bones out for the birds—the other birds. Lunch, dinner Tue–Sat. Closed Sun–Mon. Takeout only. No credit cards. Limited wheelchair accessibility. (Central)

## PROVIDENCE CAFE
**110 Perrin Place, Charlotte**
**704/376-2008**
**$$-$$$**
See listing for Providence Bistro & Bakery under North Charlotte heading.

## SONOMA ON PROVIDENCE
**801 Providence Rd., Charlotte**
**704/377-1333**

# TRIVIA

The Dilworth location of Castaldi's is known for the ghosts that haunt the former boardinghouse built in 1900. Late at night, the spirits have been known to make strange noises, send dishes flying across the kitchen, and crack a series of mirrors in the exact same spot.

As a boardinghouse, the home was also the site where Carson McCullers wrote *The Heart Is a Lonely Hunter*.

**$$$**

Winner of *Wine Spectator*'s Award of Excellence since 1994, Sonoma on Providence pays homage to its California namesake with more than 300 varieties of wine to accompany its fresh, healthy, and uniquely combined cuisine. Sonoma sets up shop in a 1920s Myers Park home with coral faux-finish walls, a lemon yellow wine bar with leather sofas, and a lovely shaded patio where patrons can eat or sip while waiting for a table. The California cuisine is multicultural, with entrées such as grilled salmon with honey barbecue glaze, sun-dried tomato couscous, *brunoise* vegetables, and carrot broth. Menu changes seasonally; desserts made in-house daily. Lunch Mon–Fri; dinner nightly. Reservations recommended. & (Central)

## SOUTHEND BREWERY & SMOKEHOUSE
**2100 South Blvd., Charlotte**
**704/358-4677**
**$$**

Some restaurants are places to see and be seen; others are frequented for their good eats. But Southend Brewery & Smokehouse can boast both. The unofficial gathering place of Carolina Panthers fans and players (a team owner also has a percentage of

the restaurant), Southend Brewery believes in big. Big tailgate parties and post-game bashes. Big glasses of handcrafted, microbrewed beers (a popular choice: Carolina Blonde Ale). And of course, big NFL-sized portions. Look for spicy sandwiches and burgers, mixing bowls of pastas tossed with seafood, thin-crust yet piled-high pizzas, and platters of nachos heaving with heaps of barbecue. Lunch and dinner daily; Sunday brunch. Additional location: Jetton Village, Jetton Road and N.C. 73 near The Peninsula in Cornelius. Live entertainment seven nights a week. Reservations accepted for groups of 10 or more. & (Central)

## SULLIVAN'S STEAKHOUSE
**1928 South Blvd., Charlotte**
**704/335-8228**
**$$$-$$$$**

Fashioned after a traditional 1940s Chicago-style steak house, Sullivan's is one of several high-profile beef houses new to the Queen City. This one is named for bare-knuckle boxing champion John L. Sullivan, whose historic photos are displayed along with a replica of his jewel-encrusted championship belt. Outside, the wraparound windows depict Sullivan and the swing musicians of his era. House specialty is the 20-ounce Kansas City strip with au gratin potatoes, but the menu also features seafood, veal, pork, lamb, and chicken entrées as well as soups and salads. Live jazz begins at 5:30 nightly. Dinner Mon–Sat. Closed Sun. Reservations recommended. ♿ (Central)

## SWING 1000
**1000 Central Ave., Charlotte**
**704/334-4443**
**$$$**
It don't mean a thing if you ain't got that swing. Charlotte's only Big Band restaurant and dance hall swings with all the fun and flavor of the '30s, '40s, and '50s. Men don coat and tie (it's required) and women dress up for a night of fine dining and dancing to Swing 1000's own eight-piece orchestra. The art deco restaurant serves three, four, and five-course meals with gourmet choices such as foie gras, as well as basics like filet mignon and grilled salmon. The house musicians are professionals who perform at the Blumenthal; count on classics by Benny Goodman, Duke Ellington, and Nat King Cole. A great place to celebrate a special occasion. Dinner Wed–Sat. Closed Sun–Tues. $10 cover charge without dinner. Reservations recommended. ♿ (Central)

## THE TOWNHOUSE
**1011 Providence Rd., Charlotte**
**704/335-1546**
**$$$-$$$$**
Paris native and chef-owner Etienne Jaulin is the man behind the gourmet French meals served at this Myers Park corner restaurant. But even though limos and Bentleys park out front, don't expect the experience to be necessarily stuffy. Jaulin, known to eat at Bojangles and shop at flea markets, has also served his fine food on cartoon character plates. The uninitiated can try the $55, five-

course chef's choice; others may opt for beef, tuna, duck breast, and more unusual combinations such as thinly sliced ostrich or elk with wild mushrooms and fried oysters. Dinner nightly. Reservations recommended. ♿ (Central)

## VINNIE'S SARDINE GRILL & RAW BAR
**1714 South Blvd., Charlotte**
**704/332-0006**
**$-$$**
See listing for Vinnie's Southside Sardine Grill & Raw Bar under South Charlotte heading.

## WOLFMAN PIZZA & PASTA
**2839-A Selwyn Ave., Charlotte**
**704/377-4695**
**$$**
See listing for Wolfman Pizza & Pasta under South Charlotte heading.

## ZARELLI
**1801 South Blvd., Charlotte**
**704/335-7200**
**$$**
Enjoy pizza, calzones, and pasta while owner Neal Zarelli, who often table hops telling jokes and visiting patrons, stands and belts out an aria. It happens all the time at this friendly neighborhood hangout that draws families, couples, and the curious hoping to hear the well-known singer who performs at Hornets and Panthers games. Zarelli was rebuilt in 1998 after a fire, and its menu was expanded to include sandwiches, four-cheese rigatoni, more salads, and seafood as well as several combination plates. Lunch, dinner Mon–Sat. Closed Sun. Reservations for six or more. ♿ (Central)

## ZYDECO
**1400 E. Morehead St., Charlotte**

Morton's of Chicago, p. 62

**704/334-0755**
**$$-$$$**

Son of a gun, we'll have some fun on the Bayou. Cajun and Creole specialties are authentic in this 50-seat, intimate eatery with a festive feel. Crawfish étouffée, gumbo, and po' boys are standard; for the more experienced, there's a spicy crawfish and corn stew over rice called crawfish *maquechaux*. Appetizers include fried alligator tails, crawfish beignets, and unusual combinations such as alligator and tasso ham spring rolls. Stucco walls are bright yellow and orange; there's a red, S-shaped bar, and punched tin reminiscent of a washboard used as accents. From the owners of the neighboring French bistro, Marais. Lunch Mon–Fri; dinner Mon–Sat; Sun brunch. Reservations for six or more. ⅛ (Central)

## EAST CHARLOTTE

**BLUE MARLIN**
**2518 Sardis Road North, Charlotte**
**704/847-1212**

**$$**

See listing for Blue Marlin under North Charlotte heading.

**CAROLINA COUNTRY BARBECUE**
**2522 N. Sardis Rd. in Crown Point**
**Shopping Center, Charlotte**
**704-847-4520**

**$**

Never tried North Carolina barbecue? It ranges by region and is best done in one-stoplight towns, but in Charlotte, Carolina Country is favored for its consistency. Take a whiff of the smoke before you open the car door, and listen for the sounds of hickory-wood flames licking the meat. Chopped pork and beef barbecue smothered in a tomato-based sauce are the norm here; order it sliced and they'll know you're an out-of-towner. Add sweet hush puppies, sugar-water tea, and you're good to go. The kind of place where the waitress calls everybody "honey" and no one seems to mind. Lunch, dinner daily. Additional location: 838 Tyvola Rd., Charlotte, 704/525-0337. No reservations. ⅛ (East)

# Top Ten Charlotte Hangouts
By John Boy and Billy of the *John Boy & Billy Big Show* on WRFX (99.7 FM)

1. **Sandwich Construction Company, 7801 University City Blvd., Charlotte, 704/597-0008.** One of America's original racing-theme restaurants and still one of the best. Check the menu for some of NASCAR's biggest names and sample some of their favorite entrées. John Boy's infamous pink tutu hangs on the wall.

2. **Press Box, 1627 Montford Dr., Charlotte, 704/523-4981.** A sports bar when sports bars weren't cool. Legendary selections include the Matheny burger and the best French Dip in town.

3. **Village Tavern, 4201 Congress St. in The Rotunda, Charlotte, 704/553-7842.** Best patio scene around and great appetizers.

4. **Longhorn Steakhouse, 700 E. Morehead St., Charlotte, 704/332-2300.** The first authentic Texas-style steakhouse in the city and a Charlotte legend.

5. **Applebee's, three Charlotte locations.** Our favorite quick, casual dining place. Great food, and the prices are surprisingly reasonable.

6. **Mr. K's, 2107 South Blvd., Charlotte, 704/375-4318.** Three words: "Big K Burger." 'Nuff said.

7. **P.F. Chang's China Bistro, 6809-F Phillips Place Ct., Charlotte, 704/552-6644.** A tad trendier than most of our other faves—but hey, it's Phillips Place so they come by it honestly. Great Oriental with a cool Southwestern twist.

8. **Athens, 101 E. Independence Blvd., Charlotte, 704/375-3597.** Breakfast anytime? Count us in! An old Charlotte landmark where you can rub elbows with Bank of America yuppies or tattooed body piercers (depending on what time you stop by). Gotta love that.

9. **The Coffee Cup Grill, 914 S. Clarkson St., Charlotte, 704/375-8855.** In the shadow of the bank towers Uptown, a real authentic Southern soul food kitchen. Highly recommended.

10. **Green's Lunch, 309 W. Fourth St., Charlotte, 704/332-1786** and 811 E. Trade St., Charlotte, 704/376-8954. In the heart of Uptown, legendary hot dogs and a pretty decent cheeseburger, too.

## PIKE'S OLD FASHIONED SODA SHOP
**2133 Shamrock Dr., Charlotte**
**704/568-1636**
**$**

More than a pharmacy-inspired soda shop, Pike's is a place to experience history and nostalgia with a marble-topped counter, drugstore stools, apothecary items, fountain Cokes, and a huge array of ice cream treats. William Joseph Pike opened the family's first pharmacy and soda shop in Concord in 1919; third-generation pharmacist Jesse Pike and his wife, Elizabeth, opened the east Charlotte pharmacy in 1982. An old-fashioned soda shop followed a few doors down, and now Charlotteans pour in for sandwiches, burgers, soup, quiche, fresh-cut and batter-dipped onion rings, scratch biscuits, and the long list of ice cream treats. Nothing over $5. Voted Best Ice Cream in Charlotte. Lunch, dinner Mon–Fri. Breakfast, lunch Sat. Closed Sun. No reservations. ⅋ (East)

## JOCKS & JILLS SPORTS GRILL
**4109 South Stream Blvd., Charlotte**
**704/423-0001**
**$$-$$$**

Voted America's #1 sports restaurant by *USA Today*, Jocks & Jills in the Queen City sits directly across from the Charlotte Coliseum. While some sports bars hang cheesy pennants and create a look that seems perfect for the worn-out leather recliner fans sit in at home, Jocks & Jills goes up-scale with framed, autographed jerseys and helmets, gleaming trophies, and encased game balls from national celebrities. You'll find hardwood floors, white columns, tasteful amounts of neon accents, and 95 televisions (even a few in the bathroom). Sit in the bistro, bar, or patio for a cold beer, manly-man seafood like oysters on the half shell or line-backer-sized entrées including pasta, meat loaf, steaks, and ribs. Lunch, dinner daily. Late-night menu. Reservations accepted. ⅋ (West)

# WEST CHARLOTTE

## CAROLINA COUNTRY BARBECUE
**838 Tyvola Rd., Charlotte**
**704/525-0337**
**$**

See listing for Carolina Country Barbecue under East Charlotte heading.

Charlotte Motor Speedway

# 5

# SIGHTS AND ATTRACTIONS

*People who say Charlotte isn't a destination city aren't looking around them. While it's true that other notable Southeast cities are known for their rich history, their size, or their locations next to rivers, mountains, or the sea, Charlotte boasts a little bit of all these things that, together, make it unique. A new city known for constructing rather than preserving, Charlotte still has an amazing number of historic homes, living-history museums, and plantations that demonstrate the pioneer way of life.*

*Charlotte is the perfect size. It's large enough to support a wide spectrum of interests, cultures, and attitudes, but not so big that the mere thought of navigating the city causes people to simply stay at home. And as for location, Charlotte sits just a few hours from both the mountains and the beach, with three major lakes in its backyard.*

*The attractions that bring people to Charlotte today show the full spectrum of its past, present, and future. A clanging trolley bell, a gold nugget the size of a melon, restored Victorian homes, Gothic churches, and backcountry farms bring long-ago Charlotte to life. Frescoes, tree-lined streets, art and science museums, family-friendly activities, and two professional sports teams draw 20th-century–focused visitors. And finally, Charlotte's future—new skyscrapers, lively restaurants, a thriving arts scene, and onward-and-upward plans—promises to continue Charlotte's distinction as a city with something for everyone.*

# UPTOWN CHARLOTTE

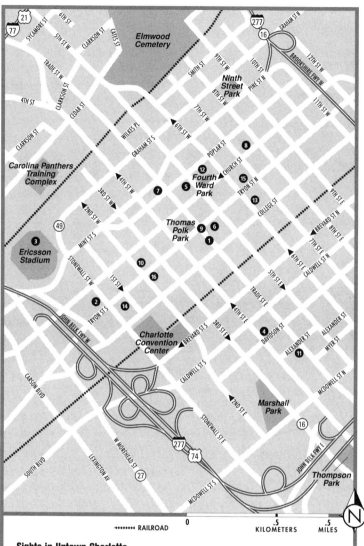

+++++++ RAILROAD

0       .5       .5

KILOMETERS    MILES

## Sights in Uptown Charlotte

1 Bank of America Corporate Center
2 The *Charlotte Observer*
3 Ericsson Stadium
4 Federal Reserve Bank
5 First Presbyterian Church
6 Founder's Hall
7 The Gallery at Carillon
8 Historic Fourth Ward
9 Independence Square
10 Latta Arcade

11 Old Mecklenburg County Courthouse
12 Old Settler's Cemetery
13 Public Library of Charlotte and
    Mecklenburg County
14 St. Peter's Catholic Church
15 Transamerica Square Building
16 Two First Union Center

# UPTOWN CHARLOTTE

## BANK OF AMERICA CORPORATE CENTER
**100 N. Tryon St.**
**Charlotte**
**704/343-2693**

The top floors of Charlotte's tallest building are no longer open to the public, but its elegant, marbled lobby and impressive artwork welcome visitors 24-7. Bank of America commissioned fresco artist Ben Long to create three related works for his first secular piece. Each measures 18 by 23 feet, and the entire project took four months for Long and his team to complete. In one panel, visitors see the construction of the corporate center; the second depicts a jostling crowd that includes a street person, priest, and toxic waste worker; the third, representing planning and knowledge, features a geometric staircase, portraits of men and women, a pyramid, a dancing girl, and a figure next to a burning tree. Many viewers try to decipher Long's message; others simply gaze at his mastery. At night, look for the city's tallest building with its illuminated "crown." Hours: Concierge on duty weekdays 8–5; lobby open 24-7. Admission: Free. & (Uptown)

## THE *CHARLOTTE OBSERVER*
**600 S. Tryon St.**
**Charlotte**
**704/358-5798**

The Carolinas' largest newspaper offers one-hour tours covering all the facets of newspaper production, from the newsroom to the printing press to the mail room, where papers are bundled and stacked on trucks for delivery. Special tours for school groups show how color is put into the newspaper, how much a typical ad costs, and how reporters work on stories. Smaller groups can see how researchers look up stories from the 1800s. In the lobby, visitors admire *The Observer*'s Pulitzer Prize display, and get a chance to compare the old (a linotype machine) with the new— four state-of-the-art presses that contain 23 computers each, print 70,000 newspapers an hour, and weigh in at 190 tons apiece. Hours: Group tours for fourth-grade to adult, Mon–Fri 9–4 by appointment. Admission: Free. & (Uptown)

## ERICSSON STADIUM
**800 S. Mint St.**
**Charlotte**
**704/358-7538**

Ericsson Stadium, home of the Carolina Panthers, has a reputation for being the most high-tech arena in the NFL, and visitors see why. One-hour tours of the $187 million facility take guests to ground-level seats, the "nosebleed section," and the sleek, sophisticated, and exclusive 50-yard-

---

## T I P

Overstreet walkways link seven of Uptown's buildings. Inspired by a system used in Minneapolis, the Overstreet allows pedestrians to avoid bad weather while also providing convenient access to restaurants and shops.

---

line lounge. Learn everything you ever wanted to know about the 73,400-seat, open-air stadium, including the number of rest rooms and TVs, the price of the most expensive luxury skyboxes, and how beer travels from tank to tap in eight miles of refrigerated beer lines. No time to tour? Check out the ferocious bronze-cast Panther statues outside—each of the seven-foot-tall, 20-foot-long, 2,800-pound cats cost $75,000. (See also Chapter 10, Sports and Recreation.) Tour hours: Tue–Thu 9, 10, 1, or 2 by reservation only; groups of 25 or more only on designated days. Admission: Under age 5 free with guardian; $2 ages 5–15, $4 adults, $3 senior citizens. $25 minimum required for tour. ♿ (Uptown)

## FEDERAL RESERVE BANK
**530 E. Trade St.**
**Charlotte**
**704/358-2500**
Visitors—and many Charlotteans—never know it, but behind the walls of this dark marble building, workers at the Federal Reserve Bank ship out $75 million daily to financial institutions in North and South Carolina. The Charlotte branch of the Federal Reserve Bank of Richmond originally opened in 1927 and grew into its present Uptown location by 1989. Visitors see check processing rooms and receiving areas where workers process the surplus currency of area banks before it is stored in a three-story vault guarded by two 15-ton doors. The Federal Reserve also inspects 4.5 million notes daily. Counterfeits are turned over to the Secret Service; worn-out bills are shredded on the spot to the tune of $17 million every day. Your souvenir is a clear bag of bills shredded like blades of grass. Hours: Prearranged group tours for high school students and

older with minimum of five people, Mon–Fri 9:30 and 1:30. Money exhibit open Mon–Fri 8:15–4:30. Admission: Free. ♿ (Uptown)

## FIRST PRESBYTERIAN CHURCH
**200 W. Trade St.**
**Charlotte**
**704/332-5123**
The first church in the city limits of Charlotte, First Presbyterian was built after town commissioners set aside a blacksmith's grove for the creation of a church and cemetery that all 300 citizens could use no matter what denomination they followed. First Presbyterian was originally known as "the brick church," and in 1857 underwent a major overhaul to its current Gothic Revival style. During the Civil War, church bells were often melted down to make guns, but Charlotteans voted to send the town bell rather than First Presbyterian's. The church bell then tolled for the town, and today it is displayed outside the sanctuary. Other interesting features of this church sitting among skyscrapers are the steeple, iron finials, Tiffany stained-glass windows, and sterling chandeliers. Tours: By appointment. Admission: Free. ♿ (Uptown)

## FOUNDER'S HALL
**100 N. Tryon St.**
**Charlotte**
**704/386-0120**
A six-story glass atrium attached to Bank of America Corporate Center, Founder's Hall is lined with unique boutiques, restaurants, and businesses catering to Uptown workers. During the holidays, Bank of America decks the hall with decorations that outshine Disney World. White lights fall from the ceiling like raindrops, a Christmas tree stretches to the stars,

and everything seems to be illuminated with holiday cheer. Arts patrons heading to shows at the North Carolina Blumenthal Performing Arts Center next door often have dinner or a glass of wine here first. It's also a good retreat from the heat in summer and a great place to find a winter garden in colder climes. (See also Chapter 9, Shopping.) Hours: Shops open Mon–Fri 10–6; Sat 10–4. Admission: Free. ♿ (Uptown)

## THE GALLERY AT CARILLON
**227 W. Trade St.**
**Charlotte**
**704/333-1296**

In a small park beside the Carillon Building and across from the lawn of First Presbyterian Church, Chicago artist Jerry Peart created a large-scale painted aluminum sculpture in bright hues to symbolize the changing seasons. *The Garden* weighs 9,000 pounds, rises 30 feet into the air, stretches 26 feet wide, and extends 22 feet deep. Constructed in 10 sections, the site-specific piece uses yellow-green for spring, brilliant blue and bright yellow for summer, and purple and Indian red for fall. Transported from Chicago to Charlotte in 10 sections loaded on three tractor-trailers, *The Garden* is Peart's 25th large-scale sculpture. (Take a peek inside the lobby of the Carillion Building while you're here. It features a 40-foot-high kinetic sculpture hovering above a black marble fountain.) Hours: Anytime. Admission: Free. ♿ (Uptown)

## HISTORIC FOURTH WARD
**Bordered by Tryon, Fifth, Graham, and Tenth Streets**
**Charlotte**
**704/331-2700**

Fourth Ward began in the mid-1800s when Uptown Charlotte was divided

*Thunder Road at Paramount's Carowinds, p. 112*

into four political areas. The Northwest quadrant, known as Fourth Ward, was the home of prosperous merchants, ministers, physicians, and others, as well as First Methodist Church, First Presbyterian Church, and St. Peter's Episcopal Church. In the early 1900s, trolley lines expanded Charlotte and Fourth Ward fell out of vogue. By 1970 many of the homes once known as "Grand Old Ladies" had been destroyed. Then the Junior League, UNCC, and several restoration pioneers stepped in to rekindle the magic of Fourth Ward. Today, the neighborhood includes vibrant Victorians, townhouses, parks, and several historic sites. Pick up a brochure from INFO! Charlotte at 330 South Tryon Street for a detailed guide through Fourth Ward. Admission: Free. ♿ (Uptown)

## INDEPENDENCE SQUARE
**Corner of Trade and Tryon Streets**
**Charlotte**

The main arteries of Uptown Charlotte meet at Trade and Tryon, known to locals as The Square. Native Americans once traded wares here while Scot-Irish settlers rolled down these paths from the Great Wagon Road in the North. In 1780, the Revolutionary War Battle of Charlotte blazed briefly in this area. Today, four Raymond Kaskey sculptures grace the square, representing industry, commerce, transportation, and vision for the future. For commerce, a 19th-century gold prospector pours his gold nuggets onto the head of a 20th-century coat-and-tie businessman. The industry statue depicts a textile worker sitting on a lightning bolt that symbolizes local power plants. Transportation is a hammer-wielding railroad worker above a locomotive headlight. For the future, a mother holds a happy infant high over her head. Each sculpture is 24 feet tall and weighs 5,000 pounds. Hours: Anytime. Admission: Free. &
(Uptown)

## LATTA ARCADE
**320 S. Tryon St.**
**Charlotte**
**704/523-0272**
You'd never know from looking at its front doors on Tryon Street, but walk inside Latta Arcade and a magical inner courtyard with an arched skylight roof, ceiling fans, old tile floors, and marble columns awaits. Entrepreneur E.D. Latta hired local architect William Peeps to build the Arcade in 1915. Prominent citizens once lived here, and skylights were used to grade cotton. The Arcade extends the length of the block; the first portion is enclosed with the skylights, the second an open-air courtyard with ornate iron gates and different storefront facades. Today the building is on the National

Register of Historic Places and was recently voted best architecture of Uptown by *Creative Loafing* magazine. Businesses include a shoe repair, barbershop, art gallery, drugstore, shoeshine station, coffeehouse, sweet shop, dry cleaner, leather shop, and various restaurants. Hours: Store hours vary; building generally open Mon–Fri 10–6. & (Uptown)

## OLD MECKLENBURG COUNTY COURTHOUSE
**700 E. Trade St. and 715**
**E. Fourth St.**
**Charlotte**
Designed by Charlotte architect Louis Asbury and built in 1928, the old Mecklenburg County Courthouse is a stark contrast to Uptown 's angled, glass-paneled skyscrapers. Now housing the Court Annex, the ornate structure is surrounded by grassy areas and flower beds, giving visitors ample opportunity to take in its Corinthian columns, detailed carvings, and heavy doors. On the Trade Street side, an obelisk erected in 1898 by the Mecklenburg Monument Association honors the signers of the Mecklenburg Declaration of Independence on May 20, 1775. A hornets' nest is carved into the stone, along with inscriptions declaring "Let Us Alone" and "When Protection Is Withdrawn, Allegiance Ceases." On the Fourth Street side, steps lead to four massive columns sitting in majestic silence. Hours: Exterior accessible anytime. Admission: Free. & (Uptown)

## OLD SETTLER'S CEMETERY
**Church and Fifth Streets**
**Charlotte**
Alexander, Davidson, Morrison, Harris, Springs. Many members of Charlotte's founding families, along with

Revolutionary War heroes, politicians, slaves, and Civil War veterans, now rest in Old Settler's Cemetery. The city's oldest public burial ground sits in the shadows of Uptown skyscrapers with more than 300 graves dating from 1776 to 1884. In recent years, vandals displaced tombstones and drifters used the graveyard for sleeping quarters. But now the Mecklenburg Historical Association is raising $250,000 to match the amount the city will provide for restoration. The project will return the cemetery to something closer to its original design and improve safety with security lighting. Hours: Anytime. Admission: Free. ♿ (Uptown)

## PUBLIC LIBRARY OF CHARLOTTE AND MECKLENBURG COUNTY
310 N. Tryon St.
Charlotte
704/336-2725
Creativity and leadership in serving the community helped the Public Library win national Library of the Year honors in 1995 from *Library Journal* magazine and Gale Research. In the Main Branch Uptown, more than 100 free programs—including films, lectures, author readings, and discussion groups—are offered monthly for adults and children. Attention to technology is apparent; the Uptown branch features a free Virtual Library with 20 computers loaded with software, CD-ROMs, and gadgets that let users compose music on the keyboard or print out customized maps. Uptown branch features include a Romare Bearden collage, the Carolina Room of local and regional history, and NOVELLO, a huge fall reading festival that draws the likes of Pat Conroy and Sue Grafton. (See also Chapter 6, Kids' Stuff.) Hours: Mon–Thu 9–9, Fri–Sat 9–6, Sun 1–6. Admission: Free. ♿ (Uptown)

## ST. PETER'S CATHOLIC CHURCH
507 S. Tryon St.
Charlotte
704/358-0050
St. Peter's, once on the edge of the city limits and now in the middle of Uptown 's building boom, is the oldest Catholic church in Charlotte and one of the oldest local churches of any denomination. Before the first cornerstone was laid in 1851, Catholics were served by missionary priests who traveled from village to village. A Confederate seal was saved from the original church, which was rebuilt in 1893 after stockpiled munitions from the Civil War were exploded nearby and damaged the foundation. Charlotte's Mercy Hospital began in the old parish house here in 1905 with 25

**TRIVIA**

Plans are in the works for the Charlotte Trolley to extend its lines throughout Uptown. Streetcar No. 85 currently runs from South End to the corner of College and Stonewall in Uptown. City officials hope to extend the current track through the Charlotte Convention Center and across Uptown to 11th Street. Additional lines would take streetcar riders to Ericsson Stadium and Fourth Ward in Uptown and as far south as Pineville.

beds and a nurses' training school. St. Peter's is also known for a three-part fresco telling the story of Easter, painted by Ben Long in 1989. Hours: Fresco viewing Mon–Sat 10–4, Sun 1–4. Services Sun 9 and 11. Admission: Free. & (Uptown)

## TRANSAMERICA SQUARE BUILDING
### 401 N. Tryon St.
### Charlotte
### 704/376-8700

The site of the latest of Ben Long's famed frescoes in Charlotte, the 10-story Transamerica Square Building features a domed lobby with a 1,047-square-foot artwork completed in early 1998. *Continuum* includes images of Bank of America CEO Hugh McColl, Jr., author Reynolds Price, musician Loonis McGlohon, and members of Long's family, along with a beach scene, tree, bridge, rockfall, and dog. The first domed fresco Long has done solo, the piece was particularly challenging because images on the top of the dome 37 feet from the lobby floor must be painted from the perspective of someone looking up. Office workers, residents of the adjacent condo building, and locals headed to Rock Bottom Brewery & Restaurant next door can often be seen craning their necks at the impressive work. Hours: Anytime. Admission: Free. & (Uptown)

## TWO FIRST UNION CENTER
### 301 S. Tryon St.
### Charlotte
### 704/383-3553

In nice weather, Uptown suits and skirts flock to the tiered patio and fountains underneath the Charlotte Hornets mural on the side of Two First Union Center. Trickling fountains with water flowing over granite surround the patio, itself dotted with huge pots

of blooming flowers, while a sculpture entitled *The Fountain* depicts children tiptoeing, splashing, and frolicking in the water. The landmark mural, now in its third version, features Hornets Anthony Mason, Vlade Divac, and Glen Rice. First Union's arched glass atrium stretches several stories and serves as a meeting place for workers and a venue for special events throughout the year. Check it out during the holidays when the atrium and patio are decorated to the hilt. Hungry? Try the Chick Fil'A kiosk, the Just Fresh bakery, or, for a sit-down, Southern-influenced gourmet meal, the Mimosa Grill. Hours: Anytime. Admission: Free. & (Uptown)

# NORTH CHARLOTTE

## CHARLOTTE MOTOR SPEEDWAY
### 5555 U.S. 29
### Harrisburg
### 704/455-3204

Ever wondered what it's like to speed around the oval track Dale Earnhardt– and Jeff Gordon–style? You won't go as fast as the NASCAR drivers, but tours of Charlotte Motor Speedway, just across the Cabarrus County line in Harrisburg, take race fans through one of the racing circuit's most respected facilities. Start at the gift shop with a 10-minute film on the speedway's history and memorable races, then hop in a 15-passenger van for a tour. Visitors hear interesting trivia and see the sprint tracks, small road courses, garage area, pit road, and winner's circle. But the real treat is riding on the 1.5-mile, 60-foot-wide track with 24-degree banks in the turns. You'll even see skid marks on the track wall, but don't worry— they didn't come from the tour van. (See also Chapter 10, Sports and

# GREATER CHARLOTTE

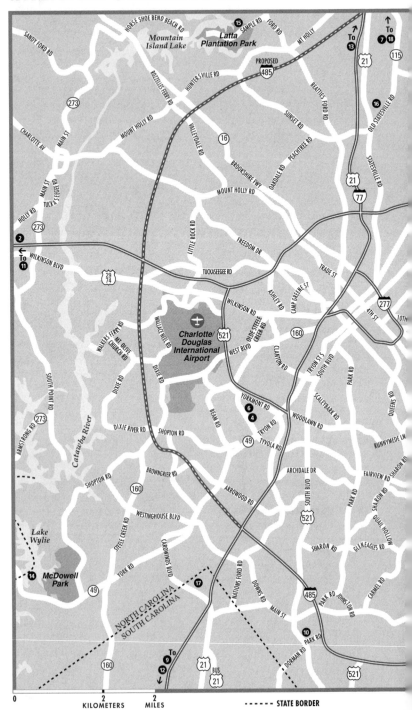

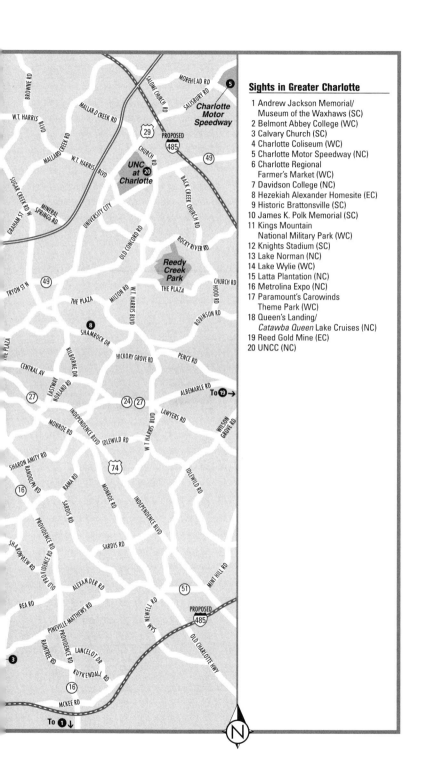

## Sights in Greater Charlotte

1 Andrew Jackson Memorial/
  Museum of the Waxhaws (SC)
2 Belmont Abbey College (WC)
3 Calvary Church (SC)
4 Charlotte Coliseum (WC)
5 Charlotte Motor Speedway (NC)
6 Charlotte Regional
  Farmer's Market (WC)
7 Davidson College (NC)
8 Hezekiah Alexander Homesite (EC)
9 Historic Brattonsville (SC)
10 James K. Polk Memorial (SC)
11 Kings Mountain
   National Military Park (WC)
12 Knights Stadium (SC)
13 Lake Norman (NC)
14 Lake Wylie (WC)
15 Latta Plantation (NC)
16 Metrolina Expo (NC)
17 Paramount's Carowinds
   Theme Park (WC)
18 Queen's Landing/
   *Catawba Queen* Lake Cruises (NC)
19 Reed Gold Mine (EC)
20 UNCC (NC)

Recreation.) Hours: Mon–Fri 9–5; during season, open weekends Sat 9–5, Sun noon–5. No tours during race weeks; groups of 10 or more should make advance reservations. Admission: $4 ages 3 and up; free under 3. Limited wheelchair access. (North)

## DAVIDSON COLLEGE
**102 N. Main St.**
**Davidson**
**704/892-2240**
Named for Revolutionary War General William Lee Davidson, this private, 1,700-student liberal arts college 20 miles north of Charlotte was founded by the Presbyterians in 1837. The 100-acre main campus features several buildings on the National Register and is designated as an arboretum, with a wide variety of tagged plant life. An antebellum quadrangle adjacent to Main Street is the heart of the historic campus. Oak and Elm Rows served as dormitories for the original 56 students, while the neoclassical, mid-1800s Eumenean and Philanthropic Halls were home to students who debated points of the day from facing balconies. The Chambers Building, the largest college structure in the South when it was built in 1860, has since been rebuilt as a massive classroom building with a beautiful dome and columns. Hours: Tours not offered; campus open to visitors. Admission: Free. ⚕ (North)

## LAKE NORMAN
**North Mecklenburg**
**Chamber & Visitors Center**
**20216 Knox Rd.**
**Cornelius**
**704/892-1922**
The largest body of fresh water in North Carolina, Lake Norman is often called an "inland sea" for its 520-mile shoreline and its surface area of more than 32,500 acres. Located 25 minutes north of Charlotte, Lake Norman was created by Duke Power in 1963 to help generate electricity. Today, Lake Norman attracts outdoor enthusiasts who like to boat, waterski, fish, and sail. Several area marinas rent pontoons, open-bow boats, ski boats, wave-runners, fishing boats, sailboats, canoes, and even a 42-foot houseboat. Want a captained cruise? Everything from a pontoon to a yacht is available. If you're content to look from the shore, try Jetton Park in Huntersville, a 105-acre facility with a beach, playground, tennis courts, walking paths, and bike trails. Ramsey Creek Park and Blythe Landing offer boat-launch ramps. (See also Chapter 8, Parks, Gardens, and Recreation Areas.) Limited wheelchair access. (North)

## LATTA PLANTATION
**5225 Sample Rd.**
**in Latta Plantation Park**
**Huntersville**
**704/875-2312**
An 1800–1837 living-history site, Historic Latta Plantation illustrates the essence of plantation life in Mecklenburg County with demonstrations in weaving, spinning, open-hearth cooking, sewing, and woodworking. The main attraction is the 1800 Federal-style dwelling house, built as part of a Catawba River plantation by merchant and planter James Latta. Visitors also see the separate kitchen, smokehouse, wash house, well house, gardens, barns, chicken coop, and log cabin. Take a guided tour with costumed docents or walk about on your own; either way, you'll leave with an appreciation of the innovative and creative ways 19th-century settlers lived and worked. Hours: Call for specific times. Admission: $4 adults, $3 students and seniors, $2 children. Limited wheelchair access. (North)

# Highland Fling

The Carolinas are rich with Scottish history and ancestors, and each April the Catawba Valley Scottish Society celebrates that heritage with the Loch Norman Highland Games.

Held 14 miles north of Charlotte, near Huntersville at the group's Rural Hill homestead, the games begin with a signal firing to call the clans. Amateur athletic competitions and children's events are held, along with bagpipe band performances, Scottish country dancing galas, a Parade of Tartans, and informal evenings of Scottish and Celtic hand-clappin', foot-stompin', sing-along entertainment.

Competitions, workshops, and demonstrations highlight Scottish heavy athletics, individual bagpipes, drums and pipe bands, dancing, Celtic harp and fiddle, wrestling, soccer, rugby, tug-of-war, kilted races, and a triathlon with battle-axe, darts, and longbow.

Tickets range from $2 for a single event to $15 for a two-day pass. For information, call 704/875-3113.

**METROLINA EXPO**
**7100 Statesville Rd.**
**Charlotte**
**704/596-4643**
Whether it's fine antiques or folk art, Majolica pottery or metal cocktail shakers from the '50s, there's something for every collector at the Metrolina Expo. Known simply as "the flea market," the Expo is held the first and third weekends of every month with additional antiques extravaganzas a few times a year that bring thousands of dealers from around the world. The first weekend show is always the biggest, but any of the flea markets here are great for cheap shopping and it-takes-all-kinds people-watching. Outdoor and indoor shopping with an-tiques, collectibles, furniture, art, home accessories, jewelry, quilts, and crafts. Hours: Fri–Sat 8–5, Sun 9–5 on first and third weekends. Admission: $2 adults, $1 seniors, children free; free parking. ♿ (North)

**QUEEN'S LANDING/*CATAWBA QUEEN* LAKE CRUISES**
**1459 River Hwy.**
**Mooresville**
**704/663-2628**
A family entertainment center on Lake Norman, Queen's Landing includes an Italian restaurant, a deli and floating dock bar, two 18-hole miniature golf courses, bumper boats, tennis courts, and souvenir and gift shops. But its main attraction is the

Latta Plantation

*Latta Plantation, p. 98*

*Catawba Queen*, a replica of a side-wheel paddle wheel Mississippi river boat. Heated and air-conditioned for year-round use, the *Queen* takes excursions on Lake Norman for sightseeing, lunch, dinner, and moonlight cruises. Private charters are also available. Call for various hours and admission prices. &. (North)

### UNCC
**9201 University City Blvd.**
**Charlotte**
**704/547-2401**
Located nine miles from Uptown, the University of North Carolina at Charlotte is a 950-acre campus with 16,000 students. Highlights include Atkins Library, the largest academic library in Charlotte; and the 200,000-square-foot Barnhardt Student Activity Center, where alumni and students gather for athletic and social events. UNCC is also well known for its botanical gardens and greenhouse, including Van-Landingham Glen, one of the leading rhododendron gardens in the South-

east; the exotic ornamental plants of Susie Harwood Garden; and the simulated rain forest and outstanding orchid collection at McMillan Greenhouse. (See also Chapter 8, Parks, Gardens, and Recreation Areas.) Hours: Campus tours offered by appointment. Outdoor gardens open to public during daylight hours. Greenhouse open weekdays 10–3. Admission: Free. &. (North)

## SOUTH CHARLOTTE

### ANDREW JACKSON MEMORIAL/ MUSEUM OF THE WAXHAWS
**NC 75**
**Waxhaw**
**704/843-1832**
One part regional history museum and one part Andrew Jackson memorial, this site 20 miles south of Charlotte is named for a Native American tribe that once populated the area. Learn about the culture of the Scot-Irish settlers who forged a new civilization in the Carolina backcountry, and see a documentation of events that took place here from 1650 to 1900. It's been a long-standing debate between North and South Carolina over exactly where the nation's seventh president was born, and this is North Carolina's tribute to Jackson. Visitors also learn about former N.C. governor William R. Davie and local crafts such as Catawba Indian pottery. *Listen and Remember*, an outdoor drama that portrays the life of early American settlers in the area, is presented each weekend in June in the museum's amphitheater. Hours: Wed– Sat 10–5, Sun 1–5. Admission: $2 adults, $1 children 7–12 and seniors, free under 6 with an adult. Limited wheelchair access. (South)

## CALVARY CHURCH
5801 Pineville-Matthews Rd.
Charlotte
704/543-1200

Sitting in a large green pasture in south Charlotte, this nondenominational church is a giant, tiara-shaped structure with pink walls and skyscraper-high glass windows across the front. The 310,000-square-foot church seats 6,000 people—4,000 in its massive sanctuary and 1,000 each in two balconies. Dedicated in December 1989, the $36 million church boasts the 13th-largest organ in the world, with five keyboards and pipes ranging from 42 feet to the size of a soda straw. Step into the beautiful marble sanctuary through one of nine entrances to see the eight floor-to-ceiling arched windows, trumpets on either side of the altar, and ceilings that soar to 80 feet. The cherry-paneled chapel seats 400, and the Word Room has a wide selection of Bibles, Christian books, recordings, and gifts. Hours: Tours available Mon–Fri 10–3, Sat 11–2 when volunteer guides are present. Visitors can see sanctuary when guides are not available. Services held Sun 8, 10:30, and 6. Admission: Free. ♿ (South)

## HISTORIC BRATTONSVILLE
1444 Brattonsville Rd.

McConnells, SC
803/684-2327

Historic homes can be found throughout the Charlotte area, but Historic Brattonsville is a complete village with 26 structures restored from the 18th and 19th centuries. Begin with the pre-Revolutionary backwoods cabin and end with the elegant Bratton Plantation Home for a look at one of the largest site restorations in the Carolinas. Located 40 miles south of Charlotte, the 25-acre York County village puts a premium on authenticity. Costumes are researched for authentic appearance and construction, down to details such as thorns used in place of buttons. Farm animals, crops, gardens, and orchards add to the living-history museum as well. Don't miss the candlelight tour, when Brattonsville is filled with the sights, sounds, and smells of an old-fashioned Christmas. Hours: First Sunday in Mar–last Saturday in Nov Tue–Sat 10–4, Sun 2–5. Admission: $5 adults, $3 students. ♿ (South)

## JAMES K. POLK MEMORIAL
NC 521
Pineville
704/889-7145

Born in 1795 on a cotton and grain farm in the hills of Mecklenburg

Crazy for coasters? If you're planning to take in the thrills and spills of Paramount's Carowinds Theme Park several times in one season, consider buying the park's season pass.

Individual passes are $79.99; family passes good for up to four family members are $209.99. Both offer unlimited visits to any North American Paramount theme park.

Season-pass holders also qualify for discounts and special offers on food and merchandise.

If you're headed to Paramount's Carowinds two days in a row, a second-day ticket is available for $11.99.

The clock tower at
Queens College, p.107

County, James K. Polk, the 11th U.S. president, spent his first 11 years here. No original buildings or articles remain from Polk's childhood, but the memorial is set up as the future president's family would have lived then. Start at the museum, which depicts Polk's family and political career, the lives of farmers in this rural area, and how the country's growth changed their world. Informative guided tours take visitors inside log buildings from the 1800s for a glimpse of how folks in the early 1800s worked, cooked, and played. Call for seasonal hours. Admission: Free. Limited wheelchair access. (South)

**KNIGHTS STADIUM**
**2280 Deerfield Dr.**
**Fort Mill, SC**
**704/36-HOMER; 803/548-8050**
Take me out to the ball game. Families, college kids, and the after-work crowd head to Knights Stadium, the 10,000-seat home of the Charlotte Knights, the top minor league farm team of the Florida Marlins. Known

locally as "the castle," Knights Stadium also includes 18 skyboxes, a full-service restaurant, two picnic areas, a playground, a miniature golf park, and a new beer garden added in 1998. For seven seasons, more than 300,000 fans have visited the stadium to watch games, test their hitting at the speed-pitch machine, and hang out with Knights mascot Homer the Dragon. Tours of Knights Stadium are also available for those who want to see the ballpark behind the scenes. (See also Chapter 10, Sports and Recreation.) Hours: Tours by request; season runs mid-April to early September. Admission: Free tours; game tickets range $5–$7. ♿ (South)

## CENTRAL CHARLOTTE

**CHARLOTTE TROLLEY**
**2104 South Blvd. at Atherton Mill**
**Charlotte**
**704/375-0850**
Step back in time to the 1930s when the neighborhoods surrounding Charlotte's Uptown were just beginning to come alive with the help of the trolley. The No. 85 streetcar, the last in its fleet to be retired, is up and running again from South End to the edge of Uptown. Folks hop inside the enclosed, heated car for a 30-minute round-trip ride full of nostalgia and local color. See the site of Charlotte's first grocery and coin laundry, the streetcar garage, factories and mills, and the place where the discovery of gold brought droves of miners long before California called. (See also Chapter 6, Kids' Stuff; and Chapter 7, Museums and Art Galleries.) Trolley hours: Fri–Sat 10–9, Sun 10–6 on hour and half-hour. Museum hours: Mon–Thu 11–2, Fri–Sun 10–6. Admission: $2 trolley round-trip; museum is free. ♿ (Central)

## HISTORIC ROSEDALE
**3427 N. Tryon St.**
**Charlotte**
**704/335-0325**

This circa-1815 plantation house now sits just three miles north of Uptown, but in its day, was out in the country along the old wagon trail that led settlers from the north and traders galore to Charlotte. Archibald Frew, a merchant, postmaster, and tax collector, built the Federal-period home that conservative locals quickly dubbed "Frew's Folly" for its outlandish appearance. While the staunch Presbyterians of the area lived in plank-and-log–style houses common to the backcountry, Frew built Rosedale in a tripartite, Palladian style with double portico, fan windows, exterior chimneys, and lemon-yellow trim on stark white paint. Today, several trees at Rosedale are documented as the largest in the county, and inside, original French wallpaper remains intact. Hours: Thu and Sun 1–4 or by scheduled appointment; closed Jan. Last tour begins at 3 p.m. (Central)

## JAMES C. DOWD HOUSE
**2216 Monument St.**
**Charlotte**
**704/398-2260**

It's a long-forgotten era in history, but in 1917, the U.S. Army created Camp Greene, a 2,000-acre site just west of Uptown that was used as a World War I military training base. As many as 6,000 soldiers at a time lived at the camp for training in trench and bayonet warfare. Fighting was still done on horseback then, and hundreds of horses were also stabled at Camp Greene. The Dowd House, a two-story Victorian built in 1879 on 250 acres of the site, served as headquarters. Originally the home of Confederate Captain James C. Dowd, the house is now furnished with 19th-century furnishings with an additional exhibit on Camp Greene's role in the economic development of Charlotte. Hours: Tours by appointment. Admission: Free. ♿ (Central)

## JOHNSON C. SMITH UNIVERSITY
**100 Beatties Ford Rd.**
**Charlotte**
**704/378-1010**

Founded in 1867 by the Catawba Presbytery, Johnson C. Smith University was originally known as Biddle Memorial Institute and later Biddle University. One of the oldest historically African American schools in the country, Smith serves 1,300 students in some 26 majors. Landmarks on the 100-acre campus include Biddle Hall, Jane M. Smith Memorial Church, and Historic Carver Hall, the original

---

# T i P

The Charlotte-Mecklenburg Historic Landmarks Commission, 2100 Randolph Rd., Charlotte, identifies and designates historic landmarks around the city and renovates and resells endangered historic properties. The group also sells a booklet with information on detailed driving tours.

For information, check local bookstores or call the commission at 704/376-9115. Open Mon–Fri 10–5 or by appointment.

# CENTRAL CHARLOTTE

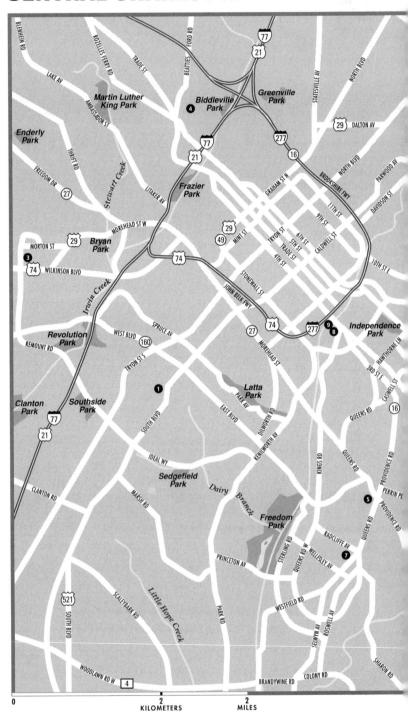

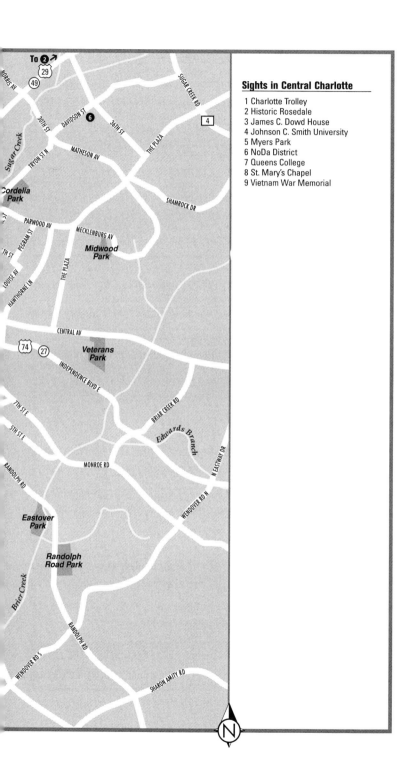

## Sights in Central Charlotte

1 Charlotte Trolley
2 Historic Rosedale
3 James C. Dowd House
4 Johnson C. Smith University
5 Myers Park
6 NoDa District
7 Queens College
8 St. Mary's Chapel
9 Vietnam War Memorial

dormitory that was reportedly built entirely by students. If you ever get a chance to see the school's energetic, funk-filled marching band perform, don't pass it up. Hours: Tours offered by appointment through the Office of Admissions. Admission: Free. &. (Central)

## MYERS PARK
**Selwyn Avenue, Providence Road, Queens Road, Queens Road West Charlotte**
Designated by the National Arbor Day Foundation as a Tree City USA

for 19 consecutive years, Charlotte is known for beautiful sweet gum trees, dogwoods, loblolly pines, redbuds, and the variety of oaks native to the area. There's no better place to see what some say are the Queen City's crowning jewels than Myers Park, one of the early suburbs of the city that is now centrally located between the historic Dilworth and Elizabeth neighborhoods. There's no set tour to follow, but the main drags of Myers Park are Selwyn Avenue, Queens Road, Queens Road West, and Providence Road with lovely, tree-shaded

---

# Medieval Merriment

*Hear ye, hear ye! Eat, drink, and be merry at The Carolina Renaissance Festival & Artisan Marketplace, a medieval celebration held 20 miles north of Charlotte over seven weekends during October and November.*

*Jousting tournaments (complete with fake blood) are held three times a day to cheering crowds, and actors dressed as kings, knights, and peasants mingle through the gallery. Street performers entertain with comedy, music, and dance, plus there's a farm-animal petting zoo, elephant rides, and face painting.*

*Games let visitors get involved in the fun themselves by shooting a bow and arrow at a target, pelting actors with tomatoes, and defending a castle with medieval weaponry.*

*As far as food goes, this festival doesn't disappoint. Think huge turkey drumsticks, desserts, and other festival fare.*

*The Carolina Renaissance Festival typically runs weekends from early October through mid-November on Poplar Tent Road, 20 miles north of Charlotte between Concord and Davidson. Admission is $10.95 adults, $4.95 children 5–12, free for kids under 5.*

*For information, call 704/896-5544.*

side streets connecting the thorough-fares. It's a place where elegant white-columned mansions with large, lush lawns sit amid Queen's College, great restaurants, and some of the city's best boutique shopping. ♿ (Central)

## NODA DISTRICT
**North Davidson Street at 35th and 36th Streets**
**Charlotte**
Dubbed NoDa for North Davidson, this mill-village-turned-bohemian-arts-community sits three miles north of Uptown. Art galleries, local watering holes, quirky shops, and a deli with live entertainment line North Davidson Street, the area's main artery. In the early 1900s, NoDa was dominated by Highland Park Mill No. 3, Charlotte's largest textile mill, the first in the state designed to run on electricity instead of steam power and, in its heyday, the country's third-largest producer of gingham. More than 1,500 mill workers lived in the surrounding village until the mill closed in 1969. Two decades later, artists began opening galleries and renovating homes in the area. Restaurants, shops, and more gal-leries followed; now NoDa is Char-lotte's hot spot for the hip, with gallery crawls, drum circles, and a lively spirit flowing through the streets. Hours: Gallery crawls held first and third Fri-day evenings monthly; galleries and shops vary with hours. Admission: Free. ♿ (Central)

## QUEENS COLLEGE
**1900 Selwyn Ave.**
**Charlotte**
**704/332-7121; 800/849-0202**
Tucked within Myers Park among some of Charlotte's most attractive homes, Queens College is a private, 1,600-student, liberal arts college af-filiated with the Presbyterian Church. Queens opened in 1857 in Uptown Charlotte as a school for girls and later became the Presbyterian Col-lege for Women. In 1912, the school moved to Myers Park and became Queens College. Highlights of the pristine, walker-friendly campus in-clude an Anna Hyatt Huntington statue of Diana near the entrance to Trexler Center (pranksters often dress Diana in everything from lin-gerie to winter coats), a 132-foot clock tower, English garden benches with history-filled plaques, and a 250,000-tile mosaic on the front of Everett Library. Hours: Tours given by appointment Mon–Fri at 9, 11, 1, and 3; Sat 9:30 and 10:30. Admission: Free. ♿ (Central)

## ST. MARY'S CHAPEL
**1129 E. Third St. at Thompson Park**
**Charlotte**
**704/333-1235**
A small brick chapel with stained-glass windows, St. Mary's is the only surviving structure of an 110-acre or-phanage that thrived in Thompson Park from 1887 to 1969. Established by the Episcopal Diocese of North Car-olina, the orphanage began with old school buildings that housed both children and staff. Over the years, dormitory-style cottages were added, along with an infirmary, superinten-dent's home, classroom building, gym, and library. Arranged in a semicircle, the orphanage built the chapel in 1892 and eventually expanded with a laun-dry, heating plant, barn, and dairy. More than 1,200 orphans called Thompson Park home over the years. The old bell that officials rang to call everyone to church or home for the evening is now displayed in the park. Hours: Fri 1–4; also available for cere-monies. Admission: Free. (Central)

## VIETNAM WAR MEMORIAL WALL
**1129 E. Third St.**
**at Thompson Park**
**Charlotte**
**704/336-4200**

One of the main attractions of this city park on the edge of Uptown and Elizabeth is the Vietnam War Memorial Wall, a curved, engraved granite wall featuring the history of the conflict and a memorial to locals who died there. Enter from Third Street, then walk among the towering oaks and flower beds as the birds' chirping overtakes the muffled sounds of traffic. The wall, dedicated in 1989, is more than a memorial. It also gives an overview of the Vietnam events that occurred under Presidents Eisenhower, Kennedy, Johnson, Nixon, and Ford. A map of Southeast Asia during the Vietnam War era adds perspective, and a list of servicemen who died in the conflict casts a reverent tone. Hours: Park open daily 6:30 a.m.–10:30 p.m. Admission: Free. ♿ (Central)

# EAST CHARLOTTE

## HEZEKIAH ALEXANDER HOMESITE
**3500 Shamrock Dr.**
**Charlotte**
**704/568-1774**

The oldest home in Mecklenburg County, this two-story rock house was built in 1774 and inhabited until the 1940s. Local chapters of the Daughters of the American Revolution stepped in to save it, and in 1970 it was designated a National Historic Property. Hezekiah Alexander was a Scot-Irish Presbyterian, planter, and justice of the peace who battled English rule of the colonies and signed the Mecklenburg Declaration of Independence in May 1775. With his wife and 10 children, he lived on 600 acres of what is now east Charlotte. Costumed docents guide visitors through the home, kitchen house, and springhouse for a look at colonial life. Heart pine floors, 18th-century furnishings, hunting rifles, a loom, cooking tools, and the home's architecture all hold clues to the settlers' way of life. Hours: Tue–Fri 10–5, Sat–Sun 2–5. Tours offered Tue–Fri 1:15 and 3:15, Sat–Sun 2:15 and 3:15. Group tours by appointment. Admission: $4. (East)

## REED GOLD MINE
**9621 Reed Mine Rd.**
**Stanfield**
**704/786-8337**

Long before California's gold-filled hills drew a rush of miners, Reed Gold Mine 25 miles east of Charlotte was the site of the first documented gold find in the United States. A former German soldier who left the British Army near the conclusion of the Revolutionary War, John Reed settled in lower Piedmont and began life as a farmer. In 1799, in a nearby creek, his son found a 17-pound yellow rock; the family used it as a doorstop for three years. A jeweler identified the rock as gold, and Reed soon started a mining operation along with many others. Today Reed Gold Mine includes tours of underground mine tunnels, gold and mining equipment exhibits, and films documenting the first gold discovery. Take a picnic, walk on trails throughout the mining area, and pan for gold yourself. Hours: Apr–Oct Mon–Sat 9–5, Sun 1–5; Nov–March Tue–Sat 10–4, Sun 1–4. Admission: Free tours; fee charged for panning Apr–Oct. Limited wheelchair access. (East)

# Top Ten Little-Known Charlotte Facts

**By Jay Rubin, owner/operator of Day Trippin'
in the Carolinas tour company**

1. Within sight of our always-changing skyline, Hollywood movie star Randolph Scott is buried.

2. Charlotte is one of the few Southern cities without a Confederate Soldier statue on its courthouse grounds. No War Between the States battles were ever fought in Charlotte.

3. Charlotte is famous for its towering native trees known as willow oaks, which line thousands of residential streets. Planting willow oaks on opposite sides of the streets gives the arched effect of Gothic church windows.

4. Charlotte has well-maintained streets, yet as recently as 1927 most city streets were paved with red clay.

5. Charlotte's Uptown has the largest collection of frescoes found anywhere in the United States.

6. Charlotte is the seat of Mecklenburg County. The city is named for the British Queen Charlotte Sophia of Mecklenburg-Strelitz, wife of King George III. Although the county is named for the German state in which she was born, no Germans founded the city.

7. Charlotte's lush fescue lawns stay green 365 days a year because the ground here doesn't freeze.

8. The frugal Presbyterians founded Charlotte on November 7, 1768. These hardy Scot-Irish fled Ulster's religious and political persecution for the 13 colonies. Back in Ulster, the Scot-Irish were never allowed to own land. This is the reason why Charlotte's old-money neighborhoods have more garden and land than oversized houses.

9. Within Charlotte, there are no buildings standing that date from the city's founding over 229 years ago. The local joke is that the average new building has a life span of 25 to 35 years because it's cheaper to bulldoze than to renovate and expand. Anything that's 50 years old in Charlotte—except people—is declared "historic," and anything 100 years old and still standing is jokingly called a "four-letter-word": rare or gone.

10. Gold was discovered under Charlotte's streets in 1800, almost 50 years before California's Gold Rush. It makes perfect sense that the city's bank skyscrapers stand where they do today: they're built on top of 54 closed gold-mine shafts.

# WEST CHARLOTTE

## BELMONT ABBEY COLLEGE
**One Abbey Place**
**Belmont**
**704/825-3711**
Founded in 1876 by Benedictine monks, Belmont Abbey College has a rich Roman Catholic heritage in an area of the South known for its abundance of Presbyterians, Baptists, and other Protestant denominations. The 600 acres that comprise this National Register of Historic Places campus were once used for farming and forestry. Today, approximately 1,000 undergrad and graduate students attend "the Abbey," which is 15 minutes from Charlotte across the Gaston County line. Landmarks include the Abbey Church, a striking German Gothic Revival cathedral erected in 1892–1893 by the monks themselves. Be sure to look at the windows: they're not stained glass; they're painted and heat-fused to allow for greater detail. Booklets available for self-guided tours at the Abbey Church. Hours: Daily 7 a.m.–7:30 p.m. Mass Mon–Fri at 5, Sat 11:30, Sun 11; vespers Mon–Sat at 7, Sun 5. Admission: Free. &. (West)

## CHARLOTTE COLISEUM
**100 Paul Buck Blvd.**
**Charlotte**
**704/357-4700**
Entertainers from circus acts to country stars perform at the Charlotte Coliseum, but most folks know it as "The Hive" because it's also home to the NBA Charlotte Hornets. The 24,000-seat arena debuted in 1988, and for several years Charlotte's loyal fans set NBA attendance records at Hornets games. Tours take visitors through the arena to the coliseum's operations areas, security stations, plush private club, visitor locker rooms, and the court. No guests enter the Hornets locker room, and tours aren't scheduled on game days when players are around. But if you get lucky, the guide may let you step onto the hardwood, take a shot, and pretend to hear the swoosh of the net and the roar of the crowd. (See also Chapter 10, Sports and Recreation.) Hours: Tours by appointment. Admission: Free. &. (West)

## CHARLOTTE REGIONAL FARMER'S MARKET
**1801 Yorkmont Rd.**
**Charlotte**
**704/357-1269**
A modern version of the roadside vegetable stand, the Charlotte Regional Farmer's Market attracts shoppers in search of fresh produce, bargain prices, and friendly barbershop banter. Like a potluck supper at a country church, this market gets Charlotteans excited—about red, juicy tomatoes the size of softballs; heaps of nearly every green vegetable God created; flower baskets bursting with the first bright spots of

*Pan for gold at Reed Gold Mine, p. 108*

Charlotte Convention and Visitors Bureau

# Rolling Out the Red for Greene

Charlotte was a city of only 40,000 people when officials recruited the federal government to create Camp Greene in the Queen City in 1917.

When Col. Leonard Wood came here to consider Charlotte as a site for Camp Greene, officials rolled out the red carpet at what are still some of the city's most impressive sites today.

Greeted by Mayor McNinch, who lived in what is now one of the city's best restaurants (Uptown's McNinch House), Wood dined at what is known locally as The Duke Mansion, one of the most beautiful private homes in Myers Park. Wood also gave a rousing speech to 5,000 Charlotteans at Uptown's First Presbyterian Church (open today for tours and regular worship services).

James Dowd, the Confederate captain who built the 1897 home that served as Camp Greene headquarters, had an interesting family: His brother, Clement Dowd, was Zebulon Vance's law partner and a mayor of Charlotte. One of James's sons served as publisher of the Charlotte News for nearly 50 years, and a second son founded Charlotte Pipe & Foundry Company, which the family still operates today.

spring; and homemade goodies the way Grandma crafted them for the county fair. (See also Chapter 9, Shopping.) Hours: Mid-March–Dec Tue–Sat 8–6; May–Aug Sun 1–6. Admission: Free. ⅋ (West)

**KINGS MOUNTAIN NATIONAL MILITARY PARK**
**2625 Park Rd. (I-85, Exit 2)**
**Blacksburg, SC**
**864/936-7921**
Revolutionary War history is the focal point of this 3,950-acre park and its several monuments. On October 7, 1780, frontiersmen from the Carolinas, Georgia, and Virginia attacked British forces on a battlefield ridge that sits near the center of this military park. The entire force of more than 1,100 Tories was killed, wounded, or captured by the Patriots, a pivotal and significant victory for the militia that wiped out a wing of Cornwallis's army and ended Loyalist dominance in the Carolinas. The park's visitors center features exhibits and an informative film, Kings Mountain: Turning Point in the South, along with a bookstore, 1.5-mile battlefield trail, and 16-mile hiking trail in the park. Living-history programs

# A Yule Jewel: Christmas Town, USA

*Each holiday season, the tiny mill town of McAdenville in neighboring Gaston County is transformed into Christmas Town, U.S.A., with millions of twinkling lights.*

*Residents and town officials decorate every tree, bush, and shrub in town with white lights, and families from across the region pack the car for a free drive-through view. A small lake in the middle of McAdenville reflects the beauty of the illuminated trees, and holiday music flows through the air.*

*Christmas Town, U.S.A., is generally on view from just after Thanksgiving through late December. For information, call 704/824-3190.*

are offered periodically. Hours: Daily 9–5; closed Thanksgiving, Christmas, and New Year's Day. Admission: Free. ♿ (West)

**LAKE WYLIE**
**Lake Wylie Chamber of Commerce**
**Hwy. 49**
**Lake Wylie, SC**
**803/831-2827**
Located on the southwest edge of Mecklenburg County, Lake Wylie covers 327 miles of shoreline through Mecklenburg and Gaston Counties in North Carolina and through South Carolina's York County. Dammed in 1904, Lake Wylie is named for Dr. W. Gill Wylie, who gave his patient J.B. "Buck" Duke the idea to generate hydroelectric power by damming the Catawba River. Special events include Fourth of July fireworks at Buster Boyd Bridge and the Lights on the Lake annual Christmas boat parade. Daniel Stowe Botanical Gardens in Gaston County also overlooks a portion of the lake. (See also Chap-

ter 10, Sports and Recreation.) Limited wheelchair access. (West)

**PARAMOUNT'S CAROWINDS THEME PARK**
**I-77, Exit 90 at**
**Carowinds Boulevard**
**Charlotte**
**704/588-2600**
Pack the Pepto and take along the beach towels. This popular theme park features roller coasters with stomach-churning drops, twists, and loops, plus water rides guaranteed to give you a shower. The 100-plus-acre park includes more than 40 rides, shows, and attractions for all ages. At the newly expanded water park, you can float down a lazy river; climb on a three-story, sprinkler-rigged jungle gym; or experience a white-water rafting adventure. Need a break? Take in live variety shows, restaurants, an amphitheater, and a special pint-size section for children. In the newest attraction, experience the air, land, and sea stunts of James Bond in a 007

motion simulator. (See also Chapter 6, Kids' Stuff.) Call for seasonal hours and varying admission prices. $5 parking cars and vans. ⅋ (West)

## TOURS

### ADAMS STAGE COACH
**8721 William Wiley Dr.**
**Charlotte**
**704/537-5342**
Step back in time to the days before streetcars and automobiles, when horse-drawn carriages carried Charlotteans throughout the city. Adams Stage Coach offers tours of Uptown Charlotte, Fourth Ward, and Dilworth for groups of up to six people. Guides with the 18-year-old company take visitors over a six-mile route, traveling past historical churches, pointing out interesting architecture, and showing folks some of the best views in town. Hours: By appointment. Admission: $17 per person, $35 per couple with minimum of six people. (Uptown, Central)

### CITY SURF'N SHUTTLE SERVICE
**631 N. Tryon St.**
**Charlotte**
**704/344-9677**
Newcomers to Charlotte and companies recruiting and relocating employees to the area are the primary customers of City Surf'n Shuttle, a customized service offering city tours. Four tours are offered daily in a luxury automobile or a 14-passenger deluxe van. For those relocating, city tours give an overview of Charlotte's government buildings, major employers, visual and performing arts facilities, schools and colleges, sports and recreation, medical centers, shopping malls, and historical sites. Apartment tours drive visitors through as many as 50 complexes to cut down legwork; those in the market to buy are often hooked up with local realtors. Hours: By appointment. Admission: $35 apartment tours; city tours $25–$65 (citywide)

### CITY TOURS OF CHARLOTTE
**8500 Barncliff Rd.**
**Charlotte**
**704/535-6518; 888/488-0578**
These two-hour tours of Charlotte take visitors by bus, 15-passenger van, or Lincoln Town Car to Historic Fourth Ward, Myers Park, Dilworth, the Mint Museum, Uptown's Financial Center, Ericsson Stadium, the Charlotte Coliseum, and Charlotte Motor Speedway. Local history—from the site of the nation's first Gold Rush to the place where Mecklenburg pioneers signed the country's

## TRIVIA

From the old (First Presbyterian Church Uptown) to the new (Calvary Church in South Charlotte), the Queen City reveres its houses of worship.

Around 650 churches can be found here, some dating back to the days when Charlotte was a small village and others reflecting the broad spectrum of religions that has arrived with the city's booming population.

*Historic Rosedale, p. 103*

first Declaration of Independence—makes the tour informative for visitors and newcomers to Charlotte. Tours are also offered to the Biltmore Estate in Asheville, the Blue Ridge Mountains, and South Carolina plantations. Hours: Daily 9:30 a.m. and 1:30 p.m., or by appointment. Admission: $20 per person with free pickup from Uptown hotels; $5 pickup charge outside of Uptown. (citywide)

### DAY TRIPPIN' IN THE CAROLINAS
**7704 Sharpthorne Place**
**Charlotte**
**704/543-1300; 800/354-2468**
Don't expect a ho-hum, look-out-the-bus-window-and-point tour; this driving and walking trip is energetic, fun, and filled with facts that make tourists more knowledgeable about Charlotte than the locals. Tours range from three to four hours, and cover the Queen City's history, current events, urban renewal efforts, politics, horticulture, architecture, and involvement in Southern history. Proprietor Jay Rubin is spontaneous

and can adapt his tour to different interests, times of the year, and even weather. You'll hear about Charlotte's founding fathers, but also the rich and poor, black and white, Catholic and Jewish, that make the Queen City unique. Instead of describing what Uptown Charlotte once looked like, Rubin passes out old photos to show you. A self-described information monster, he provides plenty of interesting facts without the pop quiz at the end. Hours: Daily 10 a.m. and 1 p.m. Admission: $20 per person. &. (citywide)

### RACE CITY TOURS
**P.O. Box 6263**
**Mooresville 28115**
**704/892-1749**
See the auto-racing sights and highlights without wasting valuable time. More than 40 NASCAR teams are based in the greater Charlotte area, along with Charlotte Motor Speedway, several auto museums, the North Carolina Auto Racing Hall of Fame, a slew of souvenir shops, and a few racing-themed restaurants. Full-day tours

include the Speedway, Backing Up Classics auto museum, Hendrick Motorsports Museum, the Hall of Fame, shops of famous drivers (such as Darrell Waltrip), and the long-awaited racing complex recently opened by Dale Earnhardt. Lunch at the Stock Car Café is not included. Custom and half-day tours also available. Hours: By appointment. Admission: $48.95 half-day; $79 full day; admission charges included. (North)

Paramount's Carowinds

# 6

# KIDS' STUFF

Take a safari, paint pottery, build a bird-feeder, zip around the ice rink, climb a 35-foot wall, or dress up in finery for an old-fashioned tea party. Charlotte offers endless possibilities when it comes to things to do with kids.

Several zoos are found in areas around the Queen City, and the region abounds with parks, gardens, and recreational facilities. Technology and science on a kid's level is the focus of a few museums, while others concentrate on art. Parents will find the ubiquitous indoor and outdoor play places across the city, but there's also plenty—from tea parties to trolley rides—that's out of the norm. Enjoy!

## ANIMALS AND THE GREAT OUTDOORS

### CHARLOTTE METRO ZOO
**4400 Cook Rd.**
**Rockwell**
**704/279-6363**
Exotic creatures such as lions, tigers, leopards, panthers, bears, kangaroos, monkeys, zebras, tropical birds, and reptiles can be seen at this 10-acre, walk-through zoo in neighboring Cabarrus County. Mostly former pets that people could no longer keep, the animals are housed in cages that allow visitors to stand as close as 12 feet away. Kids enjoy the petting zoo with more traditional farm animals such as sheep, goats, and pigs. Hours: Daily 10–dark. Admission: $6 adults, $4 children and seniors, children 2 and under free. &
(North)

### CONCORD ZOO
**1643 Simplicity Rd.**
**Concord**
**704/782-3149**
Kids love Sammy, the spider monkey that drives a golf cart, as well as the

camels, zebras, other monkeys, baboons, peacocks, and tropical birds on this 25-acre zoo in Cabarrus County. Walk through, rent a golf cart, or take a "safari" on a covered wagon pulled by a tractor. The zoo's camels, zebras, and horned African cattle often approach in search of snacks. For younger children, there's a petting zoo with baby goats, calves, and lambs, plus a picnic area with a playground of swings, slides, and seesaws. Hours: Daily 9–6. Admission: $5 adults, $3 kids. Cart rental, $10/hour. ♿ (North)

## LAZY 5 RANCH
## NC 150 E
## Mooresville
## 704/663-5100; 704/278-2618
You don't need a passport or shots to experience the thrill of a safari, thanks to the Lazy 5 Ranch, a drive-through park featuring 400 animals from around the world. Stay in your car or take a horse-drawn wagon on the 3.5-mile safari through gently sloping pastures. Animals from six continents await, including water buffalo, antelope, deer, elk, rare African cows, camels, reindeer, and zebras. Kids can get up close and touch animals in the petting zoo, monkey around at the playground, and picnic in provided areas. The only drive-through ranch of its kind in the state, the Lazy 5 has 25 years of experience working with exotic animals. Recommended as a top day trip for families by *Our Kids & Teens Magazine.* Hours: Mon–Sat 9 a.m.–one hour before sunset, Sun 1 p.m.–one hour before sunset. Admission: $7.50 adults, $4.50 children and seniors, $3.50 per person groups of 15 or more. Horse-drawn wagon rides $5 adults, $3 children and seniors, $2 per person groups of 15 or more. ♿ (North)

# ARTS AND CRAFTS

## COMMUNITY SCHOOL OF THE ARTS, SPIRIT SQUARE
## 345 N. College St.
## Charlotte
## 704-377-4187
Dedicated to providing a high-quality, comprehensive arts education to children and students, the Community School of the Arts nestles among the sophisticated galleries, marbled hallways, and grand theaters of Uptown's Spirit Square. Individual and group classes are offered in music, drama, visual arts, and dance, but it's about more than ballet and brass instruments. Parents can participate with kids to learn elements of music, including rhythm, pitch, and melody. Older kids can discover the joys of playing in an improv jazz or rock group. Drama students take everything from acting basics to applying greasepaint. Other classes teach batik, comics, origami, mixed media, famous Broadway dances, and the latest moves seen on the street. Hours: Office open Mon–Fri 9–5. Admission: Costs vary by length and type of course. ♿ (Uptown)

## FLYING SAUCERS
## 2041 South Blvd., Suite F,
## in The Pavilion at South End
## Charlotte
## 704-334-1399
Kids—and plenty of adults, too—pack this paint-it-yourself pottery studio. More than 200 pieces of pottery, from $2 refrigerator magnets to $28 centerpiece bowls, sit on shelves waiting to be painted. Choose your piece, study scrapbooks and guides for ideas, then pencil and paint your design with sponges, stencils, and brushes. When your masterpiece is finished, the shop glazes and fires it for free. To make it a

family event (or a unique date), bring in dinner and drinks. Wednesday is Mother Daughter Tea Party day, on which daughters paint for half price and tea and snacks are served. Birthday parties and group outings are also encouraged. Hours: Tue–Thu 10:30–9, Fri–Sat 10:30–10:30, Sun 12:30–5:30. Admission: $6 per hour painting time plus price of pottery. Mention this publication and paint for $5 an hour. ♿ (Central)

## IMAGINATION STATION
**1923-A South Blvd.**
**Charlotte**
**704/342-5844**
An arts school for kids ages 3 to 18, Imagination Station also conducts week-long summer camps and custom birthday parties. Exposed brick walls, primary colors, and decor that looks like the giant art-covered refrigerator of proud parents welcome kids who dress to mess. Classes are mixed media with instruction in drawing, painting, and ceramics, but there's an educational element, too. Kids' clay sculptures, masks, and papier-mâché pieces cover the walls, along with framed quotes, such as Picasso's "Painting is just another way of keeping a diary." At birthday parties, kids can paint crafts, sculpt a dinosaur, don a gold-studded crown, string a lei, make pretend scars, or paint a clay pot and plant a flower in it. Hours: Semester-long group classes offered in 45- and 90-minute increments. Admission: Class rates and party rates vary with duration and theme. ♿ (Central)

## MINT MUSEUM OF ART
**2730 Randolph Rd.**
**Charlotte**
**704/337-2000**
The oldest art museum in North Carolina and the best-known in Charlotte,

the Mint Museum includes a year-round student art gallery that shows works by youngsters in grades kindergarten through 12. The gallery, one of the most popular spots at the Mint, changes exhibits monthly and generally ties in with the museum's major exhibition. Art classes for children range from doll making to beginning sculpture to advanced drawing. Kids' summer camps offer a week-long immersion in several media or a more intense session in one area. (See also Chapter 7, Museums and Art Galleries.) Hours: Tue 10–10, Wed–Sat 10–5, Sun noon–5. Admission: $6 adults, $4 seniors and students, children 12 and under and museum members free. Free to all 5–10 Tue and second Sun each month. ♿ (Central)

## STROKE OF GENIUS
**1235 East Blvd. in Kenilworth**
**Commons**
**Charlotte**
**704/333-3473**
Charlotte's first pottery-painting studio, Stroke of Genius frequently runs

*Your hair will stand on end at Discovery Place, p. 120.*

Discovery Place, Inc.

# Cabin Fever Cure

*Kids climbing the walls? Get outside for nature-related fun. Charlotte is full of things to do with children—it's just a matter of knowing where to go. In addition to the sights and activities listed in this chapter, many outdoor destinations around the Queen City offer programs tailored to the pint-size crowd.*

*Try the three major nature preserves in Mecklenburg County— McDowell, Reedy Creek, and Latta Plantation. All offer programs for children (and adults), focusing on nature and the environment. You'll also find walking trails, lakes, boating, and picnic areas.*

*State parks, such as Crowders Mountain in Kings Mountain, Duke Power in Troutman, and Kings Mountain in Blacksburg, also offer stream studies, day hikes, wildflower walks, and programs that focus on animals, birds, and astronomy.*

*Urban gardens also offer activities for budding nature lovers. Daniel Stowe Botanical Garden in Belmont, for instance, conducts moonlight strolls through the gardens and forest, woodland walks for a look at wild plants and birds, and garden gambols through cultivated flowers, shrubs, and trees. In the garden's Kreative Kids workshop series, children make castings of animal tracks, build bird-feeders, and walk on trails to search for spring wildflowers and frogs.*

*McGill Rose Garden in Uptown Charlotte also features a children's garden where kids can plant seeds and watch their growth through the seasons.*

*For additional information on these destinations, see Chapter 8, Parks, Gardens, and Recreation Areas.*

---

after-school specials for kids who love to paint. The concept is simple: pick a ready-to-decorate piece of pottery, from picture frames to Fido bowls, then pay to paint. The shop handles the rest, including complimentary glazing, firing, and instruction. If you're short on ideas, check out the art books or try your design on sketch paper using stencils and sponges. Birthday parties and family outings are welcome. When it's quitting time, head to the yogurt shop next door. Additional locations: 8200 Pineville-Matthews Rd., Suite 700 in The Arboretum, 704/541-3531; 8662 J.W. Clay Blvd., Suite 4 in The Village at University Place, 704/548-9525. Hours: Tue–Sat 10:30–9, Sun 1–6. Admission: $6 per hour painting time, plus price of pottery. ⅚ (Central)

# FUN AND EDUCATIONAL

### CHARLOTTE TROLLEY CAROUSEL
**2104 South Blvd. at Atherton Mill**
**Charlotte**
**704/375-0850**
As if riding the Charlotte Trolley and clanging the streetcar bell weren't fun enough, a small carousel was recently moved inside the trolley's barn. Once a holiday tradition at SouthPark Mall, the carousel was taken down in 1997 to make way for bigger stores and the masses of shoppers that invade Charlotte's best-known mall. Parents complained, kids cried, and supporters searched for a new home that could house the carousel and pay thousands of dollars in operating costs each year. The Charlotte Trolley took on the job, and now the German-made carousel is back in business year-round. Kids can ride Wilbur the pig, King the lion, and horses named Beauty and Ginger, or sit in a spinning seat, between the wings of a swan, or under the watchful eye of a genie. (See also Chapter 5, Sights and Attractions; and Chapter 7, Museums and Art Galleries.) Hours: Mon–Thu 11–2, Fri–Sun 10–6. Admission: 50¢. (Central)

### DISCOVERY PLACE
**301 N. Tryon St.**
**Charlotte**
**704/372-6261**
A favorite of kids and adults who are young at heart, Discovery Place offers cool science and technology exhibits for all ages. Younger children can start at Kidsplace, an area for ages 7 and under that teaches elementary science concepts. Want to learn about the human body? Climb through the ear canal to see how people hear. Ever wonder how a seesaw and swing work? Hop on and learn about playground physics. Even toddlers have a place to climb towers and slide down chutes in Kidsplace. Older children will enjoy seeing dinosaur models move, holding iguanas in the rain forest, stroking horseshoe crabs in the touch pool, and exploring space in the planetarium. The learning possibilities are endless here; plan to stay a whole fun-filled day. (See also Chapter 7, Museums and Art Galleries.) Hours: Sept–May Mon–Fri 9–5, Sat 9–6, Sun 1–6; June–Aug Mon–Sat 9–6, Sun 1–6. Admission: Exhibit halls, OMNIMAX films, planetarium, and Challenger simulation are considered one option each. $5.50 one option ages 13–59, $4.50 one option ages 6–12 and seniors, $2.75 one option ages 3–5. Each additional option $2 per person, any age. Group rates also available. ⅚ (Uptown)

### ENERGYEXPLORIUM
**13339 Hagers Ferry Rd.**
**Huntersville**
**704/875-5600**
What puts kids to sleep in science class comes to life with neon lights, sound effects, and interactive games at the EnergyExplorium. Overlooking Lake Norman at Duke Power's McGuire Nuclear Station, the Explorium lets kids play games that show how to use energy wisely, throw switches on model power plants, and convert their own energy into enough elec-

tricity to power a television. In the Ollie's World exhibit, an osprey takes visitors through the history and features of Lake Norman. Elektri City lets kids send crews out to investigate power outages and other problems. A Geiger counter measures radiation of everyday objects, and a video leads guests on a tour through the nuclear plant. Outside, walk the mile-long nature trail for a look at Lake Norman's wildlife and natural habitats. Hours: Sat 9–5, Sun noon–5. Admission: Free. ♿ (North)

## ENERGYQUEST AT CATAWBA NUCLEAR STATION
**4850 Concord Rd.**
**York, SC**
**803/831-3609; 800/777-0006**
Science a yawner? Try a self-guided tour through high-tech exhibits at EnergyQuest, the information center of Catawba Nuclear Station located on Lake Wylie in York, South Car-

olina. Here, at one of the world's most advanced nuclear generating stations, kids and adults learn about naturally occurring radiation, how atoms are split to make electricity, and how waste is managed. Nuclear operators practice their skills in a station simulator, and visitors can watch through the window for a sense of safety measures and day-to-day operations. Films focus on the area's growth and its important ties to the past, while talks by EnergyQuest staff are tailored to age and interest. There's also a picnic area, nature trail, and free souvenir photograph of visitors inside Catawba. Hours: Mon–Sat 9–5, Sun noon–5. Admission: Free. ♿ (West)

## PUBLIC LIBRARY OF CHARLOTTE AND MECKLENBURG COUNTY
**310 N. Tryon St.**
**Charlotte**
**704/336-2409**
Even if you're visiting Charlotte and don't have a library card, there are plenty of free, educational activities for kids at the Main Library and at branches around the city. In addition to books, art is emphasized at the Children's Library through a permanent art exhibit of original pieces by well-known children's-book illustrators, soft-sculpture art hanging from the ceiling, and a reading-themed mural repainted each year by a different local school. Programs includes story-time sessions, films, author readings, and special projects on creative writing, art, drama, and science. In the computer room, log on for neat games and programs. Tours of the library are also available. (See also Chapter 5, Sights and Attractions.) Hours: Mon–Thu 9–9, Fri–Sat 9–6, Sun 1–6. Admission: Free. ♿ (Uptown)

*Mother and baby zebra at Lazy 5 Ranch, p. 117*

Lazy 5 Ranch

# CULTURE FOR KIDS

## CHARLOTTE YOUTH BALLET
P.O. Box 15098
Charlotte 28211
704/366-5133

The Charlotte Youth Ballet has offered performance opportunities to thousands of area dance students for more than 15 years. The nonprofit presented its first *Nutcracker* in 1981, giving Charlotte children a first-ever chance to perform in a locally produced version of the classic Christmas ballet. Even kids who don't take dance classes love to dress up in holiday attire and head to Ovens Auditorium to watch the show. Other ballets staged in the past include such traditional offerings as *Alice in Wonderland* and *Cinderella*. (See also Chapter 11, Performing Arts.) Hours: Generally two shows a season at holidays and spring. Admission: $9–18 adults; $6–$12 children. (Central)

## CHILDREN'S THEATRE OF CHARLOTTE
1017 E. Morehead St.
Charlotte
704/376-5745; 704/333-8983

Created 50 years ago by the Junior League, Children's Theatre of Charlotte has grown from volunteer plays on a shoestring budget to fully staged, technical productions presented to more than 180,000 families each year. Productions include classics such as *To Kill a Mockingbird*, fantasies such as *Alice in Wonderland*, and favorites including *The Wizard of Oz*. Regional theater groups specializing in mime and puppetry often present special events, while Children's Theatre's touring company, the Tarradiddle Players, take shows on the road. Classes and workshops for all ages are offered in creative drama, acting, and musical theater. (See also Chapter 11, Performing Arts.) Hours: Office open Mon–Fri 10–5; performances generally Fri–Sun. Admission: Tickets range $5–$10. &#9855; (Central)

## DANCEPLACE
800 N. College St.
Charlotte
704/372-3900

The Official School of North Carolina Dance Theatre, Charlotte's professional dance company, DancePlace offers technique classes for children, teens, and adults in ballet, modern, creative movement, and jazz. Whether for recreation or to further dance-career aspirations, Dance-Place attracts students of all levels. More advanced students can join a pre-professional program for opportunities to work with the professional company in classes, rehearsals, and performances, and on tour. Master classes and summer intensive programs are also offered, along with performance spots in the company's annual production of *The Nutcracker* and the school's Spring Showcase. Hours: Classes vary in time and day. Admission: Tuition varies by age, skill level, and frequency of instruction. (Uptown)

# STORES KIDS LOVE

## ZANY BRAINY
3345 Pineville-Matthews Rd. in The Arboretum
Charlotte
704/544-7704

Like Imelda Marcos at a shoe sale, kids go wild at Zany Brainy for its wide range of toys, games, and educational playthings. Creative children love the stickers, stamps, and creativity kits. Computer whiz-kids spend hours checking out software and trying new games on in-store terminals. Others like Zany Brainy's departments for puzzles, board games, books, electronics, sports, models, science kits, and animals of every material from plastic to stuffed to rubber. A station in the middle of the store gives kids a place to play, and the Show Time theater presents videos and music. Free daily interactive events let kids try many of the crafts, games, and toys from the store before taking them home. & (South)

## THEME PARKS

### PARAMOUNT'S CAROWINDS THEME PARK
**I-77 and Carowinds Blvd.**
**Charlotte**
**704/588-2600**
Kids love everything about Paramount's Carowinds, a 100-acre water and theme park on the North–South Carolina state line 15 minutes southwest of Charlotte. The park features six roller coasters, a 174-foot drop tower, a 12-acre water park, and thrills from mild to wild that suit all ages. At Animation Station, kids can meet their favorite cartoon characters, hop onstage in interactive shows, ride a magical carousel, and scale the three-story climbing gym and play place. At Water Works, sprayers, waterwheels, and a huge (1,000-gallon) bucket make up Splash Factory for children. New for half-pints in 1998 is Zoom Zone, a 3.5-acre playland that puts kids in the driver's seats of elevated helicopters, a miniature roller coaster, and '50s-style electric cars. Overall, the park has more than 15 attractions and shows for young visitors and their

families. Hours: Mid-Mar–mid-Aug daily 10–8, mid-Aug–mid-Oct Sat–Sun 10–8 only. Admission: $29.99 ages 7–54; $17.99 ages 4–6, children under 48" tall, and seniors; ages 3 and under free; $14.99 any age after 5 p.m.; $11.99 next-day ticket any age. $5 parking. & (West)

## PLACES TO PLAY

### CAUTION: KIDS AT PLAY
**20310 Sefton Park**
**Cornelius**
**704/892-KIDS (5437)**
An indoor play gym and more, Caution: Kids at Play offers something for everyone and every age. Older kids can tackle the "purple dinosaur," a violet-colored tube that sends them sliding to the ground from the third-story level. Daredevils can hop into the suspended bubble that rocks like a helicopter ride. Other features include climbing towers, tumbling mats, ball pits, and an obstacle course. Younger kids have their own play area and rides. When the little ones tire of the gym, send them to the arcade, snack bar, go-carts, laser tag, or miniature golf. Birthday parties and groups are welcome, too. Hours: Sun–Mon noon–8, Tue–Thu 10–8, Fri–Sat 10–11. Play gym closes at 10 p.m. Fri–Sat. Admission: weekdays $3.99 ages 1–2, $5.99 ages 3–12; weekends $4.99 ages 1–2, $6.99 ages 3–12. Free, parents and infants. Go-carts, $4 adults; $3.50 juniors. Limited wheelchair access. (North)

### CELEBRATION STATION
**10400 Cadillac St.**
**Pineville**
**704/552-7888**
Here's the fun of the fair without waiting for the carnival to come to town.

# Top Ten Day Trips for Families

**By Elaine Heitman, editor of *Our Kids & Teens Magazine***

*All trips are within two hours of central Charlotte. Check* Our Kids & Teens Magazine*'s monthly listings for current hour and rate information.*

1. **Chimney Rock State Park.** Located on U.S. 74 West just east of Asheville. Climb to the top of the rock (26 stories) and hike to view 404-foot Hickory Nut waterfall. 800/277-9611.

2. **EnergyQuest and EnergyExplorium.** EnergyQuest, at the Catawba Nuclear Station off SC 274 and Concord Road in Clover, South Carolina, offers hands-on fun and learning about electricity, energy, and nuclear power. 803/831-3612. Energy Explorium, on NC 73 in Huntersville, also offers hands-on exhibits, nature trails, and a film showing how Lake Norman was made. 704/875-5600.

3. **Historic Brattonsville.** This National Register of Historic Places site in McConnells, South Carolina, on SC 322 off Cherry Road, includes 26 restored structures and reproductions from the Revolutionary War and antebellum South eras. 803/684-2327.

4. **Kings Mountain State Park.** Off of I-85 on Hwy. 161 (Exit 8), this is the site of a 1780 Revolutionary War battle. Exhibits, hiking, and camping. 803/222-3209.

5. **Latta Place and Carolina Raptor Center.** Located on Sample Road off Beatties Ford Road in Huntersville, set within Latta Plantation Park, Latta Place is a restored and furnished Catawba River plantation house, circa 1800. 704/875-2312. The Carolina Raptor Center, also inside the park, is a conservation center dedicated to the rehabilitation and release of injured birds of prey.

6. **Lazy 5 Ranch.** On Hwy. 150 off I-77 in Mooresville, the Lazy 5 offers a drive-through safari experience in your own car or by horse-drawn wagon. Petting zoo, playground, and picnic area. 704/663-5100 or 704/278-2618.

7. **North Carolina Zoological Park.** Located in Asheboro, this natural habitat walking zoo also offers free tram rides to see the North American region, African region, and aviary. 800/488-0444.

8. **Old Salem.** Located in Winston-Salem is this 18th-century Moravian village. 336/721-7300.

9. **Reed Gold Mine.** Located on Hwy. 27 as you head toward Albemarle, Reed Mine offers exhibits, a mining tunnel tour, and hands-on gold panning. 704/786-8337.

10. **Riverbanks Zoo.** Located in Columbia, South Carolina, this self-contained metro-type zoo including an aviary, aquarium, and botanical garden. (803) 779-8717.

Celebration Station promotes family fun with three 18-hole miniature golf courses, batting cages, kid-size and adult go-carts, bumper boats, an indoor play center, snack bar, and arcade games. Pay per activity or buy an all-day pass that allows unlimited rides and games. Families often eat here at the snack bar: pizza, hot dogs, chips, breadsticks, wings, cookies, and ice cream. Birthday parties are also a treat here. Something fun for all ages and interests. Hours: Sept–May: Mon–Thu 4–9, Fri 4–11, Sat 10–11, Sun noon–9; June–Aug: Mon–Thu 10–9, Fri–Sat 10–midnight, Sun noon–9. Admission: $4 per activity; $8.99 unlimited activities kids; $15.99 unlimited activities adults. Limited wheelchair access. (South)

## CHARLOTTE CLIMBING CENTER
### 619 S. Cedar St., Suite M
### Charlotte
### 704/333-7625

Kids are natural climbers, and there's no better place to learn the basics of rock climbing than the Charlotte Climbing Center. An indoor climbing gym that offers a fun, challenging, and exciting environment for children, CCC introduces half-pints to the sport through lessons, birthday parties, walk-in sessions, and a kids-only climbing club. Beginners wear a harness and are supported by ropes and a belay person on the ground as they scamper up a 35-foot-wall or along smaller climbing walls. Summer climbing and outdoor adventure camps, Boy Scout merit badges, and field trips to rock climbs in the area are also available. (See also Chapter 10, Sports and Recreation.) Hours: Tue–Fri noon–10, Sat 10–6, Sun 1–6. Admission: $12 daily walk-in rate; $5 after 5 Wed; $20 belay for kids. Memberships, family

rates, student rates, and punch cards also available. (Uptown)

## CHUCK E. CHEESE'S
### 7701 Pineville-Matthews Rd.
### 704/541-3237

A fun, energetic restaurant with an indoor play gym, arcade, and children's theater inside, Chuck E.'s is a favorite for birthday parties and family-friendly nights on the town. Pizza, hot dogs, sub sandwiches, and salads are offered on the order-at-the-counter menu, and seating is in fast-food–style booths and tables. But the real attractions are the token-operated games—air hockey, skee ball, kids' rides, virtual reality jet skis, and gizmos that snap computerized photos. Slip off your shoes and explore the free Sky Tubes, a two-story padded jungle gym with rocking seats, tunnels, slides, and ball pits. In the back, adult-sized mechanical characters sing, dance, and play to piped-in pop music. Younger kids have their own play area, too. Additional location: 5612 Albemarle Rd., Charlotte, 704/532-9570. Limited wheelchair access. (South)

## GYMBOREE PARENT/CHILD PLAY PROGRAM
### 7427 Leharne Dr.
### Charlotte
### 704/366-9288

An international program, Gymboree pairs parents with their children from newborn to age 4 for a series of classes ranging from 12 to 36 weeks. With a new activity each week, children learn through play. In newborn classes, infants work on eye–hand coordination, balance, and strength while moms (or dads or grandparents) share their experiences. Toddlers concentrate on concepts, such as stop and go, in and out, up and down.

Preschoolers study imaginative themes and are introduced to instruments. The noncompetitive concept aims to help kids learn about themselves and their world while developing self-esteem. Because it's new every week, parents and kids can join anytime. Hours: Day and night classes offered. Admission: $108 for 12 weeks, $198 for 24 weeks, $279 for 36 weeks. First day is free. (South)

### ICE CHALET
**5595 Central Ave. inside**
**Eastland Mall**
**Charlotte**
**704/568-0772**
Charlotte's original ice skating rink, the Ice Chalet sits in the middle of Eastland Mall where shoppers watch skaters spin around the ice. Strap on figure or hockey skates, and circle the regulation-sized rink to popular and rock music. Instructors teach free beginner lessons for would-be figure and hockey skaters each weekend. Or, if you want to wing it, public skate sessions take place daily and on Wednesday through Saturday evenings. Hockey leagues are open to kids, men, and women, along with group figure-skating lessons and instruction in broomball. Birthday parties are popular, but expect big crowds on weekends. (See also Chapter 10, Sports and Recreation.) Hours: Daily; call for specific times. Admission: $6; $2.50 skate rental; $3.50 hockey rental; $4.50 senior citizens. Family Day on Sun: $26 covers admission and rental for six people. (East)

### ICE HOUSE OF CHARLOTTE
**400 Towne Centre Blvd.**
**Pineville**
**704/889-9000**
Kids in South Charlotte visit the Ice House to skate, play on hockey teams, and take figure-skating lessons. Built in 1995, the modern, freestanding facility counts children as three-fourths of its business. Hockey leagues include men's, youth, and novice, and the Ice House regularly holds how-to workshops on playing the game. Figure-skaters can sign up for group or private lessons. Newcomers to ice skating or those who just want to keep it a hobby can lace up skates every day of the week. Birthday parties are also popular here, along with a full-service eatery serving kid-friendly treats such as pizza and nachos. (See also Chapter 10, Sports and Recreation.) Hours: Daily; call for specific times. Admission: $6, rentals $2. (South)

### JUMP YARD
**4301 Park Rd. in Park Road**
**Shopping Center**
**Charlotte**
**704/522-0012**
Whether it's jumping on the bed or sliding down the stairway banister, everything outlawed for kids at home is welcomed and even encouraged at this clean, friendly play facility. A three-story tower houses a maze of slides, tubes, jungle gyms, and obstacle course runs open to kids and adults. Check your shoes at the door, then slide down chutes into pits of plastic balls, wiggle through long tunnels, and crawl up angled rope nets to the top of the tower. Younger kids can play in Sam's Side Yard, a more sedate version of the play tower, with giant rubber balls, tumbling mats, and small slides. Six party rooms await birthdays, with an arcade and snack bar serving chicken fingers, pizza, barbecue, and the like. Hours: Sun–Thu 10–7, Fri–Sat 9–9. Admission: $3.99 age 1–2, $5.99 ages 2 and up, ages 12 to adult free with younger

child. No time limits. Drop off kids for supervised care for extra $3/hour. Limited wheelchair access. (Central)

## LA-DEE-DA'S
**1942 E. Seventh St.**
**Charlotte**
**704/372-9599**

Little girls and young-at-heart ladies love La-dee-da's for their traditional tea parties, complete with beautiful china, silver tiered trays, and theme teapots. This old house in Historic Elizabeth serves breakfast and lunch plus afternoon tea, but birthday parties are an added treat. Girls ages 4 to 14 nibble teapot sandwiches, cookies, fruit, and birthday cake and dress up with vintage hats, dresses, and furs to sip tea. For the royal treatment, La-dee-da's throws in a professional photographer, limousine service, and party favors, including tea sets, sterling charm pulls, and vintage hats. Parents can browse among two floors of antiques and gifts. Hours: Tea parties by appointment. Admission: Parties range from $50 to $350. ♿ (Central)

## LASER QUEST
**5323-A Independence Blvd.**
**Charlotte**
**704/567-6707**

Cowboys and Indians, '90s style. Adopt a code name (Viper Sniper and Han Solo are popular options), get instructions on how to play, strap on a battery-charged pack, then venture bravely into the 8,500-square-foot laser-tag room with black lights, fog, and glow-in-the-dark paint. As rock music blares, players weave through the two-story maze and up ramps to the tops of four towers in search of enemies to shoot. When a light beam touches the sensors on the pack or gun, the "hit" player feels a vibration and loss of gun power for five seconds. After the game, scorecards tell players how they fared. Birthday parties are big here on Saturday mornings; arcade games entertain the kids between laser-tag sessions. Hours: Mon–Thu 6–10 p.m., Fri 4 p.m.–midnight, Sat 10 a.m.–midnight, Sun 1–10 p.m. Admission: $6 per person per 20-minute game. (East)

*An informative exhibit at EnergyExplorium, p. 120*

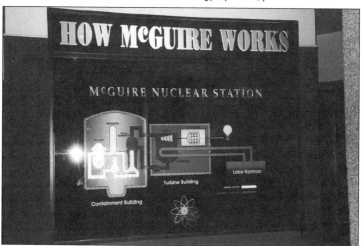

EnergyExplorium

**T**
**i**
**P**

Where do teenagers who are too old for kids' activities but not old enough to be on their own hang out?

Popular destinations for teenage Charlotte guys are laser tag centers, movie theaters, and popular play parks that offer arcade games, go-carts, batting cages, miniature golf, and bumper boats in one place.

Teenage girls often enjoy the Queen City's pottery-painting studios for creative fun.

### THE PLAYGROUND
**11325 E. Independence Blvd.**
**Matthews**
**704/845-2787**

With miniature golf, batting cages, bumper boats, go-carts, and arcade games, The Playground offers a full day of fun in one place. Choose softball or baseball in speeds from slow to pro at the batting cages, or watch from benches behind the plate. The go-cart track twists and turns for kids and adults seeking high-speed fun. For more sedate thrills, try the 18-hole miniature golf course or the bobbing bumper boats nearby. Inside, a snack bar serves pizza, wings, hot dogs, nachos, and other fair-style fare. Arcade games include pinball, skee ball, pool tables, ball tosses, air hockey, Foosball, Sega-style fighting games, and simulated motorcycle and race-car riders. Birthday parties are welcome; specials are frequent. Hours: Mon–Thu 3:30–10 p.m., Fri 3:30–midnight, Sat 10 a.m.–midnight, Sun noon–10. Admission: Go-carts: $3.50 per ride, $1 per passenger. Mini-golf: $3.50 adults, $2.50 ages 3–10, free under 3. Bumper boats: $3.50, $1 per passenger. Batting

range: $1 per token. Limited wheelchair access. (South)

### ZONES
**11210 Brigman Rd.**
**Matthews**
**704/847-5222**

The largest indoor recreation area in the Southeast, Zones features bumper cars, a carousel, a moon-walk maze, a rotating dragon ride, and nearly 100 video games. Carolina Lanes bowling, in the same building, is just a step away. Birthday parties camp out in the theater, which includes large tables and moving characters that sing and dance to music. Arcade games, which spit out tickets redeemable for prizes and candy, include skee ball, football-passing games, simulated driving games, virtual reality fighters, home-run derby games, and a simulated bowling lane. A snack bar inside Carolina Lanes serves sandwiches, pizza, and other snacks. Hours: Mon–Thu 4–9 p.m., Fri 4–11 p.m., Sat noon–11, Sun noon–9. Admission: 25¢ game tokens; $1 rides; $5.95 unlimited rides; $10.95 unlimited rides and 20 tokens. Limited wheelchair access. (South)

# 7

# MUSEUMS AND ART GALLERIES

*Controversy has plagued the city's performing arts scene for years, but Charlotte's visual-arts community thrives with well-established, well-known museums and walk-on-the-wild-side galleries that are expanding, renovating, and opening with a renewed vigor. Many museums, cultural centers, and established galleries have set up shop Uptown to be steps away from professionals, tourists, convention-goers, and business travelers, and the trend doesn't seem to be fading.*

*For instance, Bank of America is spending $7 million to restore the burned-out old First Associate Reformed Presbyterian Church at North Tryon and 11th Streets Uptown and create an artists' center. The artists' colony will have 33 artists within five years, and will give visual artists (particularly painters) individual studios for working, teaching, and exhibiting. Plans call for the facility to be completed by spring 1999.*

*The Museum of the New South, Uptown at College and Seventh Streets, also plans a $7 million expansion and renovation of its building by 2001.*

*A third, The Mint Museum of Art on Randolph Road, will open an Uptown branch for craft and design in the former Montaldo's building on North Tryon Street near Sixth. The 80,000-square-foot space is expected to open in early 1999.*

*Specialty museums—from race cars to raptors—tend to pop up all over town. For instance, South End, a growing community just off Uptown at Dilworth, includes a historical trolley museum and several galleries in its emerging restaurant and shopping scene.*

*But the cutting-edge arts community today lies north of Uptown on North Davidson Street in the 35th and 36th Street blocks. Nicknamed NoDa, the North Davidson corridor changed from a boarded-up, rundown, abandoned mill village to a revitalized arts community with new galleries, restaurants, shops, and a performing-arts theater. Arts patrons also explore NoDa and Uptown during gallery crawls that blend creativity, curiosity, and community spirit with the local arts scene.*

# ART MUSEUMS

### AFRO-AMERICAN CULTURAL CENTER
**401 N. Myers St.**
**Charlotte**
**704/374-1565**
See African artifacts, hear sizzling jazz, beat bongo drums, tour a "shotgun house." A showcase for African American art, music, theater, film, and cultural education, the Afro-American Cultural Center features permanent and changing exhibits as well as local, regional, and national performers. Started at UNCC, the museum now thrives in a building with stained-glass windows from the former Little Rock AME Zion Church. Facilities include a theater, art gallery, amphitheater, and meeting space. Two "shotgun houses" (narrow, inexpensive homes most common in African American neighborhoods earlier in this century) are restored at the side of the church. (See also Chapter 11, Performing Arts.)

Hours: Tue–Sat 10–6, Sun 1–5. Admission: Free. & (Uptown)

### THE LIGHT FACTORY
**809 W. Hill St.**
**Charlotte**
**704/333-9755**
This renovated warehouse in Uptown's Third Ward behind Ericsson Stadium showcases the latest in light-generated media, including photography, film, video, and digitally produced images. Founded in 1974 as an artists' cooperative, the noncollecting museum houses four galleries with changing exhibits. The Light Factory is best known for contemporary photography and new media; its more-than-20 exhibits a year include a juried member show. The gallery's urban design of concrete floors, exposed brick walls, and high ceilings houses photography and new media courses for adults and children, community darkrooms, lectures and panel discussions, and exhibit-related performing arts events. Hours: Wed and Fri 10–6, Thu 10–8, Sat–Sun noon–6. Admission: Free. & (Uptown)

### MINT MUSEUM OF ART
**2730 Randolph Rd.**
**Charlotte**
**704/337-2000**
Charlotte's premier art museum, the

---

**TRIVIA**

The Charlotte Hornets mural on the side of Two First Union Center in Uptown has undergone three overhauls since debuting in January 1995.

The first mural featured Muggsy Bogues, Larry Johnson, and Alonzo Mourning, all of whom have since been traded. Hugo, the Hornets' mascot, appeared to burst through the brick building later that year.

By October 1997, the third (and current) mural was unveiled, showing Anthony Mason, Vlade Divac, and Glen Rice.

Mint is also the oldest in the state. Local-interest pieces include portraits of Queen Charlotte, paintings by Mecklenburg County native Romare Bearden, and gold coins produced at Charlotte's U.S. Mint. The 81,000-square-foot museum features American and European paintings; African, pre-Columbian, and Spanish Colonial art; and one of the country's best-known collections of ceramics and porcelain. An Uptown branch will open in early 1999 featuring regional crafts and art, including glass, ceramics, wood, fiber, and North Carolina pottery. Year-round programs include independent film series, lectures, symposiums, art classes for all ages, live summer jazz, and the Charlotte Film & Video Festival. (See also Chapter 6, Kids' Stuff.) Hours: Tue 10–10, Wed–Sat 10–5, Sun 12–5. Admission: $6 adults, $4 seniors and students, free for children 12 and under and museum members. Free to all Tue 5–10 p.m. and second Sun each month. ♿ (Central)

## SPIRIT SQUARE CENTER FOR ARTS & EDUCATION
**345 N. College St.**
**Charlotte**
**704/372-9664**
Arts education takes precedence at this community arts center that includes three galleries, two theaters, nine classrooms, four acoustically isolated music practice rooms, and offices for several local arts organizations. Five buildings make up Spirit Square; the 700-seat McGlohon Theatre was originally First Baptist Church (built in 1909), and Knight Gallery was once a printmaker's shop. Renovated in 1989, Spirit Square showcases professional local, regional, and national artists working in such media as neon, metal, wood-

carving, paintings, and sculpture. Curated exhibits change every other month; call for adults' and kids' class schedule. (See also Chapter 11, Performing Arts.) Hours: Tue–Fri 11–6, Sat 11–5, Sun 1–4. Admission: Free. ♿ (Uptown)

# SCIENCE AND HISTORY MUSEUMS

## CHARLOTTE MUSEUM OF HISTORY
**3500 Shamrock Dr.**
**Charlotte**
**704/568-1774**
Opening Spring 1999, the new Charlotte Museum of History preserves a permanent collection of 15,000 regional artifacts—rare maps, books, photographs, toys, quilts, furniture, and clothing—ranging from the pre-Colonial era to the 20th Century. The museum also houses the 3,600-volume

*Science is never boring at Discovery Place, p. 133.*

Discovery Place, Inc.

# Top Ten Must-See Public Art Pieces

1. Raymond Kaskey statues on four corners of The Square at Trade and Tryon Uptown depict Charlotte's industry, commerce, transportation, and vision for the future.

2. The Charlotte Hornets mural on Uptown's Two First Union Center features Anthony Mason, Vlade Divac, and Glen Rice.

3. North Carolina native Ben Long created incredible frescoes in Uptown's Bank of America Corporate Center, Charlotte-Mecklenburg Law Enforcement Center, and St. Peter's Catholic Church, and on the domed lobby ceiling of the Transamerica Square building.

4. A statue of Martin Luther King, Jr., overlooks Uptown's Marshall Park.

5. *Queen Charlotte*, an illuminated fountain and 1990 Raymond Kaskey sculpture of the city's namesake, extends her crown to welcome visitors at the Charlotte/Douglas International Airport.

6. A bronze forty-niner panning for gold at UNCC's Main Administration Building represents Charlotte as the site of the country's first gold rush, in 1799.

7. At the Charlotte International Trade Center on College Street Uptown, a regal, jewel-adorned Queen Charlotte is about the only thing standing still in this bustling business area.

8. A kinetic, hanging sculpture by world-famous artist Jean Tinguely incorporates colored light bulbs, wheels, wrought iron, and a cow's skull, among other objects, inside the Carillon Building Uptown.

9. Jerry Peart's large-scale aluminum sculpture outside the Carillon Building at 227 W. Trade St. Uptown uses bright green, yellow, blue, purple, and red to symbolize the changing seasons of the Carolinas' weather.

10. Charlotte artist Jack Pentes created a kinetic wind sculpture on West Trade Street with six steel rings arranged in a pyramid shape. Each season, the circular panels within the steel rings are replaced with different symbols of the Queen City's surroundings.

Lassister Research Library and a gift shop. The museum serves as a gateway to the oldest house in Mecklenburg County, "the Rock House"—the Revolutionary War-era home of Hezekiah Alexander, signer of the Mecklenburg Declaration of Independence. The home site, which also includes a log cabin kitchen and a springhouse, is fully furnished with period pieces dating between 1750 and 1800, and represents one of the largest collections of Southern Piedmont furniture in the area. Hours: Tue–Fri 10–5, Sat–Sun 2–5. ♿ (Central)

## DISCOVERY PLACE
301 N. Tryon St.
Charlotte
704/372-6261

Bored by science? You won't be at Discovery Place, one of the nation's top hands-on science and technology museums. Examine creatures of the sea and rain forest; explore space in the country's largest planetarium dome; power a hair dryer by riding a bike. Work your way through the Polymer Maze; find out how cyclones form; hear dinosaurs roar. Groups work together in the Challenger Learning Center to maneuver the Space Station Horizon into the tail of Halley's Comet. Discovery Place offers wide-eyed wonder and learning opportunities for all ages. Movies in the OMNIMAX theater also make great dates. (See also Chapter 6, Kids' Stuff.) Hours: Sept–May Mon–Fri 9–5, Sat 9–6, Sun 1–6; June–Aug Mon–Sat 9–6, Sun 1–6. Admission: Exhibit halls, OMNIMAX films, planetarium, and Challenger simulation are considered one option each. $5.50 one option ages 13–59, $4.50 one option ages 6–12 and seniors, $2.75 one option ages 3–5. Each additional option is $2 per person, any age. Group rates are also available. ♿ (Uptown)

## MUSEUM OF THE NEW SOUTH
324 N. College St.
Charlotte
704/333-1887

A museum like no other, this fun, interactive history museum examines Charlotte and the Carolina Piedmont from the end of the Civil War to the present. Study economic development through a cotton gin and old photos of textile mills; don the hats and gloves ladies wore for Uptown shopping; hear early country music recorded locally; see a Ku Klux Klan mask up close. A radio exhibit highlights Charlotte's musical tastes from 1920 to 1980; another focuses on a local WWII Mobile Army Surgical Hospital (MASH) unit. Record your own radio show. Research Charlotte history as you examine editorial cartoons and black-and-white photographs. This place is top-notch. Hours: Tue–Sat 11–5. Admission: $2 adults; $1 seniors, students, and educators; free kids under 5, members, and all tour/school groups. ♿ (Uptown)

Gallery crawls—street-festival-meets-exhibit-opening block parties with art, musicians, drum circles, tarot card readers, and street vendors—are held the first and third Fridays evenings of each month in the NoDa art district on North Davidson Street between 35th and 36th.

Crowds of up to 2,500 hang out in galleries, stores, eateries, and watering holes to soak up not only art but also the creative, cutting-edge energy of this revitalized art district.

Uptown gallery crawls are on first Fridays.

## SCHIELE MUSEUM OF NATURAL HISTORY AND PLANETARIUM
**1500 E. Garrison Blvd.**
**Gastonia**
**704/866-6900**

A 30-minute drive that's worth it, the Schiele features exhibits on North Carolina's natural history, the history of earth and evolution of life, Native American artifacts, and North American habitats. Study the stars in the 50-foot-domed planetarium or explore nature at the 16-acre facility's nature trail. Behind the museum, visitors learn about the lives of Indians and pioneers 250 years ago. See how people made clothing from deerskin, hunted small game with rivercane blowguns, made clothing from sheep's wool, and built log homes. Hours: Mon–Sat 9–5, Sun 1–5. Admission: Free to museum. Planetarium shows: $2 adults, $1 senior citizens and museum members, free children 4 and under. & (West)

## SPECIALTY MUSEUMS

### BACKING UP CLASSICS AUTO MUSEUM

**4545 Hwy. 29**
**Harrisburg**
**704/788-9500**

Just past Charlotte Motor Speedway, the Backing Up Classics Auto Museum attracts car-lovers of every kind. You'll see more than 50 cars, including classics, antiques, '50s race cars, and muscle cars, along with a mountain of memorabilia, at this self-guided museum. There's a stainless-steel DeLorean with flip-up doors; a Model T; a one-door, egg-shaped BMW; a '57 Chevrolet Bel-Air convertible with fins and whitewalls; a 1923 Bonnie-and-Clyde touring car; even a Chinese pedal cab. Race fans should look for the exhibit that shows racing's evolution from moonshine-runners to modern-day NASCAR. Hours: Mon–Fri 9–6, Sat 9–5, Sun 10–5. Admission: $5.00 adults, $10 families, $4 students and seniors, free under 6 with adult, $4 per person for groups over 12. & (North)

### CAROLINA RAPTOR CENTER
**Latta Plantation Park**
**Charlotte**
**704/875-6521**

Classified as a living-history mu-

---

## TRIVIA

A rich deposit of gold nuggets found outside Charlotte in 1790 resulted in nearly 100 gold mines within 20 miles of the city. In 1836, the U.S. Congress chose Charlotte as the first branch of the U.S. Mint.

Originally in Uptown on West Trade between Mint and Graham Streets, the Mint operated until the Civil War, when it became Confederate headquarters and a hospital. Eventually the building fell into disrepair, and preservationists stepped in to save it.

In 1934, the original Mint building was demolished and its materials used to build the Mint Museum of Art on Randolph Road. The Mint Museum opened in 1936 as North Carolina's first art museum.

## Top Ten Things to Discover at Discovery Place
### By Freda Nicholson, executive director

1. Films in the *Charlotte Observer* OMNIMAX Theatre offer a thrilling, five-story experience in the region's only theater of its kind.

2. Water Play Table in Kids Place allows children up to age 7 to explore, discover, and learn in a hands-on environment.

3. See exciting and colorful poison-dart frogs in an exotic, three-story tropical rain forest.

4. Challenger Learning Center features an unforgettable simulation of space exploration.

5. In the aquariums, place a starfish in the palm of your hand, pick up a horseshoe crab in the Touchpool, and meet marine life native to the Atlantic Coast.

6. The World's Largest Anatomically Correct Eyeball lets you step into your world of vision.

7. Kelly Space Voyager Planetarium re-creates the stars and the solar system as seen from any point on Earth.

8. Rat Basketball; a 100,000-volt, hair-raising generator; and reactions, explosions, and chemical changes are featured in daily floor programs.

9. Collections Gallery features 30,000 geological, anthropological, and zoological items.

10. The convenient parking deck is connected to the museum, and an overstreet walkway keeps you safe from traffic.

seum, the Carolina Raptor Center promotes conservation of and public education about birds of prey such as eagles, hawks, falcons, owls, and osprey. Injured or orphaned raptors come here to be nursed back to health and, if possible, released. Disabled raptors that could not survive in the wild remain at the museum as teaching tools. Most are in large cages, but a fenced-in ring allows staff members to give up-close demonstrations at weekend programs. New at the center is a 40-foot-tall, 100-foot-wide, tree-filled aviary that will allow guests to see raptors in flight. Hours: Tue–Sat 10–5, Sun noon–5. Admission: $4 adults, $2 seniors and students, free for members. ♿ (North)

**CAROLINAS AVIATION MUSEUM**
**4108 Airport Dr.**
**Charlotte**

**704/359-8442**

Aviation history comes alive at this museum, housed in the first hangar of Charlotte's airport. A replica of the Wright Brothers' Glider is on display, along with under-restoration birds, including a P-80 Shooting Star, a T-33 jet trainer, an F-84 Thunderjet, and an F-86 Sabre. Military buffs enjoy the Huey helicopters, T-28 Trojan, A-4 Skyhawk, and A-7 Corsair II with Desert Storm markings. A Piedmont DC-3 occupies most of the museum, which also displays aircraft engines, flight simulators, and other memorabilia. Volunteer guides love their hobby—and sharing it with visitors. Hours: Mon–Sat 10–5, Sun 1–5. Admission: Free, but donations accepted. ♿ (West)

## CHARLOTTE HISTORIC TROLLEY MUSEUM
**2104 South Blvd. at Atherton Mill**
**Charlotte**
**704/375-0850**

Hear the trolley bell clang as streetcar No. 85 chugs from South End to Uptown. Electric streetcars debuted in 1891, and were essential to development and now-historic neighborhoods such as Myers Park, Elizabeth, Dilworth, and Plaza-Midwood. Buses retired the fleet in 1938, but No. 85 was rediscovered in ruins in 1987. Preservationists championed restoration, and a museum was formed to share streetcar history. Photos, historical exhibits, streetcars under renovation, a carousel, and, of course, the shiny revived trolley are highlights. (See also Chapter 5, Sights and Attractions; and Chapter 6, Kids' Stuff.) Hours: Mon–Thu 11–2, Fri–Sun 10–6. Trolley runs Fri–Sat 10–9, Sun 10–6, football game days 10 a.m. until end of game. Admission: Museum is free, trolley is $1 each way. ♿ (Central)

## HENDRICK MOTORSPORTS MUSEUM
**4400 Papa Joe Hendrick Blvd.**
**Harrisburg**
**704/455-0342**

Jeff Gordon fans speed to this place faster than "The Kid" himself. See the NASCAR driver's Winston Cup championship trophies, the rainbow-colored car he drove to win the Inaugural Brickyard 400 in 1994, and the garage where mechanics fine-tune his engines. Fellow Hendrick team drivers Terry Labonte and Ricky Craven are equally represented in the museum and souvenir shop. Other highlights include a Lumina used in the movie *Days of Thunder*; the remains of a car crashed at 200 mph; and a special-edition BMW, Corvette, and Camaro. Hours: Mon–Fri 8:30–5, Sat 9–2. Admission: Free. ♿ (North)

## NORTH CAROLINA AUTO RACING HALL OF FAME
**119 Knob Hill Rd.**

---

# TRIVIA

Sometimes art appears in the most unlikely places. Ericsson Stadium, for instance, is not only home to the Carolina Panthers, it's also graced by bronze-cast Panther statues outside each entrance.

The growling, ready-to-pounce cats are each 7 feet tall, 20 feet long, and 2,800 pounds, with a price tag of $75,000 a pop.

*Backing Up Classics Auto Museum, p. 134*

**Mooresville**
**704/663-5331**
Dedicated to all types of racing, this museum displays more than 35 cars and several exhibits of uniforms, helmets, and photos. A small theater shows racing-history films, and an art gallery offers prints for purchase. Included are Rusty Wallace's first race car, Richard Petty's 1979 Chevrolet, Davey Allison's rookie Thunderbird, and Harry Gant's Skoal Bandit Lumina, among others. Admission is free in the art gallery and gift shop, which sells every imaginable racing souvenir on earth. Nearly 60 race teams are based in Mooresville; look for famous faces on the streets. Hours: Mon–Sat 9–5, with extended hours during local race weeks. Admission: $3.75 adults, $1.75 seniors and children ages 6–12, free 5 and under. ঙ (North)

**TOM CLARK MUSEUM**
**131 N. Main St.**
**Davidson**
**704/892-9213**
People go wild for the Cairn Studio gnomes, wood spirits, mountaineers, and seafaring characters sculpted in clay by Tom Clark. But many don't realize that Clark, a Davidson College professor and resident of this quaint town 25 minutes from Charlotte, operates a museum here. On the second floor, collectors can see the history of the gnomes, watch videos of Clark at work, and see valuable sculptures long-ago retired. The first floor houses gnomes and other Cairn sculptures, for sale from $18 to $675. A former drugstore, the museum retains an antiquated feel with tin ceiling tiles and pharmacy cabinets. Hours: Mon–Sat 10–5. Admission: Free. ঙ (North)

## ART GALLERIES

**BLUE PONY GALLERY & PRESS**
**3202-A N. Davidson St.**
**Charlotte**
**704/334-9390**
Contemporary, experimental artists push the limits of their media at this gallery and printmaking studio in the

revitalized art community of NoDa. Local, regional, and national artists are represented in original prints, etchings, woodcuts, lithographs, paintings, mixed media, drawings, ceramics, studio glass, and sculpture. Blue Pony hosts 10 shows a year, some featuring gallery artists and others focusing on individuals or small groups. There's also some history: the spartan, SoHo-style gallery is part of a 1926 building that once housed a bank, pharmacy, and hardware store for nearby mill villagers. Hours: 11–5 Tue–Sat. Admission: Free. ♿ (Central)

## CENTER OF THE EARTH GALLERY
### 3204 N. Davidson St.
### Charlotte
### www.centeroftheearth.com
### 704/375-5756

Voted "Best Gallery" 1995-1998 by two Charlotte magazines. In its tenth year, Center of the Earth represents 40 regional and national artists, emphasizing contemporary painting, glass, and sculpture for residential and corporate collections. Recipient of the 1996 Governor's Business Award in the Arts. Owners Ruth Ava Lyons and J. Paul Sires are also high-profile artists in the Southeast. Exposed brick, twelve-foot ceilings, and terrazzo floors complete the look of urban elegance in the NoDa district that Lyons and Sires pioneered. Hours: Tue–Fri 11–5, Sat 1–5, Sun 1–4. Admission: Free. ♿ (Central)

## FARVAN INTERNATIONAL GALLERY
### 119 E. Seventh St.
### Charlotte
### 704/375-1424

A surprising find in Charlotte, this Uptown international gallery represents artists and countries from around the world with paintings, sculpture, fine jewelry, and clay, in addition to private-collection antiques. Owner Farida Sweezy grew up the daughter of a diplomat and later traveled the world as a State Department employee. She now uses her global connections to help artists and companies reach world markets. Everything is handmade at this unusual 11-year-old

*Center of the Earth Gallery*

Center of the Earth Gallery

## Juleps & Jazz at Mint Socials

*Looking for a way to meet Charlotteans and learn about art at the same time?*

*The Young Affiliates of the Mint, a Mint Museum of Art group geared to young professionals ages 21 to 45, counts about 1,600 members in its ranks. The organization started a decade ago, and now sponsors many of the city's most popular events.*

*Derby Daze held on the early-May date of the Kentucky Derby each spring, draws thousands of young people to the lush lawn of the Mint to sip Mint Juleps, socialize, and watch the horse race on a big-screen TV.*

*In summer, people spread blankets on the Mint's lawn to listen to jazz and watch films in the Jazzy Ladies series, while Halloween brings a huge costume party.*

*The Young Affiliates of the Mint also conduct Artitudes, a series of lectures on collecting art; and Art Escapades, fun and educational trips to regional art studios and craft centers.*

*Annual memberships are $55 for individuals or $80 per household.*

gallery, featuring Spanish paintings, Syrian inlaid boxes, and Egyptian tapestries for starters. Hours: Mon–Fri 11–6, Sat 11–3. Admission: Free. ♿ (Uptown)

**GALLERY W.D.O.**
**2000 South Blvd. at Atherton Mill**
**Charlotte**
**704/333-9123**
W.D.O. stands for Well-Designed Object, and there are plenty at this fine-crafts gallery that showcases national artists. There's something for every taste, age, and budget, including quilts, hand-blown glass, metal sculpture, toy trains and planes, jewelry, leather journals, bird-feeders, pottery, handwoven scarves, black-and-white photography, ornamental baskets, clay dishes, and wooden art. The retired teacher who operates the gallery offers friendly explanations of exhibits and recommendations on other local galleries. Hours: Tue–Sat 11–6. Admission: Free. ♿ (Central)

**HODGES TAYLOR GALLERY**
**401 N. Tryon St.**
**Charlotte**
**704/334-3799**
One of the best-known galleries in town, Hodges Taylor is also the oldest gallery in Charlotte. The gallery opened 18 years ago to represent professional artists of the Southeast

who work in a variety of media—painting, sculpture, clay, metal, and glass. In its newest Uptown location in the Transamerica Square building, Hodges Taylor has three exhibition spaces. Two rooms feature solo artist's or special exhibitions on a rotating schedule, while a third showcases gallery artists. The Hodges Taylor's Fine Print Room offers an expanded inventory of prints from print publishers from around the United States and Great Britain. Informal lunchtime art discussions are held the second Tuesday of each month from noon to 1 p.m. Hours: Tue–Fri 11–6, Sat 11–3, Mon by appointment. Admission: Free. ﴾ (Uptown)

The '49er in front of UNC Charlotte's Reese Administration Building, p. 132

**JERALD MELBERG GALLERY**
**3900 Colony Rd. in Morrocroft Village**
**Charlotte**
**704/365-3000**
One of the preeminent galleries for contemporary American art, the Melberg makes its home in an upscale shopping center in SouthPark. National and international artists are represented here, with a few Charlotteans in the mix. Exhibits change every six weeks or so; themes include a glass show of goblets ranging from $200 to $12,000. Media include oils, pastels, collage, glass, bronze, and wooden sculpture. Some artists—such as Mecklenburg County native Romare Bearden—are names you're sure to recognize. Hours: Mon–Sat 10–6. Closed Sun. Admission: Free. ﴾ (South)

**NOEL GALLERY**
**401 N. Tryon St., Suite 104**
**Charlotte**
**704/343-0050**
National and international works appear in this fine gallery of contemporary American artists of African American and Latin American descent. Located in Transamerica Square Uptown, the Noel changes exhibits every two months. Collage painter Benny Andrews, abstract painter Sam Gilliam, and John Biggers (a North Carolina native who paints and creates prints) are the better-known names here. Overall, the gallery represents 27 artists with works in major American museums such as the Metropolitan, the Museum of Modern Art, and the Smithsonian. Hours: Tue–Sat 11–7, Sun 11–3. Admission: Free. ﴾ (Uptown)

**23 STUDIO**
**3205 N. Davidson St.**
**Charlotte**
**704/347-0723; 704/568-1788**
23 Studio, an alternative gallery in an area created as an alternative arts scene, operates with a "by artists, for artists" philosophy. Started as a place for emerging, unrepresented artists, 23

Studio is a lucky—and worthy—survivor among other galleries that eventually closed shop in NoDa. Artists rent space here to show works in such media as pottery, collage, acrylics, black-and-white photography, watercolors, copper sculpture, mosaics, metal, even string art. During gallery crawls each first and third Friday, look for artists creating work on sidewalks, and for impromptu drum circles in the area. Hours: Fri 1–7, Sat 1–5, Sun 1–4, Mon–Thu by appointment. Admission: Free. & (Central)

**WRIGHTNOW GALLERY**
**3211 N. Davidson St.**
**Charlotte**
**704/347-0723; 704/568-1788**

Artist and 23 Studio creator Steve Holt expanded exhibit opportunities for unrepresented local artists in October 1995 with the Wrightnow. At this NoDa gallery, just down from 23 Studio, contemporary independent or small group shows are exhibited. Look for blinking white lights framing the storefront window, or better yet, just listen for the jam sessions of musicians who gather in the middle of the gallery for after-hours practice. Great prices and the recent exhibit space of Jerry Kirk, who was named "Best Local Artist" by readers of *Charlotte's Best* magazine. Hours: Fri 1–7, Sat 1–5, Sun 1–4, Mon–Thu by appointment. Admission: Free. & (Central)

Larry Mellichamp/UNCC Biology Dept.

# 8

# PARKS, GARDENS, AND RECREATION AREAS

*In the Queen City, finding a park or garden is as simple as walking out the door. The sights and sounds of spring come alive with vibrant green lawns stretching through the city and the distant hum of mowers keeping them in check. Azaleas pop with color, tulips teeter on tiny stems, and wisteria drapes in a curtain of lilac.*

*Honored with a Tree City USA designation, Charlotte goes to great lengths to protect its natural trademark. Ancient willow oaks line the streets, forming a canopy of shade in the shape of arched church windows. Dogwoods debut with delicate flowers of pink and white. Maples erupt with the blazing hues of autumn.*

*Charlotteans love to get outside to enjoy the nature in their own backyards. Strolling the city is such a popular pastime, a few friendly homeowners have installed water fountains (and bowls of water for pups) near sidewalks. One lady even lets her cockatoo sit on a tree in her front yard to socialize with passing strollers.*

*Of course Charlotte has plenty of gardens, parks, and natural sanctuaries open to the public. More than 150 parks and six greenways are maintained by the Mecklenburg County Park & Recreation Department. Public and university gardens focus on roses, azaleas, orchids, native plants, perennials, daylilies, and birds.*

*State parks and nature preserves in the area showcase pristine woodlands, glistening lakes, rugged trails, and even a few craggy peaks.*

*So whether it's a rose garden adorning the side of a shopping center, a park adjoining a skyscraper, or a preserve where wildlife thrives, Charlotte is overflowing with natural beauty.*

# PARKS

## FREEDOM PARK
**1908 East Blvd.**
**Charlotte**
**704/353-1165**

One of the most popular parks in Charlotte, Freedom Park covers 107 acres between the historic Dilworth and Myers Park neighborhoods. Blooming cherry trees dominate the East Boulevard entrance, while a seven-acre lake and its family of ducks awaits at the other end of the park. In between, urban dwellers enjoy three youth ball fields, four soccer fields, nature trails, tennis courts, volleyball beach, basketball courts, playground, amphitheater, and picnic shelters. Paved trails around the lake and through the park bring out scores of walkers, bikers, joggers, and skaters; an old locomotive train at the playground fascinates half-pints. Hours: Daily 9–dark. Admission: Free. Limited wheelchair access. (Central)

## HORNETS NEST PARK
**6301 Beatties Ford Rd.**
**Charlotte**
**704/875-1391**

In northwest Charlotte, people head to Hornets Nest Park for its walking trails, tennis courts, athletic fields, basketball, playgrounds, lake, picnic shelters, petting zoo, and two unusual elements: an 18-hole disc golf course and a BMX track. One of the fastest growing sports in North America, disc golf is similar to traditional golf but involves throwing a Frisbee into a goal. The 1,150-foot regulation BMX track is the site of bicycle motocross competitions each Saturday. Monitored open practice sessions and teaching clinics are available. If you want to get away from traffic, however, reconsider Hornets Nest—cruising through the park

has become so rampant that police often have to redirect traffic. Hours: Daily 9–dark. Admission: Free. Limited wheelchair access. (North)

## LATTA PARK
**510 E. Park Ave.**
**Charlotte**
**704/336-2533**

For seclusion within the bustling city, try quaint Latta Park, which winds through the middle of historic Dilworth in central Charlotte. Extending for several blocks through the neighborhood, the park is lined with the lovely homes of the Queen City's first suburbs. Nearby residents visit Latta Park to let dogs roam free, to find a quiet spot in the shade, or to get some exercise on the basketball court, tennis courts, and walking trail. There's also a children's playground and a picnic area. The Dilworth Jubilee, a large family festival that draws folks from throughout the city, is held in Latta Park each summer. Hours: Mon–Fri 9–9, Sat 10–6, Sun 1–6. Admission: Free. (Central)

## MALLARD CREEK PARK
**3001 Johnston-Oehler Rd.**
**Charlotte**
**704/336-8866**

A 515-acre park, Mallard Creek attracts lots of softball leagues and soccer games with its four lighted softball fields, a softball pavilion, rest rooms, concession stand, five soccer fields, and picnic shelter. The newly developed park also features one of the best playgrounds in the county, with state-of-the-art modular units with slides, swings, tubes, and climbing stations, and a thick rubber-mat surface. Mallard Creek Park is also home to 183-acre, 18-hole Tradition public golf course and its lighted driving range. A recreation center is scheduled to open by spring 1999. Hours: 9–dark. Admission: Free. Limited wheelchair access. (North)

## MARSHALL PARK
**South McDowell and Third Streets**
**Charlotte**
**704/336-4262**
This urban park in the shadows of Uptown skyscrapers offers a city block's worth of green space, flower beds, trees, a lake, and fountains for cubicle-weary workers. Located across from the Mecklenburg County Courthouse, it's a lunch-hour favorite for folks who like to eat outdoors. The small lake, snaking from one end of the park to the other, features bridges and platforms jutting out over its edge and fountains that spew and trickle. The amphitheater has four grassy tiers and a large stage for performances. Don't miss the 1980 bronze statue of Dr. Martin Luther King, Jr. Hours: Daily 6–midnight. Admission: Free. Limited wheelchair access. (Uptown)

## MCALPINE CREEK PARK
**8711 Monroe Rd.**
**Charlotte**
**704/568-4044**
The perfect place for walking, running, and biking, East Charlotte's McAlpine Creek Park connects to James Boyce Park via the McAlpine Creek Greenway to form one large continuous recreation area. McAlpine Creek Park covers 462 acres and features soccer fields, a three-acre lake, a fishing pier, nature trails, bicycle path, and picnic areas. One of the park's more unusual amenities is its 5K cross-country course, a well-known trail often used for state and national competitions. McAlpine Creek Greenway can be accessed from the park, adjoining neighborhoods, and a parking area on Sardis Road. Together, the three entities make up more than three miles of exercise trails. Hours: 9–dark. Admission: Free. Limited wheelchair access. (East)

## NEVIN PARK
**6000 Statesville Rd.**
**Charlotte**
**704/336-8866**
In northeast Mecklenburg County, the new Nevin Park features just over 300 acres of recreational enjoyment with four lighted softball fields, a softball pavilion, a concession stand, two lighted soccer fields, a playground, two well-equipped shelters with rest rooms, four horseshoe pits, and a

shuffleboard area. A winding, tree-lined entrance leads to the state-of-the-art softball complex, central pavilion, and multipurpose asphalt trails used for walking, jogging, biking, and inline skating. An active athletic area, Nevin Park draws softball tournaments, league team play, and plenty of families who like the park's open fields and shady spots perfect for a Sunday nap. Hours: Daily 9–dark. Limited wheelchair access. (North)

**PARK ROAD PARK**
**6215 Park Rd.**
**Charlotte**
**704/643-3405**

A favorite among Charlotteans in the SouthPark area, the 124-acre Park Road Park features something for everybody. Much activity centers around the four-acre lake where visitors walk on gravel trails, cook on lakeside grills, fish for trout, feed the ducks and geese, or simply sit on the banks on Sunday afternoons. Kids love the new playground area near the lake, which features slides, tubes, jungle gyms, and swings. Others enjoy riding bikes, shooting hoops, playing tennis and softball, or gathering with friends under covered shelters. From Thanksgiving to February the park's lake is stocked with rainbow trout,

---

## Top Ten Most Unusual Finds at UNC-Charlotte Botanical Gardens
By Dr. Larry Mellichamp, director

1. The largest collection of orchid species of any university gardens in the South, and in general, a fine display of tropical orchids.

2. The largest collection of hybrid rhododendrons and native azaleas of any public garden in the South.

3. A large collection of hybrid daylilies.

4. The largest collection of plants native to the Carolinas of any public garden in the South.

5. More than 40 species and cultivars of *Viburnum*.

6. The largest winter garden of any public garden in the South.

7. The largest collection of named cultivars of *Sarracenia* pitcher plants in the United States and, overall, one of the best *Sarracenia* collections in the East.

8. More than 40 cultivars of Japanese maples (*Acer palmatum*) and related species.

9. The largest collection of plants in the South for the "Black Garden."

10. An outstanding display of tropical plants from around the world and a small tropical rain forest conservatory.

---

which normally thrive in colder waters of the mountains. The decade-long program—the only one of its kind in Mecklenburg County—allows young and old to fish for trout from the banks. Hours: Daily 9–dark. Admission: Free; $1 for daily fishing permit, $20 for yearly permit. Limited wheelchair access. (South)

## POLK PARK
**121 W. Trade St. at Interstate Tower**
**Charlotte**
**704/332-7301**
Most likely the smallest park in the city, Polk Park is a natural oasis at the foot of the 33-story Interstate Tower, overlooking The Square at the intersection of Trade and Tryon Streets. It's the busiest spot in Uptown Charlotte, but this park's waterfalls, flower beds, and outdoor seating make for a calm corner in a chaotic setting. A great place for lunch or people-watching. Hours: Anytime. Admission: Free. ♿ (Uptown)

## RAMSEY CREEK PARK
**18441 Nantz Rd.**

**Cornelius**
**704/896-9808**
Need a beach break, but don't want to drive four hours to the coast? Ramsey Creek Park overlooks Lake Norman with 46 acres of sunning beaches, boat launches and docks, a new playground, picnic shelters, nature trails, and a fishing pier. There's no promise of hunky lifeguards, but large beach-style umbrellas are available to rent for an instant picnic shelter along the lakeshore. Trails offer great places to walk and admire nature. This is one of only a few public places to launch boats at Lake Norman. Hours: Daily 9–dark. Admission: Free. Limited wheelchair access. (North)

## REEDY CREEK PARK AND NATURE PRESERVE
**2900 Rocky River Rd.**
**Charlotte**
**704/336-8866 (park), 704/598-8857 (environmental center)**
Located adjacent to Reedy Creek Park (two softball fields, soccer field, picnic shelter, basketball court, two volleyball courts) in northeast Charlotte, Reedy Creek Nature Preserve covers

*Park Road Park, p. 145*

Scott Forester

# A Hidden Oasis

*Daniel Stowe Botanical Garden in Belmont is different each time you visit, and not merely because of ever-changing flowers, plants, and woodlands.*

*Long-range plans at the garden include a permanent Visitors Pavilion, many specialized gardens, cascading fountains, quiet pools, walking trails, conservatories, an amphitheater, and an auditorium.*

*The garden's property also backs up to Lake Wylie, and future development will also feature a separate lake entrance to make the garden accessible by boat.*

807 acres of gently rolling terrain. The nature preserve contains significant natural areas and is rich in cultural history. Charlotteans come to Reedy Creek for its hiking trails, picnic tables and shelters, fishing, wildlife viewing, butterfly garden/pond, three lakes, fishing pier, and environmental center with educational exhibits and classroom. (See also Chapter 10, Sports and Recreation.) Hours: Daily 9–dark. Admission: Free. Limited wheelchair access. (East)

## RENAISSANCE PARK
**1200 W. Tyvola Rd.**
**Charlotte**
**704/583-1196**
A park for active Charlotteans, Renaissance Park (west of Uptown) is part of a recreation complex that includes the 18-hole Renaissance golf course and the Jeff Adams Tennis Center. Other amenities include soccer fields, a softball complex, and rugged bike trails. With 17 lighted courts, including a stadium court with grandstands, Jeff Adams Tennis Center is the Charlotte area's premier facility. Private lessons and clinics are available for all ages; the center also hosts sanctioned and non-sanctioned tournaments throughout the year. Hours: Park open daily 9–dark. Hours vary for golf course and tennis center. Admission: Free; fees for golf, tennis courts. Limited wheelchair access. (West)

## RIBBONWALK
**Charlotte's Botanical Forest**
**4700 Hoyt Hinson Rd.**
**Charlotte**
**704/372-9594**
A 150-acre hardwood forest, Ribbon-Walk offers an inner-city escape for nature photographers, bird watchers and those who love the outdoors. Developers somehow missed this prime piece of property off of Nevin Road in North Charlotte, and now it's a botanical forest with several mile-long trails, ponds, gardens and a ravine filled with hundreds of ancient beech trees. Picnic facilities and rest rooms on site. Hours: Sat, 9–2. Admission: Free. Limited wheelchair accessibility. (North)

# A Natural Home

*In creating Wing Haven, the garden and bird sanctuary they called home, Elizabeth and Edwin Clarkson started in 1927 with a single tree in a sea of red clay.*

*Today that sapling is a towering willow oak surrounded by three acres of trees, wooded natural areas, formal gardens, fountains, and flower beds.*

*On birthdays, anniversaries, and holidays, the Clarksons exchanged gifts such as bricks, rosebushes, fountains, statues, and 3,500-pound truckloads of sunflower seeds and grains for the birds.*

*Elizabeth Clarkson was a concert pianist, and often entertained at the piano in her elegant and unique home. Decorative mirrors replaced artwork on the walls, and draperies never went up. Candles provided their only light. The Clarksons believed the beauty of nature brought inside was the only decorating they needed.*

*Today, the bricks from the paths that wind through the gardens and from the tall brick walls that surround the property would build 10 brick homes.*

---

**WILLIAM R. DAVIE PARK**
**4635 Pineville-Matthews Rd.**
**Charlotte**
**704/643-3405**
Southeast Charlotte is one of the area's fastest growing places, and now there's a new park for the many families and professionals who call Pineville, Matthews, and South Charlotte home. One of the biggest draws of the recently opened 106-acre park and recreation facility is a 4,000-square-foot indoor conference center with a patio, playground, tables, and barbecue grill. The rental facility is ideal for corporate events, conferences, reunions, receptions, and special events. A one-acre lake, sand volleyball court, soccer fields, ball fields, picnic shelters, multipurpose sport court, and horseshoe pits are a short stroll away. Hours: Daily 9–dark. Admission: Free; rental charge for conference center. Limited wheelchair access. (South)

## GARDENS

**DANIEL STOWE
BOTANICAL GARDEN
6500 S. New Hope Rd.
Belmont
704/825-4490**
An impressive sight even in its early stage of development, Daniel Stowe

Water, water everywhere and nowhere to swim. Although Mecklenburg touches three lakes, county policy states no swimming is allowed off its banks.

Lake swimming is available at a 33-acre lake within Duke Power State Park, north of Charlotte at 159 Inland Sea Lane in Troutman. For information, call 704/528-6350.

Botanical Garden in Belmont has been featured in *Southern Living* and many gardening magazines for its current offerings and far-reaching future plans. A 350-variety perennial garden displayed in 1.5 acres is the focal point; others are the Four Seasons Garden, Kitchen Garden of vegetables and herbs, Butterfly Garden, and serene Woodland Trail. From May through October, more than 275 varieties of daylilies provide continuous blooms. There's also a gift shop within a rustic cabin and a great series of speakers, nature studies, kids' programs, and workshops. Hours: Mon–Sat 9–5, Sun noon–5. Admission: Donations suggested for individuals; $2/person groups 10 or more. Limited wheelchair access. (West)

### GLENCAIRN GARDEN
### Charlotte Avenue and Crest Street
### Rock Hill, SC
### 803/329-5620
An award-winning, six-acre oasis of flowering beauty in Rock Hill, Glencairn Garden displays nature's finest colors, textures, and shapes. Stately oaks, vibrant azaleas, delicate dogwoods, fragrant wisteria, thousands of blooming flowers, fountains, lily ponds, and walking paths grace the garden that's still unknown to many Charlotteans. The highlight of the town's "Come See Me" Festival each April, Glencairn is best known for its azaleas, 7,000 daylilies, warm-weather annuals and summer-blooming perennials. Hours: dawn–dusk, daily. Admission: free. (South)

### MCGILL ROSE GARDEN
### 940 N. Davidson St.
### Charlotte
### 704/333-6497
One of the best-kept secrets in Charlotte, the McGill Rose Garden began in 1955 when the late Helen McGill planted two rose bushes at her husband's business, Avant Fuel and Ice Company. Over the years, she added beauty to the blighted area with roses along the fences and railroad track and in any other space she could find. By 1967 the spruce-up project had snowballed to 500 rosebushes, and the public was invited to a Mother's Day Open House that remains popular today. The 1.3-acre urban garden, which is also the oldest coal yard in Charlotte, features 1,100 roses, an herb garden, children's garden, fountains, grassy areas, and benches for sitting and relaxing. In late 1997, the garden received the prestigious All-America Rose Selections Public Garden honor. Blooms appear May through late October; peak season May and October. Ask about picnics, teas, horticulture workshops, and other special events. Hours: May–Oct Tue–Fri 9–3; Sun 2–5 and by appointment. Nov–April 9–1 and by appointment. Admission: Free; donations accepted. ♿ (Central)

*The award-winning McGill Rose Garden, p. 149*

## UNC-CHARLOTTE BOTANICAL GARDENS
**Mary Alexander and Craver Roads on UNCC campus**
**Charlotte**
**704/547-2555**

When a benefactor moving from Charlotte to Honolulu donated her extensive orchid collection to UNCC, the university built a greenhouse to hold it; two other gardens followed. Today McMillan Greenhouse features one of the largest orchid collections of any public garden in the South. Hundreds of the delicate, unusual blooms fill the greenhouse, which has rooms of differing climates to showcase carnivorous plants, pitcher plants, desert cacti, and a two-level tropical rain forest. Botany and horticulture students and professors lead pre-arranged tours. Peak blooming season for orchids is February through April; a huge plant sale is also held each spring. Across the street, VanLandingham Glen covers seven acres of natural woods with more than 3,000 hybrid rhododendrons, 1,000 trees, and the region's largest

collection of native plants. Rhododendrons' peak is late April through Mother's Day. Adjacent is the Susie Harwood Garden with exotic and ornamental plants from around the world. The three-acre site has an Oriental feel, with pagodas, Japanese maples, arched bridges, and gardens to attract butterflies and hummingbirds. Hours: McMillan Greenhouse Mon–Fri 9–4, Sat 10–3, closed Sun. Gardens: Daily daylight hours. Admission: Free; group tours $25 except for schools. Limited wheelchair access. (North)

## WING HAVEN GARDENS AND BIRD SANCTUARY
**248 Ridgewood Ave.**
**Charlotte**
**704/331-0664**

Perhaps thousands of people have driven down this Myers Park street without ever realizing what awaits in the backyard. Elizabeth and Edwin Clarkson built the two-story clapboard home in 1927 when this central neighborhood was merely an open, empty field. Elizabeth began gardening, but fell in love with the birds that the plants and flowers attracted. Her bluebird, Tommy, bathed in a big soup tureen in the bathroom and never spent a night outside after finding Wing Haven. Daphne the rabbit hopped through the home as she pleased. A duck returned each spring. The garden kept growing, and soon people showed up to take a look. The Clarksons died several years ago, but their legacy and love of gardens and birds lives on at this three-acre sanctuary of formal gardens, wooded areas, pools, and fountains. Enjoy self-guided or guided tours, children's programs, lectures, and workshops. Hours: Tue 3–5, Wed 10–noon, Sun 2–5, or by appointment. Admission: Free; donations accepted, guide booklet $1. Limited wheelchair access. (Central)

## RECREATION AREAS

### ANDREW JACKSON STATE PARK
**196 Andrew Jackson Park Rd.**
**Lancaster, SC**
**803/285-3344**

Controversy over whether Andrew Jackson was born in North or South Carolina has brewed since the seventh U.S. president died in 1845. South Carolinians maintain "Old Hickory" was born and raised at what is now a state park 35 minutes from Charlotte near Lancaster, South Carolina. The 360-acre park and museum focuses on

---

# Preservation Education

*The nature preserves managed by Mecklenburg County Park & Recreation Department cover about 4,200 acres of undeveloped land and offer a wide range of environmental programs for all ages. These open-to-the-public events often focus on nature walks, birds, wildflowers, or environmental issues such as composting.*

*During the school year, teachers often bring students to the nature preserves for stream studies and information about ponds, plants, trees, and food webs. The preserves also offer a year-round Ecology Club and a summertime Ecology Camp for youngsters.*

*Adults can visit for various workshops or get involved with Senior Excursions, a series of hiking and garden trips to significant natural areas around the Carolinas.*

*Natural Connections, a quarterly newsletter on environmental programs and related issues, is available for free.*

*For information, call Reedy Creek Nature Preserve at 704/598-8857, Latta Plantation Nature Preserve at 704/875-1391, or McDowell Nature Preserve at 704/588-5224.*

---

backcountry pioneer life from 1750 to 1850. There is an antique-filled museum, an 18th-century schoolhouse replica, and a bronze Anna Hyatt Huntington statue of Jackson on a horse. The park has two nature trails, an 18-acre lake, picnic shelters, 25 campsites, and an amphitheater that hosts the Carolina Legends folk music festival each May. (See also Chapter 3, Where to Stay.) Hours: Apr–Oct daily 9–9. Oct–Apr daily 8–6. Admission: Free; fee for camping, activities. Limited wheelchair access. (South)

## CROWDERS MOUNTAIN STATE PARK
### 522 Park Office Ln.
### Kings Mountain
### 704/853-5375

Crowders Mountain State Park, about 30 miles west of Charlotte in the Kings Mountain Range, covers nearly 3,000 acres. Within the saddle-shaped park, Crowders Mountain stretches 1,625 feet in the northeast, while 1,705-foot Kings Pinnacle is in the southwest. In between are 15 miles of connecting trails, picnic areas, and a nine-acre lake where fishing, canoeing, and just looking for toads, dragonflies, and crappie make for a day of fun. Great programs highlight such subjects as streams, astronomy, animal tracks, canoeing, hiking, orienteering, wildflowers, native birds, and

the history of all-healing springs. Canoe rentals available June through Labor Day; open for primitive pack-in camping. (See also Chapter 3, Where to Stay.) Hours: Nov–Feb daily 8–6; Mar and Oct daily 8–7; Apr–May and Sept daily 8–8; June–Aug daily 8–9. Admission: Free; fees for shelters, canoes and camping. Limited wheelchair access. (West)

## DUKE POWER STATE PARK
### 159 Inland Sea Lane
### Troutman
### 704/528-6350

Rolling hills, relaxing picnics, easy hiking trails, and a 33-acre lake with swimming, canoes, rowboats, and paddleboats await at Duke Power State Park, nearly an hour north of Charlotte. The 1,458-acre park also features two picnic sites, a tent-only group camping facility, 13 miles of shoreline, fishing, boat access to Lake Norman, and an area for family tents and trailers. Programs focus on nature studies at the lake, wildflower walks, bird-watches, and night hikes. Duke Power's 33-acre lake and sandy beach area is also the only lake swimming available to the public in the area. In 1999 the park will open an enclosed community building-plus-kitchen facilities for corporate meetings and family reunions. (See also Chapter 3, Where to Stay.) Hours: Nov–Feb daily

8–6; Mar and Oct daily 8–7; Apr–May and Sept daily 8–8; June–Aug daily 8–9. Admission: Free; fee for camping, swimming, boat rentals. Limited wheelchair access. (North)

## JETTON PARK ON LAKE NORMAN
19000 Jetton Rd.
Huntersville
704/896-9808

Who needs a boat to enjoy the beauty and fun of Lake Norman? Jetton Park, opened in July 1992, is a 105-acre lakefront park with picnic sites, gazebos, a sunning beach, bike rentals, lakefront decks, concession stands, formal gardens, playgrounds, tennis courts, and paved multipurpose trails. Observe the flora and fauna along the park's shaded trails, ride bikes or walk along the waterfront, then enjoy a spectacular Lake Norman sunset. Families often rent Waterfront Hall, an 1,100-square-foot building with central heat and air conditioning, while couples plan outdoor weddings here. Each September, Jetton Park hosts LakeFest, a North Mecklenburg community celebration. Hours: Daily 9–dark. Admission: $3/vehicle, county residents; $5/vehicle, non-county residents. Fees apply only on weekends

---

# Top Ten Tree-Lined Streets in Charlotte
By Don McSween, city arborist

1. **Wilkinson Boulevard, from Berryhill:** Willow Oaks and Dogwoods (spring and fall).

2. **Sharon Amity Road, from East Independence Boulevard to Hickory Grove Road:** River Birch.

3. **The Plaza, from Central Avenue to Parkwood Avenue:** Crape Myrtle, Sugar Maple, and flower beds.

4. **North Tryon Street, from Stonewall Avenue to Seventh Street:** Willow Oaks, Yoshino Cherries (spring and fall), flowers and perennials.

5. **Wendover Road, from Randolph Road to Sharon Road:** Willow Oaks, Dogwoods, and Bradford Pears (spring and fall).

6. **Wilkinson Boulevard, from Berryhill Road to Donald Ross Road:** Crape Myrtle and Zelcovas.

7. **Airport Connector Road, from Billy Graham Parkway to Charlotte/Douglas International Airport:** Bradford Pears.

8. **Colville Road, from Laurel Avenue to Providence Road:** Willow Oaks, Elms, and Sugar Maples.

9. **Colony Road, from Sharon Road to Fairview Road:** Red Maple, Crape Myrtle, flowers, and perennials.

10. **Freedom Drive, from Thrift Road to Ashley Road:** Bradford Pears, Crape Myrtle, and Hollies.

---

## War Against the Worms

*Those large bands of greenish-brown goo wrapped around many of Charlotte's tree trunks aren't an invading life form—they're the city's latest attack on pesky cankerworms.*

*The lime-green inchworms' favorite meal seems to be the leaves of dogwoods, cherry trees, and especially the massive old willow oaks that impressively line the streets of many central neighborhoods.*

*The sticky bands around the trunks trap the wingless female moths as they climb the tree to lay eggs on twigs and branches. If the moths aren't caught, the eggs hatch in the spring and the small green caterpillars feed for weeks, leaving small holes or eating the entire leaf. Losing foliage could cause the tree to die.*

*City arborists have battled the cankerworms in areas such as Eastover and Myers Park for years. Since then, the pests have spread to Freedom Park, Dilworth, and Elizabeth.*

*The city has also called in the "bomb squad" to spray the leaf-eating worms with an organic bacterium from low-flying airplanes.*

---

and holidays Mar–Oct. Limited wheelchair access. (North)

### KINGS MOUNTAIN STATE PARK
**1277 Park Rd.**
**Blacksburg, SC**
**803/222-3209**
Don't let the name fool you. The "mountains" here look more like molehills, but there's plenty of recreational fun nonetheless. Located about 45 minutes west of Charlotte, the 6,832-acre Kings Mountain State Park is adjacent to the history-oriented Kings Mountain National Military Park. Camping is available on 119 sites with electric and water hookups and two dump stations. Enjoy the trading post, putt-putt course,

swimming lake, fishing boat rentals, picnic shelters, scenic driving, 17-mile hiking trail, horseback trail, and living-history farm with 13 restored buildings. (See also Chapter 3, Where to Stay.) Hours: Easter–Oct daily 7–9; Oct–Easter daily 8–6. Admission: Free; Memorial Day– Labor Day, $2 per vehicle. Fee for activities. Limited wheelchair access. (West)

### LATTA PLANTATION NATURE PRESERVE AND VISITOR CENTER
**5225 Sample Rd.**
**Huntersville**
**704/875-1391**
The largest park facility in Mecklenburg County, Latta Plantation Nature Preserve in the northwest includes

more than 1,000 acres to form a green peninsula extending into Mountain Island Lake. The huge park features a visitor center with exhibits and classrooms, hiking and horse trails, picnic tables and shelters, wildlife viewing, fishing, seasonal boat and canoe rentals, a playground, butterfly garden/pond, and bird-feeding stations. Latta Plantation is also home to the Carolina Raptor Center, Historic Latta Place, and the Latta Equestrian Center. (See also Chapter 10, Sports and Recreation.) Hours: Daily 9–dark. Admission: Free; fees for Raptor Center, Latta Place, Equestrian Center. Limited wheelchair access. (North)

## MCDOWELL NATURE PRESERVE AND NATURE CENTER
**15222 York Rd./NC 49**
**Charlotte**
**704/583-1176**

Overlooking Lake Wylie in southwest Mecklenburg County, McDowell Nature Preserve encompasses 931 acres of tree-covered, rolling terrain. More than 90 percent of the nature preserve has been left undeveloped, so wildlife viewing and hiking opportunities are prime. McDowell Nature Preserve offers environmental and nature programs, hiking trails, picnic tables and

*UNC-Charlotte
Botanical Gardens, p. 150*

Larry Mellichamp/UNCC Biology Dept.

shelters, fishing, seasonal boat and canoe rentals, a playground, large picnic pavilion, a nature center, and nature hikes by appointment. Overnight camping is available in 88 campsites including rented 12-by-12 platform tents, RV parking spots, and tent camping in a drive-up gravel site or a primitive walk-in site. (See also Chapter 3, Where to Stay.) Hours: 9–dark. Admission: $3 county vehicle, $5 non-county vehicle; fee for activities. Limited wheelchair access. (West)

Century

# 9

# SHOPPING

Long ago, shopping in Charlotte meant putting on your hat and gloves, donning your Sunday best, and making the trek to Uptown boutiques and department stores. As residents moved to the city's first suburbs and eventually out to the area's still-booming residential developments, shopping has followed.

For the most part, shops reflect the neighborhoods they inhabit.

Myers Park, one of Charlotte's oldest neighborhoods, tends to be traditional, upscale, and refined. Dilworth and South End, both old areas made new again, feature an eclectic mixture of shops and urban markets with contemporary home accessories and clothing. Just beginning its rebirth, Plaza-Midwood offers storefront window shopping and a funky mix of antiques, vinyl records, wild clothing, skateboard gear, and African artifacts.

South Charlotte, thanks to the upscale SouthPark Mall, has experienced a flood of high-end stores that draw people from throughout the city. New retail stores continue to pop up in growing areas at Lake Norman and University in the north, and near Ballantyne, Pineville, and Matthews in the south.

Shopping in Charlotte may also be coming full circle. Plans are in the works for a new Uptown mall with upscale tenants the city has never seen. Get out those hats and white gloves . . .

## SHOPPING DISTRICTS

### SouthPark Area

SouthPark Mall, Charlotte's largest and most upscale mall, lures plenty of shoppers on its own merit, but there are no less than four other major shopping centers surrounding this merchandise mecca.

Sharon Corners Shopping Center, which boasts a Barnes & Noble; Specialty Shops on the Park, an upscale shopping center adjacent to

The Park Hotel; Morocroft Village, a red-brick shopping center with high-ceilinged stores and domed roofs; and Phillips Place, the town's newest shopping destination, are where you'll find this community's businesspeople and exclusive residents spending their spare time.

Plan to spend all day shopping in SouthPark and prepare to max out the Gold Card.

## B.D. JEFFRIES
**6822-F Phillips Place Ct. at Phillips Place**
**Charlotte**
**704/556-0019**
A boutique specializing in alligator and crocodile pieces, this masculine store with a Ralph Lauren look is a great place to find gifts for the has-everything guy. You'll find cigar cases in honey, chocolate, and black tones; classic alligator and croc belts; desk and business accessories; wallets; money clips; picture frames; and cufflinks. Ladies love the crocodile belts with silver buckles in the shape of spaniels and retrievers, tortoiseshell jewelry and accessories, and unique serving utensils. The perfect place for unusual groomsmen's gifts. Mon–Sat 10–6, closed Sun. (South)

## BEDSIDE MANOR
**6822 Phillips Place Ct.**
**in Phillips Place**
**Charlotte**
**704/554-7727**
A magazine layout come to life, Bedside Manor indulges with fine European linens for the bed, bath, and table; French and Italian tableware; and delicate yet comfortable sleepwear. The Phillips Place store spent five years in Myers Park, and has continued its tradition of beautiful things near SouthPark: scented candles, fluffy towels, soft chenille throws, iron beds, high-threadcount linens, bath products, and baby gifts. It's the way you wish your bedroom looked instead of the way it does, but not to worry. Bedside Manor also features in-home design consultation. Mon–Sat 10–6 and by appointment, closed Sun. (South)

## THE CARRIAGE
**6401 Morrison Blvd. in Specialty Shops on the Park**
**Charlotte**
**704/364-0474**
The fact that The Carriage features a fur salon within its store says plenty, and the upscale look continues throughout the spacious, two-store boutique. Most women shop here for special-occasion dresses for weddings, balls, and parties, but there is a wide selection of dressy casual and relaxed styles, too. Sales staff, known for creating complete wardrobes for clients, are courteous and more down-to-earth than you might expect for such an upscale store. Mon–Sat 10–6, closed Sun. (South)

## CRADLE AND ALL
**6822-A Phillips Place Ct. at Phillips Place**
**Charlotte**
**704/643-2700**
Cradle and All's sky-blue walls with puffy clouds and twinkling stars hint of the possibilities at this shop that specializes in wall murals, hand-painted furniture, and custom bedding for babies and children. Mothers may come here for whimsical comforters and co-ordinating window treatments, but most leave with the whole shebang. Themes include Noah's ark, Bambi, Winnie the Pooh, bunnies, jungles, beach scenes, underwater life, or Humpty Dumpty. A great place for

gifts. Mon–Wed and Fri–Sat 10–6, Thu 10–8, Sun 1–5. (South)

## ELIZABETH BRUNS JEWELERS
**6401 Morrison Blvd. in Specialty Shops on the Park**
**Charlotte**
**704/365-3700**

With an in-store security guard, soft-spoken sales staff, and atmosphere that could make Donald Trump feel uncomfortable, Elizabeth Bruns isn't the place to go to borrow fine jewelry on Oscar night. But the jewels are fine nonetheless, along with Herend and Tiffany china, Baccarat crystal, silver plate and sterling pieces, and unique gifts. Worth it if you can stomach the icy service. Mon–Fri 10–5:30, Sat 10–4:30, closed Sun. (South)

## HAROLD'S
**6401 Morrison Blvd. in Specialty Shops on the Park**
**Charlotte**
**704/366-8303**

You know from the get-go this is a different kind of place, with bowls of candy by the door and young, friendly sales staff offering soft drinks while you browse. The Oklahoma-based Harold's features classic women's clothing with preppy leanings and a Southwestern twist. Great wardrobe-building basics and accessories that can go easily from career to casual make the investment worth it. Voted Charlotte's best women's casual clothing three years running. Mon–Wed and Fri 10–7, Thu 10–8, Sat 10–6, Sun noon–5. (South)

## LION'S LTD. FINE JEWELERS
**4732 Sharon Rd., Suite P, in Sharon Corners Shopping Center**
**Charlotte**
**704/556-7747**

With one of the largest selections of David Yurman jewelry in the region, Lions Ltd. is an upscale jeweler with top lines such as Rolex and Tag Heuer, a large inventory of loose diamonds, and gifts including Limoges miniatures, Fabergé eggs, humidors, jewelry boxes, caviar-and-vodka sets, and martini glasses. Most jewelry needs can be serviced here; the store has an on-site gem lab, master goldsmith, certified gemologist, and hand engraver. Additional location: Jetton Village, Exit 28 off I-77 at Lake Norman. Mon–Fri 10–6, Sat 10–5:30, closed Sun. (South)

## MARDI'S
**4732 Sharon Rd., Suite S, in Sharon Corners Shopping Center**
**Charlotte**
**704/643-5333**

The sister store of Lions Ltd., Mardi's specializes in home accessories: Lynn Chase china, Fabergé, Limoges, hand-painted linens, party and wedding invitations, stationery, mirrors, artwork, floral arrangements, and furniture. (South)

## OUR PLACE
**4732 Sharon Rd.**
**in Sharon Corners Shopping Center**
**Charlotte**
**704/554-7748**

The name says it all at this friendly, low-key boutique where owners, sales staff, and customers dish while sipping coffee and trying on clothes. A 22-year tradition in Charlotte, the contemporary store carries Isabel Ardee, Garfield & Marks, Renfrew, BCBG, and Helen Hsu, among others. A great upscale shop for jackets, sportswear, and accessories, with some dressy beaded shells and sheer blouses as well. Mon–Sat 10–6, closed Sun. (South)

## RESTORATION HARDWARE
**6815 Phillips Place Ct. in Phillips Place**
**Charlotte**
**704/556-0180**

Here men and women can actually shop together. Handyfolk around the house love the gadgets, hardware, and "manly-man" items, but there's plenty for the Martha Stewarts of the manse, too. Iron and wooden sleigh beds, clawfoot tubs, great gardening accessories, home decorating books, and lots of inexpensive finds (like drawer pulls) to completely change the look of a room. Wooden floors, high ceilings, bright lights, and lots of windows invite customers in—and make them want to stay. Mon–Sat 10–9, Sun noon–6. (South)

## WAVERLY HOME
**6809-D Phillips Place Ct. in Phillips Place**
**Charlotte**
**704/643-7111**

One of only five Waverly Home stores in the country, this shop features home furnishings, furniture, and accessories with a traditional look. Florals, stripes, and prints in bright, cheerful hues dominate the store, with its several living and sleeping areas. Waverly offers ready-made window treatments, bedding, and shower curtains, but does big business in custom upholstery with coordinating linens and draperies. Furniture ranges from iron accent tables to distressed, hand-painted pieces. At-home and in-store design consultations available. Mon–Thu and Sat 10–6, Fri 10–8, Sun noon–5. (South)

## Uptown

*For the most part, Uptown shopping is geared to businesspeople on the go.*

*You'll find a few boutiques, gift shops, and well-known chains, but most places provide needed services such as dry cleaning, alterations, shoe shines, printers, and florists. It's weekday working hours that draw these crowds; don't be surprised to find most Uptown shops closed by 6 p.m.*

*City officials and local developers hope to change shopping habits Uptown with a plan to bring upscale department stores such as Nordstrom, Saks Fifth Avenue, and Neiman Marcus to the old Charlotte Convention Center.*

## FOUNDERS HALL AT BANK OF AMERICA CORPORATE CENTER
**100 N. Tryon St.**
**Charlotte**
**704/386-0120**

Inside a six-story glass atrium, Founders Hall includes two restaurants and more than 20 specialty shops and services catering to Uptown workers. Burke & Co. carries fine jewelry, accessories, and women's apparel; Express and Julie's Too sell moderately priced ladies' clothes; and Jos. A. Bank focuses on men's work attire. For fresh-cut flowers and plants, try The Blossom Shop. Candy!Candy! features self-serve bins of hard candy and sweets. Founders Hall also includes a bookstore, shoe-shine station, sundries shop, printer, photo developer, tailor, dry cleaner, and posh athletic club. Most shops open Mon–Fri 10–6, Sat 10–4, closed Sun. (Uptown)

## OVERSTREET MALL
**Tryon Street, College Street and Caldwell Street**

A series of shops linked by corridors and skywalks, Overstreet Mall stretches from City Fair through the N.C. Blumenthal Performing Arts Center, Bank of America Corporate Center,

Bank of America Plaza, Two First Union Center, One First Union Center, and Bell South Plaza. Most shops are service-oriented for grab-and-go Uptown workers, but some fill specialty niches. Belk Express carries cosmetics, hose, and perfume; and Feathers features unique ladies' clothing. For gifts try The Beehive, or for books and home furnishings with an antique look, MacNeil's. In-and-out restaurants outnumber the shops. In the adjacent Charlotte Plaza shops within the Wachovia building, there's a Starbucks, Rainbow Café, florist, sundries shop, dry cleaner, and printer. Most shops open Mon–Fri 10–6, Sat 10–4, closed Sun. (Uptown)

## Shopping in Dilworth

*Dilworth's shopping scene mirrors the area's refurbished cedar-shake cottages, elegant homes, and eclectic mix of restaurants. With a decidedly funky flavor, Dilworth is home to many of Charlotte's cutting-edge home accessories stores, book and gift shops, and clothing boutiques, plus the largest concentration of consignment shops in town. All mixed together are stores that attract club-hoppers, career climbers, carpool moms, and contemporary couples. East Boulevard is the main drag, with other shops on Morehead Street and Park Road.*

### CRAZY JANE'S
**1235 East Blvd., Suite 7, in Kenilworth Commons**
**Charlotte**
**704/332-5454**
Step into *Metropolitan Home* magazine at this Dilworth shop with custom bedding and upholstery, home accessories, unique lighting, wow window treatments, and in-house design consulting. The look is cutting-edge yet

elegant, with contemporary pieces next to French antique armoires and old Russian bookcases. Find iron beds, washable silk linens, chiffon-draped lampshades, and great gifts. With all the bold, rich colors and wonderful textures, you'll want to live here. Mon–Sat 10:30–6 or by appointment, closed Sun. (Central)

### HONEYCHILE
**1235 East Blvd. in Kenilworth Commons**
**Charlotte**
**704/343-2730**
Like bunnies? Hop on over to Honeychile, nicknamed "the rabbit store" for its wide selection of beautiful home accessories, many featuring our floppy-eared friends. This Southern-charming Dilworth-area shop carries Arthur Court pewter and Limoges boxes, plus handblown crystal, wall furnishings, garden plaques, pillows, silk flowers, frames, Caswell-Massey products, notecards, and gifts galore. Great service and free gift wrap complete the package. Mon–Sat 10–6, closed Sun. (Central)

### I.C. LONDON
**1419 East Blvd., Suite F, in The Shops at Twin Oaks**
**Charlotte**
**704/377-7955**
Designer, European, and fine sleepwear, loungewear, lingerie, and accessories await at this Dilworth shop, itself named for the familiar childhood rhyme. Elegant and luxurious, this is lingerie you'll enjoy wearing, not uncomfortable pieces you'll bury in a drawer. Cotton, silk, satin, and chiffon basics and special-occasion pieces draw brides (a registry is available) and women who need fine foundation undergarments. Mon–Sat 10–6, closed Sun. (Central)

## METRO
**911 E. Morehead St.**
**Charlotte**
**704/375-4563**

The polar opposite of Lexington Furniture and Waverly Home, this "classic contemporary" shop in Dilworth features furniture and home accessories with an attitude. You could just about furnish your entire home at this two-story shop with its iron beds, interesting furniture, hundreds of unusual fabric selections, contemporary lighting, and great accessories. Metro is also the only Charlotte store carrying Calvin Klein, Versace, and Tricia Guild china and bed linens. Bridal registry available. Mon–Thu 10–6:30, Fri 10–6, Sat 10–5, closed Sun. (Central)

## PAPER SKYSCRAPER
**330 East Blvd.**
**Charlotte**
**704/333-7130**

One of the best selections of irreverent, offbeat, and alternative greeting cards can be found in this hard-to-categorize Dilworth shop. Many folks stop in on the way to parties, knowing they'll find everything from the card to the gift to the wrapping in mere minutes. Books are big here, including coffee-table editions on art, photography, architecture, and design, while the moderately priced gifts lean toward funky: candles, frames, vases, home accessories, bath products, toys, and gag gifts. Mon–Fri 10–7, Sat 10–6, closed Sun. (Central)

## POSITIVE
**1419-B East Blvd.**
**in The Shops at Twin Oaks**
**Charlotte**
**704/338-1400**

The only U.S. store to carry Greek designer Anna Makris Omirly's line, Positive features career clothes, casuals, and many progressive looks. Suits, often in linen, viscose, or Tencel, typically show jackets, pants, and suits in two styles or lengths each. Also find contemporary sheath dresses, slightly sheer twin sets, and great accessories, including glass-bead jewelry, hand-painted scarves, and alligator cuffs.

*Find a wide variety of wares (and wears) at Century, p. 168.*

Century

Mon–Fri 10:30–6:30, Sat 10:30–6, or by appointment; closed Sun. (Central)

## P.S. HOME
**326 East Blvd.**
**Charlotte**
**704/333-7150**
Paper Skyscraper owners opened P.S. Home after repeated customer requests for home furnishings and occasional pieces with attitude and flair. You'll find cut-velvet sofas in hot hues such as eggplant and crimson; plush leather chairs; and interesting, clean lines in this price-conscious shop. The two stores don't duplicate items, but P.S. Home has plenty of Paper Skyscraper–style accessories, including lamps, linens, hardware, and throws. With more than 400 fabrics, shoppers can custom-order from the floor or give new life to an old piece. Mon–Fri 10–7, Sat 10–6, closed Sun. (Central)

## RUN FOR YOUR LIFE
**1412 East Blvd. in Dilworth Gardens**
**Charlotte**
**704/358-0713**
Charlotte's full of jumbo sports stores, but Run For Your Life offers an alternative for athletes from beginning walkers to experienced marathoners. Expect quality gear, training tips, and knowledgeable advice on dealing with injuries and preparing for the city's upcoming road races. All of the shop's staff are runners themselves, and are known for removing customers' shoes and examining their feet to determine proper fit. Running shoes and clothing are the staples, along with energy products, training equipment, and specialty publications. Mon–Fri 10–7, Sat 10–5, closed Sun. (Central)

## TREEHAUS SAMPLES
**1609 East Blvd. in the Dilworth Co-op**
**Charlotte**
**704/375-0152**
If you wear a size 8, run—don't walk—to Treehaus Samples for one-of-a-kind designs that end up here after manufacturers have placed their orders for coming seasons. Good prices on silk jackets and shells, career clothes, casual linens and knits, sweaters, social occasion dresses, and size 6 shoes. Two big parking-lot sales each year draw in-the-know shoppers. Mon–Wed and Fri–Sat 10–5, Thu 10–6, closed Sun. (Central)

## *Shopping in South End*

*South End dates back to 1892, when Atherton Cotton Mills began a trend of industrialization in the area. By the 1920s, businesses, industries and mills filled South End, drawing newspaper comparisons to England's industrial city, Liverpool. Over the years, however, South End came to be a sore spot on the edge of Uptown. Buildings closed and fell into disrepair, crime increased, and many Charlotteans* wrote off the dilapidated corridor for good. But in the late 1980s, visionaries and preservationists began transforming the community, first with the renovated Charlotte trolley and car barn, and soon after with shopping complexes carved out of beautifully designed buildings. Restaurants opened in old knitting mills, a microbrewery followed, and, eventually, people did, too. Today, South End's old buildings and warehouses have come alive once again with innovative shops, trendy eateries, cutting-edge galleries, and new living spaces, such as lofts and live-work townhomes.

## ECLECTIX
**2102 South Blvd.**
**Charlotte**
**704/372-8485**
Just across the parking lot from Interiors Marketplace in a converted industrial factory is Eclectix, an urban market selling art, furniture, and home accessories for the more sophisticated home. Wander through the store's simple "departments" and find racks of heavily discounted designer fabrics, stacks of dinnerware, home furnishings, and bedding. Eclectix also offers a design service, complete with a resource library and

on-staff designer. After shopping, stop for a spot of tea at Tea Rex, one of several teahouses in the city. Mon–Sat 10–6, Sun 1–5. (Central)

## INTERIORS MARKETPLACE
**2000 South Blvd. at Atherton Mill**
**Charlotte**
**704//377-6226**
Charlotte's original home market, Interiors Marketplace is a collection of more than 85 unique shops specializing in art, antiques, and home accessories. Carved out of an old cotton mill, the marketplace features exposed brick walls, creaky hardwood floors, soaring ceilings, and an open, airy atmosphere. Designers, antique dealers, and specialty shops rent space without having to staff the booth. Shoppers browse the building, then pay for purchases from throughout the marketplace at the front desk. It's an interesting mix of hand-painted pottery, antique linens, menacing gargoyles, traditional antiques, prints, and specialty items (like old golf clubs and bookshelves made from canoes). Mon–Sat 10–6, Sun 1–5. (Central)

## THE PAVILION AT SOUTH END
**2041 South Blvd.**
**Charlotte**

Saturday mornings offer the widest selection of shopping in the city, thanks to the hundreds of garage and attic clearances local folks know as "yard sales."

The daily newspaper lists yard sales a few days prior and on Saturdays; other one-day merchants simply tack up neighborhood signs.

Most yard sales plan to begin around 7 a.m., but there's inevitably a crowd that arrives, flashlights in hand, before the sun rises. The early birds don't want to miss the "good stuff," which typically is bicycles, furniture, lawn mowers, and clothes in good condition.

# . . . 'Til You Drop

*Consignment shops are so plentiful in the central Charlotte areas of Dilworth, Elizabeth, Plaza-Midwood, and South End that owners could form their own mall of lovable leftovers. But even though the resale shops appear on nearly every corner, each seems to have its own niche.*

**1. Very Terry Contemporary Consignments, 310 East Blvd. in Dilworth, 704/375-0655.** Organized by color, this funky, hip shop accepts nothing from the sisters Poly and Ester. Only natural fibers such as silk, cotton, linen, and wool will do. Named Best Bargain Shopping by two Charlotte magazines. Mon–Fri 10–6, Sat 10–4, closed Sun.

**2. Sweet Repeats and Sweet Repeats Kids, 300 East Blvd. in Dilworth, 704/374-0002.** Find upscale names such as St. John, Carlisle, Doncaster, Dana Buchman, and Escada. Next door, moms in the know buy dresses, shoes, strollers, and toys at Dilworth's only consignment shop for children. Mon–Fri 10–6, Sat 10–4, closed Sun.

**3. The Resale Shop, 1920 E. Seventh St. in Elizabeth, 704/376-1312.** Upscale consignment clothing for men, women, and children, plus household items, accessories, and furniture. In business since 1952. Mon–Fri 10–5, Sat 10–4, closed Sun.

**4. The Classy Closet, 1605-B East Blvd. in Dilworth, 704/372-6249.** Missy sizes 2–18, petites 2–16, talls 4–18. New and still-tagged items are the norm, not the exception. Mon–Fri 10–5:30, Sat 10–4.

---

**704/376-5880**
A small South End shopping center, The Pavilion is home to several artsy clothing and home-accessories stores, along with a pottery-painting studio, bookstore, day spa, art gallery, and neighborhood deli. N-Squared bills itself as a "lifestyle boutique" with one-of-a-kind, stylish treasures for the home. Article, a home-accessories and clothing store, leans to the unique and contemporary. Flying Saucers lands lots of budding artists at its pottery-painting studio, and Lulu's serves up sandwiches, espresso, and a wide variety of vino. Hours vary. (Central)

## Shopping in Myers Park

*The old flavor and old money of Charlotte, Myers Park is an upscale neigh-*

**5. A Closet Full, 1729 Garden Terrace in Dilworth, 704/372-5522.** Charlotte's only consignment and sample shop for women sizes 14 W–32 W. A great place for social-occasion dresses.

**6. Catwalk, 4600 Monroe Rd. near Elizabeth, 704/375-2090.** A cool consignment boutique with threads that are funkier and younger than those in most Charlotte shops. Sellers can get money instantly. Mon–Fri, 11–7, Sat 11–5.

**7. The Dilworth Consignment Shop, 310 East Blvd. in Dilworth, 704/332-0668.** If you can't find it here, it can't be found. Dilworth's first consignment shop carries ladies' clothes, vintage and estate jewelry, hats, high-quality scarves, shoes, home accessories, books, and greeting cards. Don't like the look of Charlotte's closets? This shop carries lovable leftovers from across the United States, and offers something different every time you visit. Tue–Fri 10–6, Sat 10–4, closed Sun–Mon.

**8. JB's Hole in the Wall, 3813 South Blvd. in South End, 704/522-7505.** Antiques, collectibles, consignment.

**9. Clearing House, 701 Central Ave. in Plaza-Midwood, 704/375-7708.** Home furnishings and accessories. Antiques, silver, crystal. Ever-changing inventory. Better merchandise at reasonable prices. Mon–Fri 9:30–4:30, Sat 9:30–4, closed Sun.

**10. Purple Picket, 3115 South Blvd. in South End, 704/527-7008.** Not technically a consignment store, but unique market samples often marked down by half. Additional location at 4506 Monroe Rd., 704/342-2060. Mon–Sat 10–6, Thu 10–8, closed Sun.

borhood with stately homes, lush lawns, and the city's best selection of boutiques and gift stores. Long before SouthPark, Phillips Place, and the Specialty Shops arrived, Myers Park was the place to find classic home furnishings, distinctive jewelry, one-of-a-kind boutiques, and shops with gifts for the special people on your list. For those with traditional taste and an eye for quality, Myers Park still is.

**ASHLEY'S ON PROVIDENCE**
**1035 Providence Rd.**
**Charlotte**
**704/332-4546**
You'll find a little of everything at this Myers Park home decor and gift store. Known for its large selection of miniature porcelain boxes, Ashley's has gifts from $10 to $300. Every nook and cranny is stuffed with traditional items for the home—pillows, throws,

lamps, candlesticks, frames, pewter ware, and serving accessories, for starters—and it's a great place for finding graduation and baby gifts. Ashley's sets itself apart from other Myers Park shops with its comfortable atmosphere and friendly staff. Mon–Fri 10–5:30, Sat 10–5, closed Sun. (Central)

### THE BAG LADY: PROVISIONS FOR THE WILD WOMAN
**2904 Selwyn Ave.**
**Charlotte**
**704/338-9778**
A one-of-a-kind find in Charlotte, The Bag Lady: Provisions for the Wild Woman nurtures the Queen in all of us with what the owner likes to call "wonderful whimsical womanstuff." The Selwyn Avenue shop sells mostly books, but has an eclectic mix of gifts you'll want to give and receive: unusual jewelry, aromatherapy products, greeting cards, T-shirts, journals, desktop fountains, jackets, magnets—anything that celebrates women. Irreverent, laugh-out-loud bumper stickers, too. Mon–Sat 10–6, closed Sun. (Central)

### THE BUTTERCUP
**343 Providence Rd.**
**Charlotte**
**704/332-5329**
The Buttercup is best known for the thousands of printed invitations, announcement cards, and stationery that give it one of the largest inventories south of Washington, D.C. Paper products are upstairs, while the bottom level features gifts for babies, for brides and, by the time you browse around, for yourself, too. The Buttercup is known for attentive service, great presents, and free gift wrap. Mon–Sat 9:30–5:30, closed Sun. (Central)

### CIEL HOME
**601 Providence Rd.**
**Charlotte**
**704/372-3335**
A shabby-chic, casual elegance runs through Ciel Home, an unusual furniture and home accessories store that takes its name from the French word for sky. Cozy and comfortable with high ceilings, vibrant paint, and a sunny look, Ciel Home carries antiques that are a far cry from the traditional cherry often seen elsewhere in Charlotte. Pieces from India, Indonesia, Italy, and France actually seem livable, not stuffy. Notable accents include sit-and-sink-in chairs and bright mosaic tables that depict a set tabletop of plates, cups, and flatware. Mon–Sat 9–6, closed Sun. (Central)

### JOHN DABBS LTD.
**759 Providence Rd.**
**Charlotte**
**704/334-5040**
For 25 years John Dabbs has been one of the top shops for elegant wedding gifts, baby presents, and traditional home accessories. Upscale china patterns include Lynn Chase, Herend, Tiffany, and Raynaud, with a good selection of Mariposa pewter, Armetale, Waterford crystal, and Lucite acrylic serving pieces. For babies, try monogrammed pillows and Tiffany rattles. Registry and free gift wrap. Mon–Fri 9–5, Sat 10–5, closed Sun. (Central)

### PAUL SIMON CO.
**1027 Providence Rd.**
**Charlotte**
**704/372-6842**
Named one of the top 30 independent men's clothing stores in the country, Paul Simon has provided top-of-the-line sportswear, suits, and formal wear in Myers Park for 23 years. Look for

updated traditional lines such as Brioni, Zegna, Hickey-Freeman, Southwick, and Samuelsohn on the rack, while on-premises tailors offer custom clothing for an added touch. Exceptional service without the snooty attitude. A new Paul Simon for women is a few doors down. Mon–Sat 9–5:30, closed Sun. (Central)

Additional location: 3900 Colony Rd., Charlotte, 704/366-4523; Mon–Sat 9–6, closed Sun. (South)

### SHELAGH
### 102-B Middleton Dr.
### Charlotte
### 704/376-8171

Step into this Myers Park boutique with its forward-fashion, contemporary designs, shoes, and accessories, and you'll think you're in New York City. Names like Nanette Lepore, Theory, Anni Kuan, and Vivian Tam make for a look that's young, hip, and straight out of *Melrose Place*. (Unfortunately for many of us, most of the clothes also require a TV-type figure.) An energetic, friendly shop where shoppers model and sales staff give

*A cozy couch at Ciel Home, p. 166*

Photography by Gerin Choiniere

advice as only girlfriends can. Mon–Sat 10–6, closed Sun. (Central)

### SUITE 106
### 605 Providence Rd.
### Charlotte
### 704/333-0094

With a Myers Park location and look without the Myers Park cost, Suite 106 carries a variety of casual, career, and special-occasion styles at affordable prices. You'll find colorful Michael Simon sweaters, sleek Kenar dresses, and other brands, including Laundry, Finity, Jones New York, Cambridge Dry Goods, and Garfield & Marks. Enjoy friendly service and a comfortable atmosphere with reasonable prices. Mon–Sat 10–6, closed Sun. (Central)

### THE VILLA
### 715 Providence Rd.
### Charlotte

Wealthy and eccentric society maven Blanche Gourmajenko built this Myers Park mansion in the 1920s after falling in love with Mediterranean and Tuscan architecture in Europe. Her lavish parties and dinners were famous for years, and later the tiled-roof home housed a series of restaurants. Today the property is a unique shopping center with four distinctly different stores offering niceties from upscale fashions to chic interior designs. Villa owner Carl Walker occupies the living room with sophisticated sportswear from Giorgio Armani, Hermès, and Sergio Pellari. Next door, Jenko's combines antiques and gifts in a design that resembles rooms in a private home. And in the former garage, Charlotte's Garden carries fresh flowers, garden accessories, and antique garden furnishings. Stores open Mon–Sat, closed Sun. (Central)

# Keeping Up with the Malls

*Concord Mills, the region's largest mall, began construction in early 1998 in next-door Cabarrus County. With 1.4 million square feet and approximately 220 stores, the megamall will be bigger than SouthPark Mall (1.2 million square feet), Eastland Mall (1.1 million square feet), and Pineville's Carolina Place Mall (1.1 million square feet). Developers plan to open Concord Mills in Fall 1999.*

*But SouthPark, long the most upscale mall if not the largest, has expansion ideas in mind. Its Dutch owners have been approved to add 140,000 square feet of space, which rumors say will be a Saks Fifth Avenue.*

*SouthPark officials are also reportedly looking into the possibility of another 300,000 square feet on top of that. Together, the two additions would expand SouthPark by one-third.*

## *Shopping in Plaza-Midwood*

*One of the few remaining places in Charlotte with storefront windows and sidewalk shopping, Plaza-Midwood is experiencing a rebirth. Spaces once boarded up or occupied by unsavory businesses are being filled again and replaced with new cafés, coffee shops, boutiques, and specialty stores. About as far away from a mall atmosphere as possible, Plaza-Midwood is a cutting-edge eclectic mix of alternative clothing, vinyl records, comics, posters, skateboarding gear, African artifacts, and '50s antiques.*

**CENTURY**
**1508–1510 Central Ave.**
**Charlotte**
**704/344-1005**
Originally a pawnshop and a photo lab, owners merged two stores to create one large space that now houses the wares of 23 merchants selling everything from traditional antiques to classic items from the '50s. As in other urban markets, each vendor sublets space, and the customer pays at one place. A diverse crowd shops here, from 20-year-olds furnishing a first apartment to designers in search of eclectic items for their clients. Shoppers with a specific item in mind—whether it be old band instruments or Barcelona chairs—can list it in the store's Wish Book that buyers check against their inventory in hopes of making a match. Very little advertising makes Century a well-kept secret. Mon–Fri noon–8, Sat 10–7, Sun noon–6. (Central)

**FRESH PRODUCE**
**1221 Thomas Ave.**
**Charlotte**
**704/372-1890**
Urban streetwear for men and women

attracts club-hoppers, skate rats, teenagers, Gen X'ers, the pierced, and the tattooed. The mood is friendly and laid-back, and a skateboard attitude prevails. Styles are tight, tiny T-shirts for girls; baggy pants and shorts for guys; sunglasses; silver jewelry; and skateboard logos. A live DJ spins in a back-of-the-store booth several times a week. Mon–Sat 11–8, closed Sun. (Central)

## HEAVEN
**1500 Central Ave.**
**Charlotte**
**704/376-3338**

Formerly known as Superior Feet, this cutting-edge clothing boutique carries wild, out-on-the-town getups that most folks wouldn't dream of wearing. But the club crowd, drag queens, and trendsetters love Heaven for its small, independent labels and hard-to-find fashions. Within the revamped boutique, another shop called Faster Pussycat features a makeup and beauty bar, along with a line of 60+ wigs in Easter-egg hues. The shop sells its own brand of makeup along with alternative lines such as Cookie Puss and Urban Decay. A far cry from the Clinique counter, Faster Pussycat also has one salon chair for bleaching, coloring, and wig consultation. Mon–Sat 10–9, Sun 1–6. (Central)

## HOUSE OF AFRICA
**1215 Thomas Ave.**
**Charlotte**
**704/376-6160**

Senegal-born, Paris-educated Pap Ndiaye stumbled upon the flea market in Charlotte while driving from Atlanta to his home in New York and thought he'd try to make a few sales. His African art, jewelry, clothing, and herbal products went over so well,

he decided to stay. Nearly every inch of wall space is covered with authentic African antique masks, while lion and zebra pelts cover the floor. In between the beaded jewelry, drums, clothing, and dolls, don't be surprised to find Pap in the back mixing up black soap or shea butter, a lotion made from the karita tree. Daily 10–8. (Central)

## Shopping in NoDa

*NoDa, the North Davidson Street area between 34th and 36th Streets, has a great reputation for contemporary art galleries, neighborhood hangouts, and block parties that bring out a mixture of Charlotte folks. Interesting shops also pop up in NoDa, from alternative clothing to furnishings from the '50s. You'll find quirky home accessories, wild-child fashions, and even a store with hemp clothing and products. Note that most stores keep gallery hours and are closed on Monday and sometimes Tuesday as well.*

## SUNSHINE DAYDREAMS
**3225 N. Davidson St.**
**Charlotte**
**704/332-2800**

One of only a few hemp stores in the state, Sunshine Daydreams sells anything and everything ever made of hemp—casual clothing that's surprisingly attractive, shoes, hats, bags, wallets, jewelry, shampoo and conditioner, balms and salves, snack bars, cookies, baking products, and even shade-grown coffee with hemp seeds. The fact that hemp comes from the same cannabis family as marijuana confuses some people, but its low THC levels mean hemp is a distant cousin to the buzz-inducing weed and is better used for its durability and environmentally friendly aspects. Aside from hemp products, here you'll find women's clothing, sterling silver jewelry, and handblown glass tobacco accessories. Mon–Sat 11:30–7:30, Sun 3–6. (Central)

## Shopping in South Charlotte

*South Charlotte shopping reflects the suburban families that live here. Except for a few boutiques and one notable urban market, you'll find mostly department stores, mall shops, and huge chains in power centers that surround areas such as Carolina Place Mall. Carolina Place in Pineville and The Arboretum on Providence Road are South Charlotte's major shopping centers.*

### B NATURAL
**8038 Providence Rd.**
**at The Arboretum**
**Charlotte**
**704/544-0074**
When hot, humid Charlotte summers hit, this is where you want to shop for casual, contemporary, and comfortable clothes, all made from natural fibers. The washable linens, hand-painted knits, and embroidered T-shirts go nearly anywhere while maintaining a polished look. Additional location: Eclectix Urban Marketplace at Atherton Mill, 2102 South Blvd., Charlotte, 704/377-6226. Mon– Sat 10–6, closed Sun. (South)

### BLACKLION
**10605 Park Rd.**
**Charlotte**
**704/541-1148**
This is Charlotte's largest urban market, with 157 interior designers and merchants under one roof. Each vendor is in an open-room setting with divider walls; customers shop throughout the market and pay at the front. BlackLion features unique gifts, decorative accessories, art and prints, home furnishings, a Christmas shop, lamps and rugs, antiques, and lawn and garden accents. The in-house café makes for a good lunch break. Mon–Wed and Fri–Sat 10–6, Thu 10–9, Sun 1–6. (South)

### FINEE
**8040 Providence Rd.**
**at The Arboretum**
**Charlotte**
**704/544-1188**
Ladies in South Charlotte shop this boutique for its casual sportswear, unique accessories, and wide selection of styles with a limited number of sizes. The look is Cambridge Dry Goods and Eileen Fisher; friendly, personal service. Mon–Sat 10–6, closed Sun. (South)

### FONTANA
**8600 Crown Crescent Ct.**
**Charlotte**
**704/814-4006**
One of the few places in the Queen City where the highest-priced international designer labels can be found. With ready-to-wear upscale fashions for men and women that are a notch above the bridge designers found in most boutiques and a few department stores, Fontana fills a void in the Charlotte clothing market. Familiar apparel and footwear labels include Armani, Versace, Gucci, Fendi, Bruno Magli, Ungaro, and Cole Hahn. Expect to pay around $1,000 for a complete outfit; if that's not in the budget, you can escape with a $200 silk scarf. Mon–Wed and Fri 10–6, Thu 10–8, Sat 10–2, or by appointment; closed Sun. (South)

# NOTABLE BOOKSTORES AND NEWSSTANDS

## EARFULL OF BOOKS
**601 S. Kings Dr. in Kings Pointe**
**Charlotte**
**704/343-0090**
The Blockbuster of audio books on cassette and CD, EarFull of Books carries around 10,000 titles and specializes in unabridged versions. Categories include mystery, classics, history, philosophy, personal growth, business, short story, humor, sports, and biography; kids also have a large selection for those long car trips. Books are for sale, but most folks rent them for an average of $3.50 per day and up to $12 for 30 days. Annual memberships $10. Additional location: 7868 Rea Rd., Charlotte, 704/341-0794. Mon–Sat 9–8, Sun 1–6. (Central)

## LITTLE PROFESSOR BOOK CENTER
**4139 Park Rd. in the Park Road Shopping Center**
**Charlotte**
**704/525-9239**
A locally owned, full-service alternative to the big chains, Little Professor prides itself on customer service with free gift wrap, special orders, computerized title searches, and order by phone. Speed of delivery is key (Little Professor can get hard-to-find books in two or three days), and if you don't like it, return it within 30 days with no questions asked. Magazines, out-of-town newspapers, and book signings are also a plus. Mon–Fri 9–9, Sat 9–6, Sun noon–6. (Central)

## NEWSSTAND INTERNATIONAL
**5622-128 E. Independence Blvd. in Independence Shopping Center**
**Charlotte**
**704/531-0199**
Hang out with Bob, the bookstore cat, while browsing through 5,000 magazines, 200 newspapers, and 500 foreign publications at this bookstore/ newsstand that's been a Charlotte favorite for more than 20 years. Aside from the fact that it's the Queen City's best source for magazines, Newsstand International boasts a knowledgeable staff and a focus on customer service with special orders and shipping. Mon–Sat 9–9, Sun 9–6. (East)

# MARKETS, GOURMET GROCERIES, AND HEALTH FOOD STORES

## BERRYBROOK FARM
**1257 East Blvd.**
**Charlotte**
**704/334-6528**
Natural foods and supplements, juice bar, take-out salads and sandwiches. (Central)

## CHARLOTTE REGIONAL FARMER'S MARKET
**1801 Yorkmont Rd.**
**Charlotte**
**704/357-1269**
Fresh fruits and vegetables, homemade desserts and jams, crafts, plants and flowers. Open mid-March through December. (See also Chapter 5, Sights and Attractions.) (West)

## DEAN & DELUCA
**6907 Phillips Place Ct. in Phillips Place**
**Charlotte**
**704/643-6868**
Martha Stewart showed up for the opening celebration of this gourmet grocery that also offers take-out meals. (South)

*Charlotte Regional
Farmer's Market, p. 171*

**Charlotte**
**704/377-5467**
Gourmet groceries and meats; second
location Uptown will give the area its
only grocery. (Central, Uptown)

**SALUTE WINE AND PROVISIONS**
**2912 Selwyn Ave.**
**Charlotte**
**704/343-9095**
Italian meats, cheeses, and wines.
(Central)

**TALLEY'S GREEN GROCERY**
**1408 East Blvd.**
**Charlotte**
**704/334-9200**
Organic food shopping. (Central)

## MAJOR DEPARTMENT STORES

**BELK**
**SouthPark Mall, 4400 Sharon Rd.**
**Charlotte**
**704/364-4251**
A venerable department store, Char-
lotte- based Belk has 225 locations
in 13 southeastern and mid-Atlantic
states. Since 1888, the department
store has carried fashions for the
whole family, plus shoes, accessories, home furnishings, and, in
many stores, a wide selection of
china, crystal, and silver gifts. Customer service is a top priority, and it
shows. Additional locations: Carolina
Place Mall, Pineville, 704/543-9888;
Eastland Mall, Charlotte, 704/568-
4251; Overstreet Mall—Bank of
America Plaza, Charlotte, 704/331-
2676. Hours vary by location. (South)

**DILLARD'S**
**SouthPark Mall, 4400 Sharon Rd.**
**Charlotte**
**704/365-3111**

**THE HOME ECONOMIST**
**5410 E. Independence Blvd.**
**Charlotte**
**704/536-4663**
Health foods, bulk staples, cheeses
and candy; great selection of sauces
and unusual packaged foods. (East)

**MECKLENBURG COUNTY MARKET**
**1515 Harding Place**
**Charlotte**
**704/392-5948**
A 60-year tradition on Wednesday
and Saturday mornings. A smaller
version of the regional Farmer's Market. (Central)

**THE NATURAL MARKETPLACE**
**8206 Providence Rd. at The**
**Arboretum**
**Charlotte**
**704/542-1444**
Natural-foods grocery with large selection of vitamins, herbs, hair and
skin care; to-go lunches. (South)

**REID'S SUPERMARKET**
**707 Providence Rd.**

Found in most area malls, Dillard's gives Belk a run for its money with the same merchandise (for the most part). Clothes, shoes, and accessories for the family; some stores have home accessories, too. Additional locations: Carolina Place Mall, Pineville, 704/544-0113; Eastland Mall, Charlotte, 704/568-3111. Service falls short of Belk. (South)

**HECHT'S**
**Carolina Place Mall, 11011**
**Carolina Place Pkwy.**
**Pineville**
**704/542-7800**
The third major department store in the city, Hecht's stores are typically smaller and more cluttered than Belk and Dillard's. Fashions for the family, shoes, and accessories; Hecht's home department has great sales. Additional

locations: SouthPark Mall, Charlotte, 704/365-1000. (South)

## MAJOR SHOPPING MALLS

**THE ARBORETUM**
**Providence Road**
**at Highway 51**
**Charlotte**
A large strip shopping center in South Charlotte, the Arboretum includes mostly familiar chains with a few interesting boutiques. But with a Harris Teeter grocery store, Wal-Mart, Bed Bath & Beyond, Old Navy, and several quick lunch spots, it's a good place for one-stop shopping. Store hours vary. (South)

**CAROLINA PLACE MALL**
**11025 Carolina Place Pkwy.,**

---

# Upscale Shopping Moves Uptown

*Charlotteans are excited about a long-discussed idea to create a $300 million retail complex within the old convention center at South College and Trade Streets Uptown.*

*After nearly three years on the market, the old convention center was sold to a Michigan developer with hopes of luring stores that make Charlotte shoppers salivate—Nordstrom, Saks Fifth Avenue, and Lord & Taylor.*

*The three- or four-block retail development could also calm the critics who say there's not much to do Uptown for convention-goers and locals after the work whistle blows at 5 p.m.*

*But don't look for upscale fashion in Uptown anytime soon. Developers have until early in the year 2000 to come up with a plan and recruit those top-of-the-line tenants never before seen in the Queen City.*

**Pineville**
**704/543-9300**
The region's newest mall, Carolina Place is popular with South Charlotteans and those in outlying towns who have easy accessibility via the I-485 outer belt. The 1.1-million-square-foot mall counts Belk, Dillard's, Hecht's, JC Penney, and Sears among its anchors, plus 115 specialty stores—the same stores you see in malls across the country, but a large selection nonetheless. For lunch, try Atlanta Bread Company or Spinnaker's. Mon–Sat 10–9, Sun 12:30–6. (South)

## COTSWOLD MALL
**300 S. Sharon Amity Rd.**
**Charlotte**
**704/364-5840**
Overshadowed by neighboring South-Park Mall, Cotswold is attempting to expand and revamp its image. The mall opened in 1963 and led the charge for retail shopping outside of Uptown. Then megamalls and power centers of the suburbs came into vogue, and strips like Cotswold fell out of favor. Stores include Carmen Carmen Salon e'Spa, Storehouse, Rack Room, Old Navy, Starbucks, and David's Ltd. jewelers. Store hours vary. (South)

## EASTLAND MALL
**5431 Central Ave.**
**Charlotte**
**704/537-2626**
Eastside shoppers head to this older mall for familiar department stores such as Belk and Dillard's and for the usual offering of chains. The rest of Charlotte pretty much only shows up for the ice-skating rink. Store hours vary. (East)

## SOUTHPARK MALL
**4400 Sharon Rd.**

**at Fairview Road**
**Charlotte**
**704/364-4411**
Charlotte's best-known, biggest, and most upscale mall, the 100-plus-store SouthPark offers something for everyone. Higher-end stores include Tiffany & Co., Garibaldi & Bruns, St. John Boutique, Coach, Brooks Brothers, and Rangoni of Florence, but the average Joe and Jane find fashion at J. Crew, Eddie Bauer, The Gap, Golf America, and Banana Republic. Home furnishings are at Pottery Barn, The Bombay Company, and This End Up; and one of Charlotte's best-known specialty shops, Sharon Luggage & Gifts, is also here. Department stores Belk, Dillard's, Hecht's, and Sears serve as anchor tenants, but there's talk of expanding the mall to bring in another upscale tenant such as Saks Fifth Avenue. Food court plus several good sit-down restaurants. Mon–Sat 10–9, Sun 12:30–6. (South)

## UNIVERSITY PLACE
**W.T. Harris Boulevard at Highway 29 and J.W. Clay Boulevard**
**Charlotte**
**704/549-9614**
Suburban shoppers head to this North Charlotte cluster of stores, but they don't get any surprises: standard American chains including Wal-Mart, Best Buy, Sam's Club, Pier 1, Old Navy, Michael's, T.J. Maxx, Office Depot, and Rooms to Go. A lake in the middle of the shops offers scenery along with paddleboat rentals. In addition to fast-food chains and shops selling bagels, doughnuts, and ice cream, the noteworthy Providence Bistro restaurant overlooks the water here. Hours vary, but most shops open daily. (North)

# FACTORY OUTLETS

## CANNON VILLAGE
**200 West Ave.**
**Kannapolis**
**704/938-3200**

Outlet and specialty shopping with a twist. Cannon Village in nearby Kannapolis combines its factory-direct shops with colonial charm and special events such as the Scarecrow Festival in late October and Christmas in the Village during the holidays. The outlet store of Fieldcrest Cannon, a local maker of towels, linens, and bedding, is the anchor tenant. Century and Baker furniture, Karastan rugs, and Waccamaw pottery are also featured, along with several specialty gift stores, women's clothing chains, and a bookstore with some 30,000 titles. At the visitors center, watch a 20-minute slide show on the history of Kannapolis. Hours: Store hours vary; bigger outlets open Mon–Sat 9–7, Sun 1–6. Visitors center open Mon–Sat 9–5, Sun 1–6. (North)

## OUTLET MARKETPLACE
**I-77 at SC Exit 90, Carowinds**
**Boulevard**
**Fort Mill, SC**
**704/377-8630**

Located on the North–South Carolina border beside Paramount's Carowinds Theme Park, Outlet Marketplace is a quick drive down I-77 from central Charlotte. The one-level mall features 35 outlets and factory stores selling shoes, men's and women's clothes, antiques, home furnishings, books, fragrances, jewelry, videos, and leather goods. Carolina Pottery, the largest anchor, is a huge warehouse of home accessories. An eight-shop food court sits in the middle, while a farmer's market sets up in the parking lot. Mon–Sat 10–9, Sun 1:30–6. (West)

Charlotte Convention and Visitors Bureau

# 10

# SPORTS AND RECREATION

*The only city in the Carolinas with major professional sports, Charlotte loves its Carolina Panthers, Charlotte Hornets, and numerous NASCAR teams. Charlotte is also home to minor-league teams and events in golf, baseball, hockey, softball, and soccer. But Queen City residents aren't content to remain a bunch of spectators.*

*Teams, clubs, and organizations can be found in nearly every imaginable sport, from the traditional basketball, baseball, and soccer to the more unusual orienteering, lacrosse, windsurfing, archery, and disc golf.*

## PROFESSIONAL SPORTS

### Auto Racing

With the massive Charlotte Motor Speedway, nearly 40 NASCAR teams, race car museums, art galleries, and theme restaurants, Charlotte could be the capital of auto racing. Some 240,000 fans attend each Winston Cup at the speedway, with thousands more visiting for smaller races and for tours throughout the year.

Just a few blocks from the speedway, Backing Up Classics Auto Museum showcases more race cars

from the 1950s and other classics, antiques, and muscle cars. Also in Harrisburg, the Hendrick Motorsports Museum features the cars, trophies, and memorabilia of Jeff Gordon, Terry Labonte, and Ricky Craven.

North of Charlotte, in the Mooresville area, legendary driver Dale Earnhardt draws thousands of NASCAR loyalists with his new shop and garage. Mooresville is also home to the North Carolina Auto Racing Hall of Fame, a museum dedicated to all types of racing, with 35 display cars; exhibits of uniforms, *helmets, and photos; a small theater; and an art gallery.*

## CHARLOTTE MOTOR SPEEDWAY
**5555 U.S. 29**
**Harrisburg**
**704/455-3204**
Charlotte Motor Speedway's ongoing renovations have boosted capacity to 200,000-plus, and big NASCAR races continually pack the house. By the year 2000 the seating capacity will be increased to allow even more fans to watch as drivers battle, bump, and breeze to the finish line. Tours take the curious around the 1.5-mile, 60-foot wide oval track, through its 24-degree banked turns. (See also Chapter 5, Sights and Attractions.) Hours: Race dates and ticket prices vary. Tours offered Mon–Fri 9–5; during season, open weekends Sat 9–5, Sun noon–5. No tours during race weeks; groups of 10 or more should make advance reservations. Admission: $4 ages 3 and up; free under 3. Limited wheelchair access. (North)

## Baseball

### CHARLOTTE KNIGHTS
**2280 Deerfield Dr.**
**Fort Mill, SC**
**704/36-HOMER; 803/548-8050**
The Charlotte Knights are a top-level minor-league farm team affiliated with the Florida Marlins. For the past seven seasons, more than 300,000 fans have visited the 10,000-seat stadium to watch ball games, test their hitting at the speed-pitch machine, and hang out with the Knights' mascot, Homer the Dragon. The stadium also has a full-service restaurant, two picnic areas, a playground, a miniature golf park, a new beer garden, and 18 skyboxes. (See also Chapter 5, Sights and Attractions.) Hours: Season runs Apr–Sept;

evening games on weekdays and day games on weekends. Admission: Game tickets range $5–$7. ♿ (South)

## PIEDMONT BOLL WEEVILS
**2888 Moose Rd.**
**Kannapolis**
**704/932-3267**
What's a boll weevil? A cotton bug and a mascot for a Single A minor-league baseball team in a textile-driven town. The Piedmont Boll Weevils play at the 4,500-seat Fieldcrest Cannon Stadium. An affiliate of the Philadelphia Phillies, the Boll Weevils have 71 home games April through August. The games are popular with families and with UNCC students who come out for the WEND (106.5 FM) Thirsty Thursdays when beers and sodas are a buck a pop. Hours: Games played weekday evenings and Sunday afternoons. Admission: $3–$7.50. ♿ (North)

## Basketball

### CHARLOTTE HORNETS
**100 Hive Dr.**
**Charlotte**
**704/357-0252**
When the Charlotte Hornets played their first home game in 1988, they lost by 40 points but earned a standing ovation from a crowd elated to finally have its first major-league team. The Hornets led the NBA in attendance eight of their nine seasons; however, support has wavered a bit since then and tickets are now easier to come by. The season runs October through April, and games are played at the Charlotte Coliseum (also known as "The Hive"). Web site: www.nba.com/hornets. (See also Chapter 5, Sights and Attractions.) Hours: Season runs Oct–Apr. Admission: Single game tickets $11–$53. ♿ (West)

**CHARLOTTE STING**
**2709 Water Ridge Pkwy., Suite 400**
**Charlotte**
**704/424-WNBA**
One of eight inaugural WNBA teams introduced in 1997, the Charlotte Sting plays 14 home games at the Charlotte Coliseum. A refreshing change of pace in professional sports, players wave to fans and sign autographs for anyone who asks—kind of like the NBA before it became driven by money, deal-makers, and lawyers. Hours: Summer season; game times vary. Admission: Single game tickets $8–$50. ఈ (West)

### Football

**CAROLINA PANTHERS**
**Ericsson Stadium, 800 S. Mint St.**
**Charlotte**
**704/358-7800**
Charlotte is crazy about the Panthers, who began playing in the NFL in 1995

---

# Launching on the Lakes

*Looking for a public place to launch a boat at one of the Charlotte area's three lakes?*

*At Lake Norman, try Blythe Landing (15901 NC 73, Huntersville, Exit 25 off I-77, 704/896-9808) or Ramsey Creek Park (18444 Nantz Rd., Cornelius, Exit 28 off I-77, 704/892-7852). There are no boat-launch sites at Lake Norman's waterfront Jetton Park.*

*At Mountain Island Lake, north of the city, Latta Plantation Nature Preserve rents canoes, kayaks, paddleboats, and johnboats on a seasonal basis. Visitors may also launch their own boats and windsails at the nature preserve (5225 Sample Rd., Huntersville, 704/875-1391).*

*Lake Wylie, southwest of Charlotte, has public launch sites on its North and South Carolina banks. McDowell Nature Preserve, on the Mecklenburg County side of the lake, offers two sites: one at the nature preserve (15222 York Rd., NC 49, 704/588-5224) and one at Copperhead Island (15200 Soldier Rd., 704/588-5224).*

*Cross Buster Boyd Bridge and you're in South Carolina. Launch there at Lake Wylie Marina (Highway 29 South at Buster Boyd Bridge) and other nearby locations.*

*Most marinas at both Lake Wylie and Lake Norman also rent boats, pontoons, jet skis, sailboats, canoes, wave-runners, fishing boats, paddleboats, and houseboats. Both areas also offer captained cruises.*

and moved into $187 million Ericsson Stadium in Uptown a year later. When the team went on an eight-game winning streak and upset the defending Super Bowl champion Dallas Cowboys in 1996, the city buzzed. The team has since experienced a bit of a downturn, but home games still make for the hottest ticket in town. All games at the 73,400-seat open-air stadium are sold out, but occasionally the team releases a few hundred more tickets five days before home games. Stadium tours available. (See also Chapter 5, Sights and Attractions.) Admission: Official prices range from $35 to $50; expect to pay more on the street. ♿ (Uptown)

## *Golf*

**THE HOME DEPOT INVITATIONAL**
**TPC at Piper Glen**
**4300 Piper Glen Dr.**
**Charlotte**
**704/846-4699**

Held annually in early May at Piper Glen in South Charlotte, The Home Depot Invitational is a Senior PGA tournament that attracts the likes of host Arnold Palmer and players Lee Trevino, Jim Dent, and Larry Gilbert. Palmer designed the TPC course with a "stadium golf" concept; spectator mounds and natural amphitheaters provide unique, unrestricted views of competition. A Charlotte event since 1980, the tournament week includes two practice rounds, a pro-am, and three days of competition. Tickets range $17–$65. Limited wheelchair access. (South)

## *Hockey*

**CHARLOTTE CHECKERS ICE HOCKEY**
**2700 E. Independence Blvd.**
**Charlotte**
**704/342-4423**

Dance like a chicken, kick back with a beer, and watch the fists fly along with the pucks at the always-entertaining Charlotte Checkers games. A professional hockey team playing in the East Coast Hockey League, the minor-league Checkers draw around 7,000 fans per game at Independence Arena. Season runs October through March. Admission: Tickets range $2–$6. ♿ (Central)

## *Soccer*

**CHARLOTTE EAGLES**
**2101 Sardis Rd. North, Suite 201**
**Charlotte**
**704/841-8644**

A member of the United System of Independent Soccer Leagues since 1993, the Charlotte Eagles are a farm team for the D.C. United of Major League Soccer. The Eagles compete against South Atlantic teams in the second of the league's three tiers, and have gone to the national championship of the USISL two years running. Games are played Fridays and Saturdays April–August at Charlotte Christian High School, 7301 Sardis Road. Admission: Tickets are $6 adults, $4 youth. (South)

## *Softball*

**CAROLINA DIAMONDS**
**1001 N. Marietta St.**
**Gastonia**
**704/865-3747**

One of six teams in the newly formed Women's Professional Fast-pitch Softball League, the Carolina Diamonds play a 72-game schedule from late May through late August. The team debuted in Charlotte in 1997, but found a permanent home at Sims Legion

Park in nearby Gastonia. Other teams in the league include Durham, Virginia, Georgia, Tampa Bay, and Orlando. Admission: $5–$7. (West)

## RECREATION

### Auto Racing

**RICHARD PETTY**
**DRIVING EXPERIENCE**
**6022 Victory Lane**
**Harrisburg**
**(800) BE-PETTY**

If you've ever watched NASCAR races from the stands or on television, you've probably wondered what it's like behind the wheel. This driving school, based at Charlotte Motor Speedway, gives fans and adrenaline junkies alike the chance to hop in a stock car, peel out of the pits, and drive solo through the speedway's turns and banks. A professional instructor leads while two student cars follow at up to 145 mph. For those a

*Catch racing action at the Charlotte Motor Speedway, p.177.*

Charlotte Motor Speedway

little more timid, try riding for three laps with an instructor. Web site: www.rpde.com. Hours: Sessions offered various times Mar–Dec. Admission: $90 for ride; $330–$2,400 for driving experiences, depending on duration and complexity. (North)

### Ballooning

*The ultimate skyscraper observatory, hot-air balloon rides offer a peaceful and unmatched perspective of the Queen City and Lake Norman north of Charlotte. Balloon rallies, competitions in which pilots demonstrate flying skills, are also held in the area. The National Balloon Rally, held the third weekend of each September at the Troutman Fairgrounds north of Charlotte, is one of the closest.*

**BALLOONS OVER CAROLINA**
**4408 Hwy. 74 West**
**Monroe**
**704/556-RIDE (556-7433)**

See the Uptown skyline, the city's sprawling suburbs, and farther landmarks such as Lake Norman, Crowders Mountain, and neighboring towns. Flights usually travel 6 to 10 miles. Upon arrival, a champagne toast celebrates a successful landing, and passengers are returned to the launch site with a certificate and great memories to savor. $125/person refundable ticket. $95/person in advance buys a nonrefundable ticket that may be used within two years in case of weather-interrupted flights. (citywide)

**LAKE NORMAN BALLOON**
**COMPANY**
**21524 Delfmere Dr.**
**Cornelius**
**704/892-5929**

An upscale twist on hot-air balloon

flights, the Lake Norman Balloon Company offers privately chartered trips over the sparkling water and jagged shoreline of Lake Norman, north of Charlotte. Leisurely morning or afternoon flights often incorporate limousine pickup and dinner at a lakeside restaurant. After a post-flight champagne toast (or sparkling cider, if preferred), passengers take home the flutes and a certificate. Hours: Mornings and evenings by appointment, as weather permits. Admission: $175/person for first two passengers; $150/person additional adult passengers. Half-price, children. Limited wheelchair accessibility. (North)

## Baseball

### METROLINA BASEBALL ASSOCIATION
**10908 Fox Mill Lane**
**Charlotte**
**704/561-2260; 704/846-9283**
Weekend warriors need not apply. Former collegiate and minor-league ballplayers are divided into three branches of the MBA. Single A and AA teams are open to players 18 and up; the Roy Hobbs group (remember Robert Redford in *The Natural*?) includes men 30 and older. Play is competitive and serious, but good sportsmanship is a top priority. Each team holds its own tryouts; new teams are welcome. Games played at Charlotte-Mecklenburg high schools. Hours: Game times vary. Admission: $100–$275/season to play; free for spectators. (citywide)

### NATIONAL ADULT BASEBALL ASSOCIATION (NABA)
**704/867-0612**
Mainly a summer baseball league for experienced and collegiate players, the amateur-level NABA season runs

early June through late August, with the all-star game following championship play. Tryouts are held each April; those who are not placed on teams go into a player pool for a chance to be picked up during the season. Anyone is welcome to start a new team; currently, the local league has 11 teams with anywhere from 12 to 20 players each. Games are played at Charlotte-Mecklenburg high schools. Hours: Games Sunday afternoon and evenings Tue–Thu. Admission: $200/season to play; no charge for spectators. (citywide)

## Basketball

*March Madness has clearly set in when teachers bring televisions to class and the boss doesn't mind when everyone gathers around to watch the big game. Charlotteans love their basketball.*

*Wanna-be hoopsters also drive for goals on indoor and outdoor courts around the city. For pickup games on nice days, try nearly any of the Mecklenburg County Parks, most notably Clanton Park and Camp Greene Park. Indoor courts most accessible to the public are at YMCAs throughout Charlotte. Leagues and organizations for amateurs also thrive.*

### CHARLOTTE HORNETS BEE BALL CENTRAL AT CAMP GREENE PARK
**1221 Alleghany St.**
**Charlotte**
**704/336-3449**
Located just west of Uptown Charlotte, this one-of-a-kind full-court basketball complex features open play, tournaments, leagues, and clinics. A dozen lighted full courts and a covered stadium court, prominently featuring the Charlotte Hornets logo, offer year-round basketball for all

ages. Concessions, rest rooms, stereo/PA system, bicycle racks, and two barbecue areas surround the basketball complex. There's also a lake, playground, nature trail, and six grass volleyball courts. Hours: Late Aug–May Mon–Fri 5–9, Sat 10–10, Sun noon–10. June–early Aug Mon– Sat 10–10, Sun noon–10. Admission: Free. ♿ (Central)

## CHARLOTTE-MECKLENBURG 3-ON-3 SENIORS BASKETBALL
### 704/563-6145

Organized by the same fitness council that conducts the N.C. Seniors Games, this club for men 55 and older holds pickup games twice a week. Monday games are at Naomi Drennan Gym at Grayson Park, 750 Beal Street; while Friday games are at Latta Park, 510 East Park Avenue. Players range from 55 to 75 with a few "youngsters" in their late 40s. Pickup games are the norm, but the teams have placed in the top five of North and South Carolina tournaments on three occasions. Organizers also hope to recruit more players for a full-fledged league. Hours: Mon and Fri 5:30–7:30. Admission: Free. (Central)

## CLANTON PARK
### 1520 Clanton Rd.
### Charlotte
### 704/336-2884

*The* place to play hoops in Charlotte, Clanton Park is a lighted basketball complex with seven half-courts, three full courts and a unique new bank-shot course with a series of odd-shaped backboards to challenge shooting skills. Want to soar Jordan-style? The park's dunk-shot area includes three different heights of goals that invite players to slam it. The park, which opened in summer 1997, is operated by Mecklenburg County Park

& Recreation Department. Hours: Daily 7–dark. Admission: Free. Limited wheelchair access. (Central)

## *Biking*

## CANNONBALLS CYCLING TEAM
### 617 N. Summit Ave., Suite 211
### Charlotte
### 704/358-1123

This 40-member Charlotte club meets for on-road bike rides three times a week, with off-road treks offered periodically during colder weather. Weekday team rides average 30 miles and are held on Tuesday and Thursday. Saturday rides range from 40 to 60 miles. Out-of-town trips and social picnics are also scheduled. All skill levels are welcome; members range in age from early 20s to 60-plus. E-mail: watueng@aol.com. Hours: Rides offered Tue, Thu, and Sat. Admission: $60 first-year membership, $15 following years. (North, Central)

## TARHEEL CYCLISTS
### P.O. Box 35392
### Charlotte 28235
### 704/845-1423

For more than 20 years the Tarheel Cyclists have gathered for weekly road rides throughout the Charlotte area. The 125-member group most often schedules "show-and-go" rides, trips that follow the same route each time. Rides are offered in wee morning hours, in afternoons, and on weekends, and range from a 10-mile breakfast ride to a 70-mile trek at 20-plus mph. Charity events, overnight trips, picnics, and rides led by group members are also offered and are listed in a monthly newsletter. E-mail: 102125.2600@compuserve.com. Hours: Dates and times vary. Admission: $12/year singles; $17/year families. (citywide)

*Hornets Nest BMX track*

### HORNETS NEST BMX TRACK
**6301 Beatties Ford Rd.**
**Charlotte**
**704/875-1391**
This 1,150-foot regulation track within Hornets Nest Park hosts bicycle motocross competitions each Saturday. Monitored open practice sessions and teaching clinics let beginners and experienced riders hone their skills before race time. Hours: race registration 2:30 p.m. Sat; races start 3:30 p.m. Open practice sessions Tue and Thu 6 p.m.–dusk. Admission: $8/day racing; free for spectators; free open practice sessions. (North)

## Bowling

### CAROLINA LANES
**11210 Brigman Rd.**
**Matthews**
**704/841-7606**
This 36-lane bowling center features automatic scoring, bumper bowling for kids, extreme bowling from 11 p.m.

to 3 a.m. Friday and Saturday nights, game rooms, birthday parties, and group rates. Café serves sandwiches, pizza, and other snacks. Adjacent to Zones, an indoor recreation center with bumper cars, carousel, moonwalk maze, kids' rides, and close to 100 arcade games. Hours: Sun–Thu 9 a.m.–midnight, Fri–Sat 9 a.m.–3 a.m. Admission: Varies. (South)

### COLISEUM LANES
**2801 E. Independence Blvd.**
**Charlotte**
**704/334-0431**
A 40-lane bowling center near the old Charlotte Coliseum (now Independence Arena) in the central part of town, Coliseum Lanes offers automatic scoring, bumper bowling for kids, a snack bar and lounge, leagues, and tournaments. Extreme bowling—with colored lights, disco music, and fog—runs 11 p.m. to 3 a.m. Friday and Saturday nights. Hours Sun–Thu 9 a.m.–midnight, Fri–Sat 9 a.m.–3 a.m. Admission varies. (Central)

### GEORGE PAPPAS' PARK LANES
**1700 Montford Dr.**
**Charlotte**
**704/523-7633**
Owned by Professional Bowling Association Hall of Famer George Pappas, Park Lanes attracts some of the best scratch bowlers in town. The 32-lanes bowling center has morning and evening leagues, kids' weekend leagues, church leagues, and three leagues for scratch players, plus tournament play, bumper bowling for kids, birthday parties, pro shop, and restaurant (known for its delicious onion rings). Hours: Sun–Thu 9 a.m.–midnight, Fri–Sat 9 a.m.–2 a.m. Admission: Prices vary; midnight specials Fri–Sat. (South)

## Day Hikes

State parks in the region and many of the county-operated nature preserves and parks offer day hikes for varying skill levels.

### LATTA PLANTATION NATURE PRESERVE AND VISITOR CENTER
5225 Sample Rd.
Huntersville
704/875-1391

More than 1,000 acres make up this nature preserve that overlooks Mountain Island Lake in northwest Mecklenburg County, with hiking and horse trails, picnic areas, wildlife, fishing, boat and canoe rentals, playground, and visitors center with an extensive offering of nature programs. In addition to park amenities, Latta Plantation is also home to the Carolina Raptor Center, Historic Latta Place, and Latta Equestrian Center. (See also Chapter 8, Parks, Gardens, and Recreation Areas.) Hours: Daily 9–dark. Admission: Free; fees for Raptor Center, Latta Place, Equestrian Center. Limited wheelchair access. (North)

### REEDY CREEK PARK AND NATURE PRESERVE
2900 Rocky River Rd.
Charlotte
704/598-8857

Nearly 700 acres of rolling terrain make for leisurely hikes at Reedy Creek Nature Preserve in East Charlotte, including picnic areas, fishing, wildlife, three lakes, and an environmental center with recreation facilities in adjacent Reedy Creek Park. (See also Chapter 8, Parks, Gardens, and Recreation Areas.) Hours: Daily 9–dark. Admission: Free. Limited wheelchair access. (East)

## Disc/Frisbee Golf

One of the fastest growing sports in North America, disc golf involves throwing a Frisbee-like disc into an elevated goal on 18-hole courses similar to those used for traditional golf. Thanks to three disc golf courses run by the Mecklenburg County Park and Recreation Department, the sport's popularity has soared in Charlotte.

### CHARLOTTE DISC GOLF CLUB
5534 Albemarle Rd.
Charlotte
704/567-9006; 704/882-9420

The Charlotte Disc Golf Club helped provide finances and labor to build several disc golf courses at various county parks. The club sponsors events and maintains a calendar posted at the Reedy Creek and Kilborne Parks. The club is based at S&P Kite Store on Albemarle Road, which carries a great disc selection, and is open to all ages and skill levels; ask about their bimonthly newsletter. Admission: $10 membership; $15 with disc. (citywide)

### MECKLENBURG COUNTY PARK & RECREATION DEPARTMENT
5841 Brookshire Blvd.
Charlotte
704/336-3854

Charlotte's Park & Recreation Department operates three disc golf courses open to public play for free as long as tournaments are not underway. Hours: Daily 9–dark. Admission: Free. The 18-hole courses are at Reedy Creek Park, 2900 Rocky River Road, 704/598-8857 (East); Kilborne Park, 2600 Kilborne Drive, 704/568-4044 (Central); and Hornets Nest Park, 6301 Beatties Ford Road, 704/875-1391. (North)

## Golf

The Charlotte area is a golf-lover's paradise, with more than 50 courses within 40 minutes of Uptown. Exclusive country clubs still thrive, but in recent years golf clubs catering to younger families, semi-private courses, and upscale daily-fee courses have opened with success. Charlotte also has several respected public courses that are far from goat-track status.

### BIRKDALE GOLF CLUB
**16500 Birkdale Commons Pkwy.**
**Huntersville**
**704/895-8038**
One of the best-rated daily-rated courses, this 18-hole Arnold Palmer championship course features Bermuda fairways, bent grass greens, concrete cart paths, and state-of-the-art lighted practice facilities, including an 18-hole natural-turf putting green, driving range, and chipping area. Birkdale's 10,000-square-foot clubhouse is the focal point of the Huntersville neighborhood with Arnie's Tavern, conference facilities, a full-service pro shop, and lessons and club fittings by PGA profession-

als. Rental clubs available. Exit 25 off I-77 North. Hours: Daily 7–7. Range and putting green, daily 7 a.m.–9 p.m. Fees: Call for fee information. (North)

### CHARLOTTE GOLF LINKS
**11500 Providence Rd.**
**Charlotte**
**704/846-7990**
With a unique Scottish links–style layout, this par-71 course in South Charlotte incorporates an open design with Bermuda fairways and bent grass greens. The innovative Yardmark system provides accurate yardage from a satellite-fed readout in each cart. Clubhouse has a pro shop and restaurant, instruction from PGA and LPGA professionals, tournaments, and outings. Fully lit practice range and rental clubs available. Hours: Daily 7–7. Call for fee information. (South)

### THE DIVIDE
**6800 Stevens Mill Rd.**
**Matthews**
**704/882-8088**
Rated number one in the area by Carolinas Golf Association, The Divide challenges golfers with its traditional

design and lush, tree-lined Bermuda fairways with bent grass greens. Four sets of tees make the course accessible to all skill levels, and the Yardmark system eliminates yardage guesswork. Large practice range with putting green, short game area, lessons from PGA professionals, clubhouse, pro shop, restaurant, and rental clubs available; carts only. Hours: Daily 7:15 a.m.–dark. Call for fee information. (East)

### HIGHLAND CREEK GOLF CLUB
**7001 Highland Creek Pkwy.**
**Charlotte**
**704/875-9000**
Rated Charlotte's toughest golf course by *Charlotte Business Journal* and listed in *Golf Digest*'s Places to Play, Highland Creek is an upscale championship course carved out of the Carolina forest. With five lakes, the course also features water on 11 of its 18 holes. Includes all-grass practice facility, large putting green, and 15,500-square-foot clubhouse with golf shop, full-service restaurant, and terrace overlooking the 18th

hole. Rentals for righties and southpaws. Call for hours and fee information. (North)

### MECKLENBURG COUNTY PARK & RECREATION GOLF COURSES
The city/county Park & Recreation Department oversees two noted public golf courses conveniently located in Charlotte proper. Try Renaissance Park Golf Course, 1525 West Tyvola Road, Charlotte, 704/357-3373, for a well-manicured 18 holes. Revolution Park Golf Course, 2662 Barringer Drive, Charlotte, 704/342-1946, offers a nine-hole Bermuda-greens course with adjacent pro shop. Call for hours and fee information. (West, Central)

### OLDE SYCAMORE GOLF CLUB
**7504 Olde Sycamore Dr.**
**Charlotte**
**704/573-1000**
The centerpiece of a community near Mint Hill east of Charlotte, Olde Sycamore is an 18-hole, par-72 course created by Tom Jackson. Framed by a forest of hardwoods and pines, the soft-spike course has a reputation for

*Carolina Panthers game, p. 178*

Charlotte Convention and Visitors Bureau

a mix of long, challenging holes and shorter ones that allow some fun with shot placement. Large practice facility with putting green, sand trap, chipping area; lessons, new clubhouse. Hours: Daily 7:30–dark. Call for fee information. (East)

## Horse Racing

### CHARLOTTE STEEPLECHASE ASSOCIATION
**815 Wood Ridge Center Dr.**
**Charlotte**
**704/423-3400**
And they're off! In 1998, Britain's Princess Anne visited the Charlotte region for the third annual Charlotte Steeplechase. A day of thoroughbred steeplechase racing held each April, the event includes five races, with horses clearing four-foot-tall brush jumps at speeds up to 30 mph. The 15,000 attendees dressed in hats, sundresses, khaki pants, and ties also celebrate at tailgate and tent parties. The race benefits Hospice of Union County. Hours: Last Saturday of April, rain or shine. Admission: $40/car off-site parking; $125/car reserved infield; $275/car reserved knoll; $325/car reserved rail space. ♿ (South)

## Horseback Riding

*Green pastures and scenic trails winding through forests and along lakes are mere minutes away once you get outside Charlotte's city limits. Many stables board horses and offer equestrian lessons, but only a few feature horseback riding sessions for the public.*

### LARKSPUR RANCH
**6715 Charlotte Hwy.**
**Lancaster County, SC**
**803/547-5019**
This cowboy-flavored ranch 14 miles south of Pineville rents horses on weekends for all levels of riders. With more than 100 horses to choose from, the wide-open ranch features 2,000 acres with miles of trails. Guided tours by request; birthday parties; riders must be eight or older. Lessons available Monday through Saturday. Groups of five or more should make reservations one week in advance. Hours: Sat–Sun 8:30–5. Admission: $15/hour. (South)

### LATTA PLANTATION PARK EQUESTRIAN CENTER
**6201 Sample Rd.**
**Huntersville**
**704/875-0808**
This 25-acre facility features show grounds, lighted arenas, horse rentals, trail rides, horseback riding lessons, and a tack shop. Miles of horse trails winding through this Mountain Island Lake nature preserve make it the perfect spot for a peaceful afternoon ride. Reservations required for lessons, parties, hayrides, and trail rides. Hours: Sat–Sun 9–5. Call for price information. (North)

## Rock Climbing

### CHARLOTTE CLIMBING CENTER
**619 Cedar St.**
**Charlotte**
**704/333-ROCK (333-7625)**
An indoor climbing gym in Uptown's shadows, the Charlotte Climbing Center opened in 1993 with nine simulated rock walls and a 20-foot inverted stairwell wall nicknamed "the cave." A good place for beginners to learn and for seasoned climbers to practice, CCC also offers lessons, parties, camps, scouting activities, and two outdoor trips a

month. The 150-member Charlotte Rock Climbing Club makes three trips a month on a seasonal basis. Top destinations are Crowders Mountain, Table Rock, and Looking Glass. (See also Chapter 6, Kids' Stuff.) Hours: Tue–Fri noon–10, Sat 10–6, Sun 1–6. Admission: $12 daily walk-in rate; $5 after 5 Wed; $20 belay for kids. Memberships, family rates, student rates, and punch cards also available. (Uptown)

## Running

### CHARLOTTE HASH HOUSE HARRIERS (TRAIL RUNNING)
### 704/559-4155

A laid-back, fun-loving bunch, the Charlotte Hash House Harriers are part of an international fellowship that holds noncompetitive hare-and-hound fun runs on three- to five-mile marked trails. Short-cutting, cheating, and nefarious tricks are encouraged! Schedule includes road trips and hashes closer to home. All ages and skill levels welcome, from walker to marathoner. Hours: Winter Sun 2 p.m.; summer hours vary. Admission: $3/hash (to buy the food, dude). (citywide)

### CHARLOTTE ROAD RUNNERS
### 9508 Cedar Knoll Ct.
### Charlotte
### 704/814-6670

More than 300 local athletes of varying skill levels gather through this club for runs, races, road trips, and social activities. Group runs ranging from 6 to 20 miles are scheduled regularly. A monthly newsletter includes information on upcoming races, road trips, and charity events, as well as race results and registration forms. The decade-old club has runners from beginners to marathoners and offers a good social environ-ment for people with an interest in running. Admission: $12/year individual membership; $16/year family membership. (citywide)

### CHARLOTTE TRACK CLUB
### P.O. Box 11364
### Charlotte 28220
### 704/358-0713

Run For Your Life, a Dilworth store specializing in running shoes and gear, sponsors the 450-member Charlotte Track Club. Benefits include a monthly newsletter, store discounts, dinner meetings, sponsored races, and frequently scheduled runs. Plenty of experienced runners, but all levels and ages are welcome and encouraged. Hours: Sat 8 a.m. at Central YMCA; Sun 7, 8, and 9 a.m. at McAlpine Creek Park. Admission: $15 membership fee. (citywide)

### MCALPINE CREEK PARK
### 8711 Monroe Rd.
### Charlotte
### 704/568-4044

Runners and walkers like McAlpine Creek Park in East Charlotte for its

*In-line skating at Jetton Park*

Mecklenburg County Park and Recreation Dept.

The Coca-Cola 600, a Winston Cup race held at Charlotte Motor Speedway over Memorial Day weekend each year, is the second-largest spectator sporting event in the United States.

continuous recreation area formed by the park, McAlpine Creek Greenway, and adjacent James Boyce Park. McAlpine also has Charlotte's only 5K cross-country course, a well-known trail often used for state and national competitions. Access the greenway from the park, adjoining neighborhoods, and a parking area on Sardis Road. Hours: 9 a.m.–dark. Admission: Free. Limited wheelchair access. (East)

## Skating

*Area inline skaters often head to the concrete and asphalt trails of Freedom Park, Jetton Park, and Nevin Park to get away from traffic and enjoy nature. Others zip through Uptown and neighborhoods including Dilworth, Myers Park, Elizabeth, and Plaza-Midwood.*

*When workers abandon Uptown on weekends, skateboarders and more radical inline skaters move in for the wide selection of concrete structures they can jump and ride. But don't be surprised if you get chased off the premises.*

*Ice-skaters have two options in Charlotte: the Ice Chalet inside Eastland Mall and the Ice House near Carolina Place Mall in Pineville.*

**ALPINE SKI CENTER**
**1501 East Blvd.**
**Charlotte**
**704/332-2824**

Skiers often use inline skates to keep their legs in shape during the off-season. Alpine Ski Center sells and rents inline skates and equipment, sponsors lessons for beginners, and serves as a meeting place for inline skating clubs in the area. Hours: Mon–Fri 10–7, Sat 10–6, Sun 12–6, Closed Tue. Admission: $8 beginner lesson. Call for rental prices. (Central)

**CHARLOTTE BLADE ROLLERZ**
**704/563-0581**

This group of 55 male and female skaters gather twice a week year-round for 10- to 15-mile runs through the Dilworth and South End areas of Charlotte. Most skaters in the club are intermediate to advanced, but don't be intimidated—the idea is to have a good time and to get some exercise. Social activities include dinners, birthday celebrations, parades, and races. Meets Wednesdays at 6 p.m. at Alpine Ski Center, 1501 East Boulevard; and Sundays at 2 p.m. at Rainbow Café, 1933 South Boulevard. Admission: Free. (Central)

**METHODIST HOME SKATEPARK**
**3200 Shamrock Dr.**
**Charlotte**
**704/568-3363**

Charlotte's only facility for skateboarders and aggressive inline skaters, the SkatePark features a six-foot vertical halfpipe, six-foot bank ramps, a pyramid ramp, and other street-course challenges, with open skating, tournaments, and special events. All skaters must wear protective equipment, and those under 18 must have notarized waivers on file before they rip it. Hours: Tue, Thu, and Fri 4–8:30 p.m.; Sat 9–4:30; Sun 1–5; weather permitting. Admission: Free. (Central)

### ICE CHALET
**5595 Central Ave. inside Eastland Mall**
**Charlotte**
**704/568-0772**
Strap on figure or hockey skates and circle the regulation-sized rink to popular and rock music. Instructors teach free beginner lessons for would-be figure and hockey skaters each weekend. Public skate sessions are offered daily and on Wednesday through Saturday evenings. Hockey leagues are open to kids, men, and women, along with group figure-skating lessons and broomball instruction. Birthday parties are popular, but expect big crowds on weekends. (See also Chapter 6, Kids' Stuff.) Call for hours and admission prices. (East)

### ICE HOUSE OF CHARLOTTE
**400 Towne Centre Blvd., Pineville**
**704/889-9000**
Kids and adults in South Charlotte come here to skate, play on hockey teams, and take figure-skating lessons. The freestanding facility features public skating sessions, group or private lessons in figure skating, aerobic exercise classes on ice, hockey leagues for adults and kids, hockey clinics, and summer hockey camps. Birthday parties are a big business in the full-service eatery, which serves pizza, nachos, and other snacks; expect large crowds on weekends. (See also Chapter 6, Kids' Stuff.) Hours: Call for specific times. Admission: $6; rentals $2. (South)

## Skiing

*When snowflakes fall in the Queen City, Charlotteans head to the North Carolina mountains, just a few hours away, to shred the slopes and sip hot toddies in the lodge. Most ski resorts are the family-friendly type that cater to two sticks, but two—Ski Beech and Wolf Laurel Ski Resort—also welcome snowboarders.*

*A word to the wise: Always call ahead to check conditions, since most North Carolina resorts rely on snow-making machines when the weather turns warm.*

### APPALACHIAN SKI MOUNTAIN
**800/322-2373**
Located off U.S. 321 near the Blue Ridge Parkway, between Boone and Blowing Rock. Nine slopes; 390-foot vertical drop. Snow report 828/295-7828 anytime.

### CATALOOCHEE SKI AREA
**800/768-0285**
Off I-40 in Maggie Valley. Nine slopes; vertical drop of 740 feet. Snow report 800/768-3588 anytime.

### CHARLOTTE SKI BEES
**P.O. Box 11771**
**Charlotte 28220**
**704/552-2588**
Originally a ski club that organized in the mid-1960s, the Charlotte Ski Bees have since branched out to include boating, hiking, inline skating, running, scuba diving, biking, and any other activity members want to try. One of the largest recreational groups around, this 800-member organization is open to all ages and skill levels. In fact, beginners outnumber the advanced athletes, making this a club where everyone feels comfortable. The club features a learn-to-ski program, a monthly newsletter, char-

ity work, and programs focusing on fun, culture, entertainment, and the community. Meets second Tuesday of each month at 7 p.m. at Charlotte Hilton Executive Park, 5624 Westpark Dr. at Tyvola Rd. Admission: $45/year singles, $35 annual renewal; $65/year families, $55 renewal.

## SAPPHIRE VALLEY SKI AREA
**828/743-1164**
Off U.S. 64, east of Cashiers. Three slopes; vertical drop of 425 feet. Snow report 828/743-1162 anytime.

## SKI BEECH
**800/438-2093**
One of North Carolina's most popular ski resorts. Located off NC 194, north of Banner Elk. Fourteen slopes, with halfpipe for snowboarding; vertical drop of 830 feet.

## SKI HAWKSNEST
**800/822-HAWK**
Off NC 105, south of Boone. Fourteen slopes, vertical drop of 669 feet.

## SUGAR MOUNTAIN SKI AREA
**800/SUGARMT (784-2768)**
The biggest area ski resort, with 18 slopes and a 1,200-foot vertical drop. On NC 184, east of Banner Elk.

## WOLF LAUREL SKI RESORT
**828/689-4111**
Fifteen slopes, with one set aside for snowboarders; 700-foot vertical drop. Off NC 23, north of Mars Hill.

## *Ski Rentals*

### ALPINE SKI CENTER
**1501 East Blvd.**
**Charlotte**
**704/332-2824**
Many Charlotteans rent skis and the related gear from Alpine Ski Center before heading to North Carolina

mountain slopes. Car racks are also available for rent. The shop sells skis, equipment, and clothing. Hours: Mon–Fri 10–7, Sat 10–6, Sun noon–6. Closed Tue. Call for rental prices and package information. (Central)

## *Soccer*

### CHARLOTTE WOMEN'S SOCCER LEAGUE
**704/366-5361**
Mecklenburg Park & Recreation Department sponsors this indoor/outdoor league for amateurs 18 and older. Season runs from late February through May and picks up again in August for a fall session. Open registration and practices are held at the start of each season. Players are ranked by skill level and distributed evenly across teams. Games at 7 and 8:30 Thursday at Renaissance Park, 1536 Tyvola Road. Indoor play at Soccer City, 5001-G South Boulevard. Admission: $25/season. (West, South)

### PREMIER SOCCER ACADEMY AT THE SPORTS WAREHOUSE
**10930 Granite Street**
**Charlotte**
**704/583-1444**
The Sports Warehouse, an indoor play facility for volleyball, basketball, and soccer, also conducts a year-round indoor soccer school called Premier Soccer Academy. Lessons for kids and adults run in six-week increments, and cover technical fundamentals. Indoor soccer leagues, clinics and camps are also regularly scheduled. Hours: Open seven days a week; public play and lesson times vary. Admission: Lessons $75/six weeks. (South)

## *Swimming*

*When summer turns hot and humid, Charlotteans take to swimming pools* and lakes for relief. *Year-round swimming, open to nonmembers and visitors, are most often found at health clubs, YMCAs, and recreation centers operated by the Mecklenburg County Park & Recreation Department.*

## MARION DIEHL RECREATION CENTER POOL
**2219 Tyvola Rd.**
**Charlotte**
**704/527-3175**

This 25-meter, six-lane indoor pool is kept at an inviting 88 degrees year-round. Schedule includes public swim times, water aerobics for senior citizens, and varied special instruction for adults and children with physical disabilities. Call for hours information. Admission: $1 children, $1.50 seniors, $2 adults. (West)

## MECKLENBURG COUNTY AQUATIC CENTER
**800 E. Second Ave.**
**Charlotte**
**704/336-DIVE (336-3483)**

A nationally known indoor swimming facility where large meets are held, the Aquatic Center has one-meter and three-meter diving boards, an instructional pool, competition pool, hot tub, fitness center, swimming and diving instruction, plus water exercise classes for all ages. Hours: Swimming and class times vary. Admission: Day pass $1; three-month pass good at any county pool, $92 individual, $127 family. (Uptown)

## YMCA OF CHARLOTTE
**400 E. Morehead St.**
**Charlotte**
**704/333-7771**

The YMCA features nine indoor pools and three outdoor pools among its 10 Mecklenburg County branches. Swimming lessons are offered at all of them, and many also include water aerobics and other exercise classes. Hours: Vary by location. Admission: Metro membership good for all activities at all 10 locations, $54/month individual, $76/month family. Site-specific memberships also available. Day pass $10; week pass $20. (citywide)

# 11

# PERFORMING ARTS

In Charlotte, the arts are A-1 newspaper stories, the lead on the evening news, and the topic of conversation around water coolers citywide. But it wasn't always that way.

In 1996 the Charlotte Repertory Theatre staged the Pulitzer Prize–winning play Angels in America, a controversial choice to some because it portrayed gays and lesbians sympathetically. Right-wing extremists picketed, and the theater company had to obtain a court order to do a brief nude scene. The ruckus raised eyebrows, generated a lot of ink and air time, and hasn't died down since.

In 1997 Mecklenburg County commissioners yanked the county's $2.5 million annual contribution to the Charlotte-Mecklenburg Arts and Science Council, a nonprofit, proactive organization that provides leadership, direction, and funding to 40 affiliates. Four conservative Republicans and one renegade Democrat banded together to stamp out what they saw as smut. Several of the most powerful CEOs in town spoke out in support of censorship-free arts, and vowed to recruit pro-diversity candidates for local politics. Letters to the editor on the controversy ran for months, and a group of two dozen gays and lesbians "outed" themselves on the front page of the Charlotte Observer, using the Angels controversy as their rallying point.

Finally, arts supporters opened their wallets and helped the Arts and Science Council's fund drive top $6 million.

Aside from the cultural growing pains, Charlotte has a wide range of performing-arts options, including well-attended symphony orchestras, cutting-edge professional and community theater, familiar Broadway traveling productions, classic operas, and innovative dance productions.

# MULTI-ARTS FACILITIES

## AFRO-AMERICAN CULTURAL CENTER
401 N. Myers St.
Charlotte
704/374-1565

Find sizzling jazz, rhythmic bongo drums, African artifacts, and cultural exhibits at this showcase for African-American art, music, theater, film, and cultural education. The center showcases the attitudes, struggles, and talents of the African and African American experience through performances by local, regional, and national groups; visual arts exhibits; and ongoing education programs. Started at UNCC, the museum now thrives within the stained-glass windows of the former Little Rock AME Zion Church. Facilities include a 200-seat theater, art gallery, amphitheater, and meeting space. (See also Chapter 7, Museums and Art Galleries.) Hours: Tue–Sat 10–6, Sun 1–5. Admission: Free. & (Uptown)

## NEIGHBORHOOD THEATRE
Charlotte
704/358-9298

When Charlotte's arts community and its funding fell under a black cloud a few years ago, Paul McBroom, a real estate agent and NoDa historic property renovator, stepped up with the Neighborhood Theatre. Once known as the Astor Art Theater, the 50-year-old landmark in funky North Davidson was looking worse for wear until McBroom refurbished it for live performances. Theater productions, plus national music acts such as Junior Brown, Doc Watson, and Robert Earl Keen perform here. & (Central)

## NORTH CAROLINA BLUMENTHAL PERFORMING ARTS CENTER

130 N. Tryon St.
Charlotte
704/372-1000 (box office); 704/333-4686 (administrative office)

Adjacent to the 60-story Bank of America Corporate Center, the Blumenthal is the premiere performing-arts venue in Charlotte. Renowned architect Cesar Pelli designed the center, which opened in 1992 with a curved glass front and a large glass dome that looks up to the illuminated "crown" atop the Bank of America building. The impressive, European-style 2,100-seat Belk Theater features performances by touring Broadway companies and local groups, including Charlotte Symphony Orchestra, Opera Carolina, North Carolina Dance Theatre, Charlotte Choral Society, and Carolinas Concert Association. The cozy 430-seat Booth Playhouse hosts Charlotte Repertory Theatre shows and smaller, more intimate performances. & (Uptown)

## SPIRIT SQUARE CENTER FOR ARTS & EDUCATION
345 N. College St.
Charlotte
704/372-9664

Primarily an arts education center for the community, Spirit Square includes three galleries, two theaters, nine classrooms, four acoustically isolated music practice rooms, and offices for several local arts organizations. Five buildings make up Spirit Square, and its history adds to the character of the center. In the 700-seat McGlohon Theatre (formerly known as NationsBank Performance Place), visitors can see stained-glass windows from First Baptist Church built in 1909; Knight Gallery was once a printmaker's shop; the 180-seat Duke Power Theatre originally served as the church auditorium. First opened in 1976, Spirit Square

*Grey Seal Puppets performance of Emperor's New Clothes, p. 196*

underwent an extensive renovation in 1989. Today the facility showcases professional local, regional, and national artists in a variety of media. Changing exhibits; arts classes for kids and adults. (See also Chapter 7, Museums and Art Galleries.) Hours: Tue–Fri 11–6, Sat 11–5, Sun 1–4. Admission: Free. &. (Uptown)

## THEATER

### ACTOR'S THEATRE OF CHARLOTTE
**P.O. Box 12325**
**Charlotte 28220-2325**
**704/342-2251**
Presenting a diverse, thought-provoking collection of comedy and drama, Actor's Theatre is a contemporary professional company dedicated to producing works by new, cutting-edge playwrights and recent, classic, and daring American plays. Shows run at The Duke Power Theatre at Spirit Square, a 180-seat venue first built in 1923 as a church auditorium. &. (Uptown)

### BARE BONES THEATRE GROUP
**3200 Wesley Ave.**
**Charlotte**
**704/347-4298**
More into minimalist theater than ritzy uptown gigs? Try Bare Bones Theatre Group, a new company of Queens College theater grads who put on open-air shows behind Fat City Deli in the NoDa district. Folding metal chairs, a wooden platform stage, exposed brick walls patched with concrete, and chugging trains make for a quirky atmosphere, but where else can you watch creative theater while wearing jeans and sipping a beer? Recent shows included James McLure's Pvt. Wars and Edward Albee's Zoo Story. Tickets are under $5. &. (Central)

### BROADWAY LIGHTS SERIES
**130 N. Tryon St.**
**Charlotte**
**704/372-1000 (box office); 704/333-4686 (administrative office)**
Presented by the North Carolina Blumenthal Performing Arts Center and Best of Broadway, Broadway Lights brings in high-profile traveling shows such as *Peter Pan, Riverdance, Bring in 'Da Noise/Bring in 'Da Funk,* and *Rent.* It's a big draw for many Charlotteans who generally go to the theater only for well-known names such as these. Shows are held in Belk Theater of the Performing Arts Center and at Ovens Auditorium. &. (Uptown, Central)

### CENTRAL PIEDMONT COMMUNITY COLLEGE SUMMER THEATRE
**P.O. Box 35009**
**Charlotte 28235**
**704/330-6534; 704/330-6568 (office)**

When other performing-arts companies break for the summer, Central Piedmont Community College steps in with musicals and farces presented by a mix of young professionals and advanced students. Recent offerings were *Annie Get Your Gun*, *Will Rogers Follies*, and *Tommy*. Summer season includes five shows at Pease Auditorium on Elizabeth Avenue at Pease Lane. Tickets: $13. & (Central)

## CHARLOTTE REPERTORY THEATRE
**129 W. Trade St.**
**Charlotte**
**704/372-1000 (box office); 704/333-8587 (administrative offices)**
This premiere professional theater company in Charlotte presents eight full productions and staged readings of four new scripts each spring in the annual Charlotte Festival/New Plays in America. Repertoire ranges from Broadway fare to contemporary works and classics. At the New Plays in America festival, audiences participate by giving their opinions and playwrights comment on ideas. Shows run in Booth Playhouse in the Blumenthal Performing Arts Center. Tickets range $16–$23.50. & (Uptown)

## CHILDREN'S THEATRE OF CHARLOTTE
**1017 E. Morehead St.**
**Charlotte**
**704/376-5745; 704/333-8983**
Created 50 years ago by the Junior League, Children's Theatre of Charlotte has since grown from volunteer plays on a shoestring budget to fully staged, technical productions presented to more than 180,000 families a year. Productions include classics such as *To Kill A Mockingbird*, fantasies such as *Alice in Wonderland*, and favorites including *The Wizard of Oz*. Regional theater groups specializing in mime and puppetry often present special events, while the Children's Theatre's touring company, the Tarradiddle Players, take shows on the road. Classes and workshops for all ages are offered in creative drama, acting, and musical theater. (See also Chapter 6, Kids' Stuff.) Office open Mon–Fri 10–5; performances generally Fri–Sun. Tickets range $5–$10. & (Central)

## DAVIDSON COMMUNITY PLAYERS
**P.O. Box 76**
**Davidson 28036**
**704/892-7953**
Community theater at its best. For 35 years, the Davidson Community Players have put on two summer productions and treated folks in Lake Norman to several small dinner theater shows. The lineup runs from musicals to drama—with everything in between. Summer shows are staged at Davidson College's Cunningham Fine Arts Building; dinner theater is at Vail Commons on campus. Tickets are $8–$10 per show; $21 for dinner and theater. & (North)

## GREY SEAL PUPPETS
**225 W. Fourth St.**
**Charlotte**
**704/374-0346**
The internationally acclaimed Grey Seal Puppets make their home in Charlotte, but travel North America to perform in theaters and on TV. The company writes, designs, builds, and performs each unique show, most of which cater to children with a few aimed at mature audiences. Performances often focus on Hans Christian Andersen stories, well-known writers, and familiar tales. Shows run at The Children's Theatre of Charlotte and other community venues. (citywide)

**OMIMEO MIME THEATRE**
P.O. Box 221267
Charlotte 28222
704/553-0032

Celebrating its 20th anniversary this year, Omimeo (say oh-my-me-oh) Mime Theatre stages up to five productions for kids and adults at Children's Theatre of Charlotte and Spirit Square. Forget the annoying, white-faced, beret-wearing park mimes and imagine a blend of mine, vaudville, spoken words, dance, and circus techniques. Tickets range $6–$10. &#x267F; (Uptown)

**SPECIAL ATTRACTIONS**
130 N. Tryon St.
Charlotte
704/372-1000 (box office); 704/333-4686 (administrative office)

A second series of the North Carolina

---

# Music for Everyone

*The Charlotte Symphony offers a wide range of programs and performances to introduce patrons to the orchestra.*

*Starbucks Pre-Concert Talks are held at 7 p.m. in the Booth Lobby before Classics shows on Friday and Saturday nights. Get the inside scoop plus a cup of Starbucks java as conductors share funny and informative insights on the upcoming program.*

*Family Matinees, on weekend afternoons, are economically priced concerts for the whole family. Familiar tunes are presented, along with commentary from the conductor.*

*Lollipops concerts delights young listeners and their parents with programs under one hour, designed to help children make friends with great music and the orchestra.*

*Mostly Mozart is a fairly new series that travels to churches and synagogues for charming, intimate concerts. They're inexpensive, convenient, and scheduled throughout the community.*

*"What to Listen For in Music" is a four-week short course held on Monday evenings in the fall at Metropolitan Bakery, led by Peter McCoppin and the CSO conducting staff.*

*Finally, Casual Fridays is a Charlotte tradition welcoming patrons who would like to attend concerts directly from work on Fridays.*

*For more information on the Charlotte Symphony, call the office at 704/332-0468 or the box office at 704/332-6136.*

*Oratorio Singers of Charlotte with the Charlotte Symphony*

Blumenthal Performing Arts Center, Special Attractions includes a variety of musical theater, dance performances, and individual performers. The 1998-1999 season featured Tom Jones, Patty Loveless, Wynton Marsalis and the Lincoln Center Jazz Orchestra, A Christmas Carol, Sandi Patty and Bill Cosby. Shows performed in the Belk Theater of the Performing Arts Center. 🕭 (Uptown, Central)

### THEATRE CHARLOTTE
**8501 Queens Rd.**
**Charlotte**
**704/376-3777**
North Carolina's oldest community theater, Theatre Charlotte dates back to 1927. Volunteers stage several productions each season, including popular musicals, comedies, and dramas. Recent shows included *Gypsy, Arsenic and Old Lace, An Ideal Husband, Death of a Salesman,* and *Anything Goes.* Four O'Clock Theatre features one-act plays, produced in the lobby of the group's Myers Park base on select Saturday and Sunday after-

noons. Season runs Sept–June; subscriptions range $55–$75. 🕭 (Central)

## MUSIC AND OPERA

### CAROLINA CROWN DRUM AND BUGLE CORPS
**227-A Main St.**
**Fort Mill, S.C.**
**803/547-2270; 704/338-1331**
**(Nightbeat office)**
A precision drum-and-bugle outfit, the Carolina Crown consists of youth ages 14 to 21 who use brass and percussion instruments and color guard while marching into various formations. Summers are spent touring and performing; but the big event in Charlotte is Nightbeat, an annual August show with 8–10 nationally ranked groups taking the field. Nightbeat tickets range $10–$50. 🕭 (Central)

### CAROLINA PRO MUSICA
**P.O. Box 32022**
**Charlotte**
**704/334-3468**
An ensemble dedicated to early music,

Carolina Pro Musica plays historic instruments and dresses in period costume for its five-performance, October-to-April season, held at local churches and chapels. The group has also recorded *The Angel So Did Sound It*, music of medieval and Renaissance Germany, France, and England. Individual tickets $10; season tickets $35. (citywide)

## CHARLOTTE CHORAL SOCIETY
1900 Queens Rd.
Charlotte
704/374-1564

This is an umbrella organization for four distinct choral groups: The Mainstage Choir, a 120-voice choir performing music from gospel to Gershwin; the Festival Singers, a 32-voice choir performing sacred and secular works a cappella; the Contemporary Ensemble, a 29-voice African American choir; and IMPROMPTU!, a small vocal ensemble specializing in jazz, blues, and bigband standards. The society is best known for its annual Singing Christmas Tree, a holiday concert in which chorus members stand on platforms to form the shape of a tree. (citywide)

## CHARLOTTE FOLK MUSIC SOCIETY
P.O. Box 36864
Charlotte  28236
704/372-3655

Even if you don't play a note, the Charlotte Folk Music Society welcomes anyone who loves bluegrass, old time folk, Cajun, Celtic, and the like for monthly concerts and open jam sessions September through June. Local and regional concerts are generally free to the public; bring your guitar so you can jump in on the impromptu jam after the show. ♿ (Central)

## CHARLOTTE PHILHARMONIC ORCHESTRA
P.O. Box 470987
Charlotte
704/846-2788

A semiprofessional orchestra that focuses on "the music you want to hear," the Charlotte Philharmonic presents seven shows in a September-to-May season. Performances include Romantic Fantasy, Christmas Spectacular, An American Salute, and *South Pacific*. The group also has a compact disc recording, *Timeless Moments*, with pieces from *Phantom of the Opera*, "The Blue Danube," "The Hallelujah Chorus," and "Sophisticated Ladies." Shows are at Belk Theater in the Performing Arts Center, Ovens Auditorium, and Oasis Shrine Temple. ♿ (citywide)

## CHARLOTTE REPERTORY ORCHESTRA
P.O. Box 11334
Charlotte
704/366-4499

Charlotte's only all-volunteer civic symphony is comprised of 65 auditioned musicians that present concerts to a culturally diverse audience at an affordable ticket price. Five major concerts are in venues across the city, along with outreach and chamber ensemble performances. Single-show tickets range from $6 students and seniors to $17 families. Seven-show season tickets range from $25 students and seniors to $60 families. ♿ (citywide)

## CHARLOTTE SYMPHONY
211 N. College St.
Charlotte
704/332-6136

The Charlotte Symphony, the region's full-time professional orchestra, performs in the Belk Theater of the

Blumenthal Performing Arts Center. World-renowned soloists and the great masterworks highlight the symphony's signature Classics series—featuring the music of Rachmaninoff, Beethoven, Tchaikovsky, Schumann, Debussy, Strauss, and Mahler. The Charlotte Symphony Pops series of seven concerts features high-profile entertainers like Ray Charles, Sandy Duncan, and Al Jarreau. Other Symphony series include Lollipop concerts for young people, family matinees, Cabaret, and Mostly Mozart, performed in churches and synagogues throughout the area. The Summer Pops concerts, held on the lawn at SouthPark Mall, as well as concerts in Gaston County, Matthews, Rock Hill, and Concord, are free. These starry-night concerts attract more than 50,000 listeners during the summer season. The Oratorio Singers of Charlotte, the 150-member chorus of the Charlotte Symphony, perform with the orchestra on the Classics series, as well as the annual Handel's Messiah in December. (Uptown, citywide)

**OPERA CAROLINA**
**345 N. College St.**
**Charlotte**
**704/332-7177**
Charlotte's professional opera company presents works featuring singers and artists of national and international acclaim alongside local and regional performers. Marking its 50th year in the 1998–1999 season, Opera Carolina also provides a variety of educational, training, and outreach programs in addition to OperaFest, a workshop for high-school students of diverse racial and cultural backgrounds. Recent shows included *Tosca*, *Rigoletto*, and *The Crucible*. Operas are sung in Italian with English supertitles or in English at Belk Theater in the Blumenthal Performing Arts Center. ♿ (Uptown, citywide)

**ST. PETER'S EPISCOPAL CHURCH CHAMBER MUSIC SERIES**
**115 W. Seventh St.**
**Charlotte**
**704/332-7746**
Charlotte's oldest Episcopal parish hosts free noon concerts and longer Sunday evening concerts at its Uptown site.

# DANCE

**CHARLOTTE CITY BALLET**
**8612 Monroe Rd.**
**Charlotte**
**704/536-0615**
Around 30 middle- and high-school students make up this auditioned

Want the best seats in the house?

At the North Carolina Blumenthal Performing Arts Center, try orchestra level and grand tier circle for opera, ballet, and theater. For concerts, grand tier and higher are prime spots.

To reach the Performing Arts Center box office, call 704/372-1000.

Van Miller

Dance Legends *at the North Carolina Dance Theatre*

youth ballet company that presents full-length story ballets each June and performs with the Charlotte Philharmonic several times a year. *Sleeping Beauty* and *Cinderella* are recent productions; during the holidays, the dancers perform while the Philharmonic plays music from *The Nutcracker*. A good opportunity for young dancers to learn the rigors—and rewards—of work in a dance company. Performances at Blumenthal, Ovens and Queens College. Tickets for spring show: $5. (Uptown, Central)

**CHARLOTTE YOUTH BALLET**
**P.O. Box 15098**
**Charlotte**
**704/366-5133**

The Charlotte Youth Ballet has offered performance opportunities to thousands of area dance students for more than 15 years. The nonprofit group presented its first *Nutcracker* performance in 1981, giving Charlotte children a first-ever chance to perform in a locally produced version of the classic Christmas ballet. Even kids who don't take dance classes love to dress up in holiday attire and head to Ovens Auditorium to watch the show. Other ballets staged in the past include such traditional offerings as *Alice in Wonderland* and *Cinderella*. Generally two shows a season at holidays and spring. Tickets range $9–$18 for adults, $6–$12 children. (See also Chapter 6, Kids' Stuff.) ♿ (Central)

**NORTH CAROLINA DANCE THEATRE**
**800 N. College St.**
**Charlotte**
**704/372-0101**

Charlotte's well-known, highly respected professional dance company presents both classical and contemporary works in its six-show, October-to-May season. Its artistic leadership boasts impressive credentials: Jean-Pierre Bonnefoux, Patricia McBride, and Jerri Kumery are former New York City Ballet performers. Shows include cutting-edge innovative works; pieces by North Carolina choreographers; master works; energetic, jazz-influenced performances; and classics such as *The Nutcracker* with the Charlotte Symphony and the Charlotte Children's Choir. Performances are at the Blumenthal Performing Arts Center. Dance Place is the official school of the North Carolina Dance Theatre. (See also Chapter 6, Kids' Stuff.) ♿ (Uptown)

## CONCERT VENUES

**AFRO-AMERICAN CULTURAL CENTER**
**401 N. Myers St.**
**Charlotte**
**704/374-1565**

Features a 200-seat theater and amphitheater. ♿ (Uptown)

## N.C. BLUMENTHAL PERFORMING ARTS CENTER
**130 N. Tryon St.**
**Charlotte**
**704/372-1000**
Includes Belk Theater and Booth Playhouse. ♿ (Uptown)

## OASIS SHRINE TEMPLE
**604 Daniel Burnham Way**
**Charlotte**
**704/549-9600**
Hosts performances by Charlotte Symphony (Cabaret series), Charlotte Philharmonic Orchestra, and other groups. ♿ (North)

## OVENS AUDITORIUM
**2700 E. Independence Blvd.**
**Charlotte**
**704/335-3100**
Charlotte's largest performing arts facility, with 2,600 seats. ♿ (Central)

## SPIRIT SQUARE CENTER FOR ARTS & EDUCATION
**345 N. College St.**
**Charlotte**
**704/372-9664**
Houses 700-seat McGlohon Theatre (formerly NationsBank Performance Place) and 180-seat Duke Power Theatre. ♿ (Uptown)

# BUYING TICKETS

## N.C. BLUMENTHAL PERFORMING ARTS CENTER BOX OFFICE
**Founders Hall, Bank of America Corporate Center**
**130 N. College St.**
**Charlotte**

**704/372-1000**
Open Mon–Sat 10–6. A half-hour of free parking in the Bank of America garage is available for customers purchasing tickets.

## TICKETMASTER
**704/552-6500**

## TICKET BROKERS
AAAA Ticket Pros, 800/962-2985
A-1 Ticket Service, 800/381-0595
Encore Tickets, 704/333-1640
Premiere Tickets & Tours, 704/529-1788
Primo Ticket Services, 704/523-9099
24/7 Ticket Service, 704/569-1400

# ARTS EDUCATION

## COMMUNITY SCHOOL OF THE ARTS
**345 N. College St.**
**Charlotte**
**704/377-4187**
The Community School of the Arts recently moved to the sophisticated galleries, marbled hallways, and grand theaters of Uptown's Spirit Square. Dedicated to providing a high-quality, comprehensive arts education to students and adults, CSA offers individual and group classes in music, drama, visual arts, and dance. Parents can participate with kids to learn elements of music; older kids can discover the joy of playing in an improv jazz or rock group. Other classes teach famous Broadway dances and the latest moves seen on the streets. ♿ (Uptown)

© Honour Hiers—Ri-Ra

# 12

# NIGHTLIFE

*Whether it's a martini and a cigar or two-stepping to country tunes at a cowboy bar, Charlotte's nightclub scene offers something for every interest. Watch the big game at a sports bar, take a relaxing seat on a couch for acoustic music, boogie to the best of the '80s, or hang with the drag queens 'til the wee hours.*

*One of Charlotte's liveliest entertainment districts is Uptown, where young professionals mix with college students, club-hoppers, and curious tourists. College Street is the main drag, with several dance clubs that play everything from retro to techno. On Tryon Street, the suits hang out after work for microbrews, Irish beer, and a good meal.*

*Live music can be found throughout the city, but the best-known places are The Double Door Inn for blues, Coyote Joe's for country acts, and Tremont Music Hall for rock, alternative, reggae, and other varieties from regional and national acts.*

*Charlotte also has plenty of pubs, watering holes, and neighborhood hangouts where you can grab a beer and relax in a casual setting.*

*Happy trails . . .*

## DANCE CLUBS

**THE BAHA**
**4369 S. Tryon St.**
**Charlotte**
**704/525-3343**
Voted Charlotte's best dance club, The Baha stands alone on South Tryon

Street a few miles from Uptown, close to Woodlawn Road. The crowds are young; the atmosphere high-energy. Thursday nights are Retro '80s; Fridays feature DJs spinning industrial and progressive dance tunes; Saturdays attract the largest crowds when KISS 95.1 FM broadcasts live and people come to shake their stuff until 3 in the morning. Ladies enter free before 10 on Saturdays; ages 18 and up welcome. Thu–Sat 9 p.m.–3 a.m., Sun 9–2:30. $3–$5 cover. (Central)

## BAR CHARLOTTE
**300 N. College St.**
**Charlotte**
**704/342-2557**
BAR Charlotte attracts college and twenty-something kids still into chugging beer and dancing on top of bars. Located in a strip of clubs and hangouts on North College Street uptown, BAR plays dance music from the '60s to the '90s. Trademark drink is the BAR Yard, 36 ounces of brew in one shot. Ages 18 and over welcome. Thu–Sun 9 p.m.–3 a.m. $3 cover. (Uptown)

## COPACABANA
**4110 E. Independence Blvd.**
**Charlotte**
**704/531-8486**
Popular with Charlotte's growing Latino community, Copacabana features live and DJ Latin music at the corner of East Independence and Albemarle Road. Mixed drinks, beer, and wine served, but most folks go for the hot dancing. Doors open at 8; closing time ranges 2:30 to 3:30 a.m. Thu–Sun. Cover charge varies. (Central)

## HAVE A NICE DAY CAFE
**314 N. College St.**
**Charlotte**
**704/373-2233**
Like walking into your teenage bedroom from the '70s, this fun dance club in Uptown's Entertainment District covers every imaginable space with '70s memorabilia and pinup posters from Shaun Cassidy to Charlie's Angels. The infectious atmosphere gets everybody moving with songs like "Brick House" and "Play That Funky Music." Lots of groups, bachelorette parties, and college kids. Fishbowl-sized drinks with several straws are the house specialty. Wed 9 p.m.–2 a.m., Fri–Sat 8–2. Cover varies around $6. (Uptown)

## MYTHOS
**300 N. College St.**

*Pool table at Atlantic Beer & Ice, p. 207*

© Honour Hiers

**Charlotte**
**704/375-8765**
Voted Best Late Night Club, Mythos is a progressive, cutting-edge dance club on the corner of 6th and College Streets across from the Holiday Inn Uptown. DJs spin progressive house music, techno, and European dance music; occasional live performances such as RuPaul and Big Bad Voodoo Daddy. All types of people, including straight and the open-minded community, show up when the other bars shut down. Tue–Thu and Sun 10 p.m.–3 a.m., Fri–Sat 10–4. Cover varies. (Uptown)

**THE TUNNEL**
**4120 E. Independence Blvd.**
**Charlotte**
**704/563-0888**
Formerly the Sugar Shack, The Tunnel attracts the urban crowd into hip-hop, rap, and new R&B at this shopping center club a few miles from Uptown. Live entertainment and DJs; urban contemporary station WPEG "Power 98" also does live broadcasts. Thu–Fri 10 p.m.–3 a.m., Sat 10–4. Cover varies around $3. (Central)

# MUSIC CLUBS

## Blues

*Several Charlotte steakhouses also serve up live blues music on weekdays and weekends. In addition to the following listings, try Mill Street Blues, 200 E. Morehead St., 704/375-8448; or Morehead Chop House, 300 E. Morehead St., 704/334-2655. Both are just blocks from Uptown Charlotte.*

**THE DOUBLE DOOR INN**
**218 E. Independence Blvd.**
**Charlotte**

**704/376-1446**
Look no farther than this for the best in blues, rock, old R&B, zydeco, and rockabilly. The oldest blues bar in the Queen City and home to the Charlotte Blues Society, the venerable Double Door won the prestigious W.C. Handy Award for Blues Club of the Year in 1994. The friendly, easygoing club has hosted huge names over the years, including Eric Clapton, Koko Taylor, and Buddy Guy. Mon–Fri 9 p.m.–2 a.m., Sat 8–2. Cover charge varies with show. (Central)

## Country and Western

**COYOTE JOE'S**
**4621 Wilkinson Blvd.**
**Charlotte**
**704/399-4946**
Nominated for Country Nightclub of the Year by the Academy of Country Music, Coyote Joe's is a cavernous honky-tonk with live music and dancing nightly. Big-name acts such as Merle Haggard and Tracy Byrd perform here along with the house band, Vic Rorrer & The No Name Band. The largest country-music club in the Southeast, Coyote Joe's also offers free line dancing and Texas two-step lessons for those who've yet to get their 10-gallon hat. Tue–Sun 7 p.m.–2 a.m. Cover charge varies. (West)

## Rock/Pop/Alternative

**FAT CITY**
**3127 N. Davidson St.**
**Charlotte**
**704/343-0240**
A rockin' spot in the middle of the city's cutting-edge NoDa arts community, Fat City features live rock, alternative rock, blues, reggae, and jazz. Local DJs spin laid-back beats every Monday; Tuesdays offer jazz; better-known

# UPTOWN ENTERTAINMENT

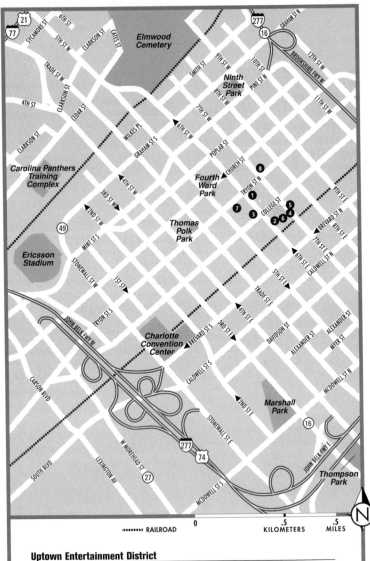

## Uptown Entertainment District

1 Atlantic Beer & Ice
2 BAR Charlotte
3 Fat Tuesday
4 Have A Nice Day Cafe
5 The Hut
6 Mythos
7 Ri-Ra—The Irish Pub
8 Rock Bottom Brewery & Restaurant

bands on weekends; open jam each Sunday. Known for great food as well, the casual Fat City gets especially packed during gallery crawls the first and third Friday of each month. Nightly 9 p.m.–2 a.m. Cover varies. (Central)

## JACK STRAW'S
**1936 E. Seventh St.**
**Charlotte**
**704/347-8960**

A college and young-professionals' hangout in the Elizabeth neighborhood, this restaurant/bar has one of the best live music lineups in Charlotte: rhythm and blues, rock, and reggae, with a slant toward laid-back, jam-happy bands. Jazz on Thursday; live bands Friday and Saturday. One-buck beer nightly. Thu 5 p.m.–1 a.m., Fri–Sat 5–2; dinner served until 10:30; closed Sun. Cover varies. (Central)

## TREMONT MUSIC HALL
**400 W. Tremont Ave.**
**Charlotte**
**704/343-9494**

*Mixing drinks at Mythos, p. 204*

© Honour Hiers

This South End music club hosts local, regional, and national music acts from alternative rock to reggae. The two-room hall features a smaller stage with capacity for 300; a larger room holds up to 1,000. Charlotte's Sugarsmack, Jolene, Our Lady Peace, Yellowman, Morphine, and Leftover Salmon are a sampling; original bands only. Fri–Sat 10 p.m.–2 a.m.; some weekday shows. $5–$10 cover. (Central)

## PUBS AND BARS

### ATLANTIC BEER & ICE
**330 N. Tryon St.**
**Charlotte**
**704/339-0566**

Known as ABI around Charlotte, this Uptown restaurant/bar draws young professionals after work and on into the wee hours. Upstairs features a cigar and scotch bar; downstairs has billiards and regional bands. Great microbrews. Jazz, blues, modern rock Friday and Saturday in the cellar. Also hosts wine-tastings and cigar dinners. Lunch, dinner; bar open until midnight Mon–Thu and until 2 Fri–Sat. No cover. (Uptown)

### FAT TUESDAY
**211 N. College St.**
**Charlotte**
**704/375-3288**

With a Mardi Gras theme and a wall of frozen daiquiri slush machines, Fat Tuesday is a fun, upbeat club with live funk, '80s retro, and rock. The world's largest selection of frozen daiquiris includes names like 190 Octane, Triple Bypass, Swampwater, Jungle Juice, and Banana Banshee. Sandwiches, salads, chicken, and appetizers at lunch and dinner; bar open until midnight weekdays and until 2 Fri–Sat. Cover varies. (Uptown)

## THE GRADUATE
**911 E. Morehead St.**
**Charlotte**
**704/377-3808**

A longtime Charlotte favorite, The Graduate in Dilworth is a two-story bar with billiards downstairs and live music at street level. Live alternative rock and upbeat cover bands appear at the Dilworth location, with Top 40 and cover rock at the South Charlotte digs. UNCC students head to The Graduate off Independence Boulevard. Lunch, dinner; bar open late. Additional locations: 8334 Pineville-Matthews Rd., Charlotte, 704/543-4020; 2014 Sharon Forest Dr., Charlotte, 704/532-2562. Hours and cover charges vary. (Central)

## THE HUT
**314 N. College St.**
**Charlotte**
**704/374-0488**

A tropical tiki lounge, this Charlotte hangout shouldn't be overlooked among its larger and louder neighbors in Uptown's Entertainment District. Thursdays offer penny drafts, 50-cent well drinks, and $1 longnecks; Fridays and Saturdays feature '80s and reggae tunes. Live entertainment with local and regional bands periodically. Thu–Sat 10 p.m.–2 a.m. Cover varies around $5. (Uptown)

## MIDTOWN SUNDRIES
**618 Kenilworth Ave.**
**Charlotte**
**704/358-3933**

At this traditional Charlotte hangout (with three locations around the city) you can relax with a beer on the large patio, belt out tunes on karaoke night, watch the big game on a large-screen TV, or jam the night away with regional bands. After about 10 p.m., the restaurant makes way for twenty-somethings drinking and hanging out around the large, brass-adorned bar. Additional locations: 3425 David Cox Rd., Charlotte, 704/597-7413; 7713 Pineville-Matthews Rd. at Carmel Commons, Charlotte, 704/541-8117. (Central)

## RI-RA—THE IRISH PUB
**208 N. Tryon St.**
**Charlotte**
**704/333-5554**

One of the most popular bars in Uptown Charlotte, Ri-Ra is an Irish pub that serves lunch and dinner before attracting the young professional crowd. A navy and yellow exterior is accented with blooming flower boxes on the second floor and large storefront windows at street level. Faux-finished paint and furnishings from Ireland complete the effect. Offers Guinness, Harp, Bass, a large selection of single malts and fine cigars, and live traditional Irish music. Lunch, dinner; late-night and dessert menu to 1 a.m.; bar open until 2 nightly. Cover charge varies. (Uptown)

## ROCK BOTTOM BREWERY & RESTAURANT
**401 N. Tryon St. in Transamerica Square**
**Charlotte**
**704/334-2739**

The jacket comes off, the sleeves roll up, and the tie is loosened. The young professionals in Uptown Charlotte head to this upscale restaurant and microbrewery straight from work for beers, snacks, and shop talk. Dinner is served on one side of the restaurant; the bar is on the other and features a menu with brick-oven pizzas and big-portion appetizers. Televisions, pool tables, cigars, and an outdoor patio offer something for everyone. (See also Chapter 4, Where to Eat.) Lunch, dinner; bar open until 2 a.m. nightly. No cover. (Uptown)

## SELWYN AVENUE PUB
**2801 Selwyn Ave.**
**Charlotte**
**704/333-3443**

Like your homecoming football game, everyone seems to know each other at this Myers Park pub and young professionals' favorite watering hole. A large patio out front makes a great setting for a cold beer and relaxation spring through fall. A good place for a casual dinner, too. Weekdays 4 p.m.– 2 a.m.; Saturdays and Sundays (11:30 a.m.–2 a.m. No cover. (Central)

## SOUTHEND BREWERY
## & SMOKEHOUSE
**2100 South Blvd.**
**Charlotte**
**704/358-4677**

A microbrewery and restaurant in the South End district just outside of Uptown, the Brewery draws big crowds to the bar adjacent to its dining room. Like many of South End's shops, condos, and urban markets, the Brewery features high ceilings and many windows from its days as a mill. Large copper tanks store the beer, and the patio is popular in warm weather and on Carolina Panthers game days. Try Carolina Blonde and other beer varieties. Live music nightly. (See also Chapter 4, Where to Eat.) Lunch, dinner; bar open until 2 a.m. Cover charge varies. (Central)

## VINNIE'S SARDINE GRILL
## & RAW BAR
**1714 South Blvd.**
**Charlotte**
**704/332-0006**

Always packed to the gills, no pun intended. Vinnie's is a popular raw bar and restaurant in South End known for

its seafood, $1 domestic beers, and pre- and postgame parties when the Carolina Panthers play in nearby Ericsson Stadium. It's a casual place with oysters, peel-your-own-shrimp, and cold beer. Additional location: 142 E. John St., Matthews, 704/849-0202. Lunch, dinner; bar open Mon–Sat until 2 a.m. and Sun until 11 p.m. (Central)

# SPORTS BARS

*With the Carolina Panthers and the Charlotte Hornets in town, sports restaurants and bars do a booming business in the Queen City. See Chapter 4, Where to Eat for entries on Jocks & Jills in West Charlotte and Champp's Americana in Central Charlotte.*

## PICASSO'S SPORTS CAFÉ
**1004 Kings Dr.**
**Charlotte**
**704/333-2255**

Pizza, beer, and the game. What more could you want? Central Charlotteans head to Picasso's Sports Café in the midtown area for its food, wide variety of draft beers, and rowdy atmosphere that make you feel like you're actually at the game. Lunch, dinner; bar open 'til 11 nightly. (Central)

## SCOREBOARD
**2500 Crown Point Executive Blvd.**
**Charlotte or Matthews**
**704/847-7678**

Named Best Sports Bar in Charlotte, Scoreboard is a sports-themed restaurant/bar with stadium seating, volume controls at each table, and four movie-sized screens with other big-screen TVs scattered inside and on an outdoor patio. Enjoy appetizers, pizza, salads, sandwiches, chicken, pasta, desserts, and of course, beer. Go early on big game days. Mon–Thu 4 p.m.–1 a.m., Fri–Sat 11–2, Sun noon–midnight. (East)

## COMEDY CLUBS

### THE COMEDY ZONE
**5317 E. Independence Blvd.**
**Charlotte**
**704/568-4242**
Voted Best Place to Take a Date by *Charlotte's Best* magazine, the Comedy Zone on East Independence Boulevard will lighten up any evening. The club features national and regional comedians Tuesday through Sunday. Country comedians Pinkard & Bowden, "The Funniest Man in America" James Gregory, and hypnotist Mike Harvey are recent offerings. Additional location: Lake Norman Comedy Zone, 455 Plaza Dr., Mooresville, 704/664-3031 (Exit 36 off I-77 North). Shows 8 Wed–Thu and Sun 8 p.m.; Fri 8 (nonsmoking) and 10:15; Sat 7, 9, and 11. Cover varies with show. (East)

### THE PERCH
**1500 Central Ave.**
**Charlotte**
**704/372-7724**
On Fridays and Saturdays, locals head to this live original sketch comedy club above a cutting-edge clothing store on the corner of Central and Pecan in Plaza-Midwood. Random couches give it a laid-back feel, and desserts and coffee are served in place of alcohol. A Comedy Zone for cool cats. Shows are rated R for verbal content. Fri–Sat 9 (nonsmoking) and 11 p.m. $7 cover. (Central)

## MOVIE HOUSES OF NOTE

*Movies are a popular pastime for Charlotteans, and choices abound.*

*The most recent trend in theaters is stadium seating, which uses stairs from the top to the bottom so all patrons have unobstructed views. Many of these theaters also have love seats, with raisable armrests.*

### CAROLINA PAVILION 22
**9541 South Blvd.**
**Charlotte**
**704/643-4262**
A huge stadium-seating multiplex, the 22-screen Carolina Pavilion features stadium seating and electronic billboards listing times and sell-out information. Expect huge crowds on weekends. (South)

### THE MANOR THEATRE
**609 Providence Rd.**
**Charlotte**
**704/334-2727**
This longtime Myers Park theater has only two screens, but is one of the few Charlotte theaters to take chances on art, foreign, and noncommercial titles. (Central)

### OMNIMAX THEATRE AT DISCOVERY PLACE
**301 N. Tryon St.**
**Charlotte**
**704/372-6261**
The largest planetarium dome in the United States (79-foot diameter), Charlotte's OMNIMAX Theatre is inside the interactive science museum Discovery Place in Uptown. Planetarium shows and films are projected onto a screen that's five stories tall. *Everest* was a popular recent offering. Hours: Call for times. Admission: Theater admission only is $5.50 ages 13–59; $4.50 ages 6–12 and seniors; $2.75 ages 3–5. (Uptown)

### PHILLIPS PLACE
**Fairview at Cameron Valley**

**TIP**

Film lovers can earn free tickets to local movie theaters with the Movie Awards Gold Card. Buy one ticket at Phillips Place, Park Terrace or Arboretum theaters to get the card, then earn a free popcorn after four shows and a free ticket after eight shows.

The three theaters also admit members free on their birthdays with one paid admission.

For more information on shows at these theaters, call the 24-hour movie hot line at 704/55-MOVIE.

**Parkway**
**Charlotte**
**704/556-6843**

A 10-screen, stadium-seating theater in upscale Phillips Place Shopping Center near SouthPark Mall, this makes for a great date after dinner at one of the many popular restaurants in the area. (South)

### SILVER SCREEN CAFÉ
**4120 E. Independence Blvd.**
**Charlotte**
**704/535-8333**

Have dinner and a movie—at the same time. The Silver Screen Café serves food, beer, and wine during movies that have been in release for a few months. *The Rocky Horror Picture Show*, complete with live cast, runs each Friday; Mondays are $1 nights with $1 admission and $1 beer. Weeknight specials. (Central)

## CONCERT VENUES

### BLOCKBUSTER PAVILION
**707 Pavilion Blvd.**
**Charlotte**
**704/549-5555**

An outdoor amphitheater off NC 29 in northeast Mecklenburg County, Blockbuster Pavilion features 19,000 seats and a huge lawn. Summer months bring a steady stream of shows such as James Taylor, Dave Matthews Band, Lollapalooza, and Tina Turner. (North)

### CHARLOTTE COLISEUM
**100 Hive Drive**
**Charlotte**
**704/357-4700**

This 24,000-seat arena is home to the Charlotte Hornets and Charlotte Sting basketball teams, and also hosts shows from country superstar Garth Brooks to Ringling Bros. Barnum & Bailey Circus. (West)

### ERICSSON STADIUM
**800 S. Mint St.**
**Charlotte**
**704/358-7538**

The NFL's most high-tech arena, Uptown Charlotte's Ericsson Stadium is a $187 million open-air stadium and home of the Carolina Panthers. The 73,000-plus–seat facility has also featured a Rolling Stones concert and a Billy Graham revival. (Uptown)

### INDEPENDENCE ARENA
**2700 E. Independence Blvd.**
**Charlotte**
**704/335-3100**

Actually the first Charlotte Coliseum before "The Hive" was built for the Hornets, Independence Arena is home to the Charlotte Checkers hockey team and other sporting events, such as AAU Junior Olympics and gymnastics events. Some smaller concerts also use the 10,500-seat arena. (Central)

## PARAMOUNT'S CAROWINDS PALADIUM
### I-77 and Carowinds Boulevard
### Charlotte
### 704/588-2600

Located inside Paramount's Carowinds Theme Park, this outdoor venue has hosted smaller concerts for decades. Some of its 13,000 seats are partially covered. Hosts Christian music concerts and gospel shows, and occasional alternative and pop rock acts. (West)

The Biltmore Estate, Asheville, NC

# 13

# DAY TRIPS FROM CHARLOTTE

## Day Trip: Blowing Rock

### Distance from Charlotte: 2 hours, 120 miles

The charming mountain village of Blowing Rock is a favorite day trip or weekend getaway for Charlotteans who enjoy its breathtaking scenery, small-town atmosphere, and friendly people. The village sits in the Western Mountains atop the Eastern Continental Divide and the Blue Ridge Parkway at an elevation of 4,000 feet. Only 1,600 people make Blowing Rock their full-time home, but in summer and fall the population jumps to 6,500.

The first visitors to the region known as the High Country were ancient Cherokee Indians who traveled here each summer for the cool climate and the abundance of deer, elk, and bear. Spanish explorer Hernando de Soto searched for gold here in the early 1500s. But European colonies formed along the coast, and the High Country's snowy winters and Native American threat discouraged much settlement for the next 150 years.

Those who did explore and settle this region were tough and fearless. Davy Crockett was born in a cabin on the Nolichucky River. Jesse James's brother, Frank, hid out in the High Country. Annie Oakley ran a trap-shooting range in Blowing Rock.

The area's most famous pioneer, however, is Daniel Boone. A resident in the 1760s, Boone guided settlers along an old buffalo path known as The Wilderness Road. The adjacent town of Boone is named in his honor.

Eventually, visitors started coming to the High Country, first by coach and later by train. By the turn of the 19th century, affluent Southern families built elegant homes or lived in luxurious hotels around the area. Snow-making technology sparked winter tourism in the 1960s, and the High Country became a popular year-round destination.

While Charlotte's humid summer lingers on into September, Blowing Rock enjoys crisp temperatures that make folks itch for autumn. When fall does arrive in the North Carolina mountains, its colors dazzle and its leaves create a confetti carpet of orange, yellow, and red.

The annual **Woolly Worm Festival** is held on a mid-October weekend in nearby Banner Elk. Fuzzy caterpillars race, and the winner is said to predict the area's winter weather by the colors of its stripes. Around 16,000 people attend the festival to enjoy craft booths, food vendors, artwork, and entertainment.

Back in Blowing Rock, **Main Street** is an old-fashioned downtown with shops, restaurants, and eateries lining both sides. Blowing Rock's park is also on Main Street, and is home to regular weekend festivals. **Art in the Park**, which includes more than 125 exhibitors, runs six Saturdays between May and October.

Rustic cabins, fully furnished condominiums, country inns, and fine resorts are all available for Blowing Rock's weekend visitors. The **Green Park Inn** is on the National Register of Historic Places, and **Chetola** is a casually elegant resort with rooms, suites, or condominiums. **The Mast Farm Inn** in nearby Valle Crucis is one of North Carolina's few remaining historic farms.

For things to do, start with the obvious: nature. Western North Carolina is home to the **Blue Ridge Mountains**, which are best seen via the **Blue Ridge Parkway**. The scenic road winds 469 miles through the mountains of Virginia, Tennessee, and North Carolina. Known as the "sanctuary of high places," the parkway passes mountain forests, old farms, rolling hills, and vast pastures of wildflowers.

It took crews 32 years to complete the parkway, except for a 7.5-mile strip around rugged **Grandfather Mountain**. After years of study, a complicated concrete bridge called the Linn Cove Viaduct was built to sweep around the mountain. Grandfather is the highest mountain in the Blue Ridge range, and features a 228-foot walk along the **Mile High Swinging Bridge**. Bears, eagles, cougars and deer in their natural habitat make for great photo opportunities, followed by hiking or a picnic.

Westglow Spa

*Native Charlotteans (and you!) can escape to Westglow Spa, p. 216.*

# CHARLOTTE REGION

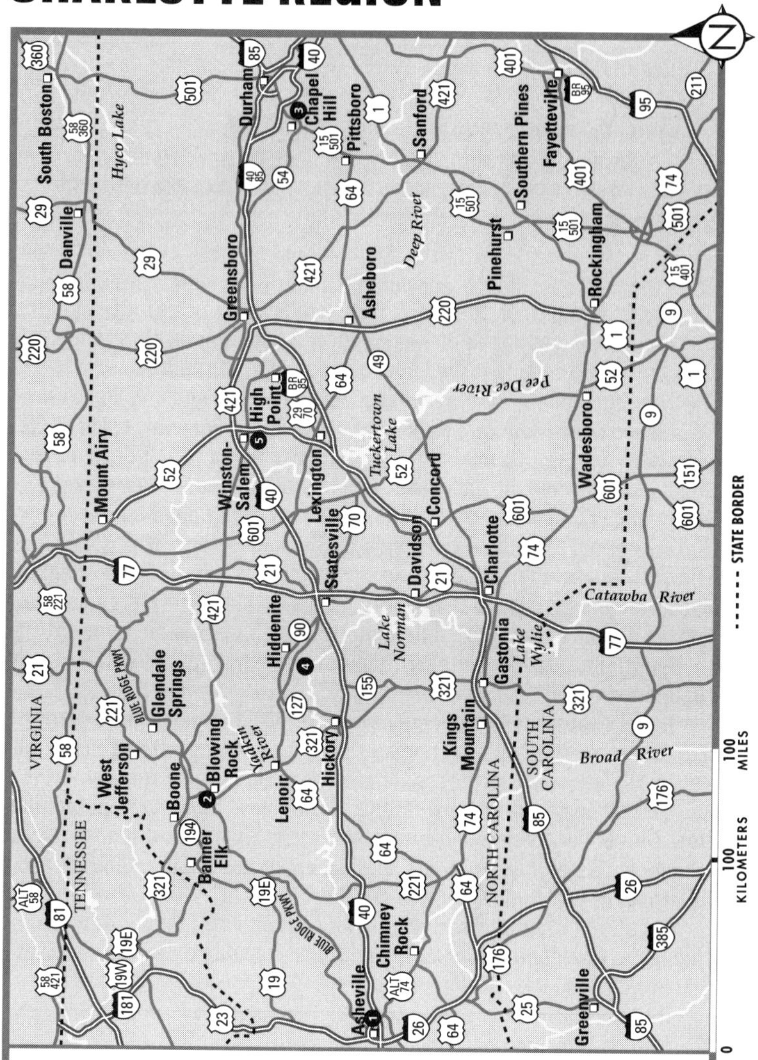

**Day Trips from Charlotte**

1 Asheville
2 Blowing Rock
3 Chapel Hill
4 Hiddenite
5 Winston–Salem

The **Blowing Rock** that gave the town its name is a protruding rock formation 3,000 feet above the Johns River Gorge. Winds blow with such force that small objects tossed over its edge are returned.

The High Country offers plenty of other things to see and do as well. **Moses Cone Memorial Park**, on the Blue Ridge Parkway, covers 3,600 acres and features 25 miles of gently graded paths which draw cross-country skiers when the snow falls. Hiking, trout fishing, and two lakes are here, along with a craft center in the historic Moses Cone Manor.

Just down the parkway outside of Blowing Rock is **Westglow Spa**, where stressed Charlotteans go for relaxing facials, body treatments, and massages. Housed in the restored mansion of an artist, the beautiful, white-columned Georgian-style home sits high upon a hill overlooking the mountain area. Tourists can stay overnight or go for a day of spa treatments.

In Valle Crucis, a few minutes away, the **Mast General Store** dates to 1883. Listed on the National Register of Historic Places, it is considered one of the nation's best representations of an old country store.

Boone, just three miles from Blowing Rock, is home to **Appalachian State University**. Performing-arts patrons can check out the university's summer series of theater, music, and dance, or see the dramatic outdoor play about Daniel Boone, *Horn In the West*.

Visitors to Charlotte will also be interested in this area's **Ben Long's Blue Ridge Mountain Frescoes**, located in tiny mountain churches in Glendale Springs and West Jefferson.

**Getting There from Charlotte**: Take I-85 South to Gastonia and U.S. 321 North to Blowing Rock.

## Day Trip: Chapel Hill

**Distance from Charlotte: 2 hours, 15 minutes; 125 miles**
Known as "Blue Heaven" in these parts, Chapel Hill is near and dear to many Charlotteans' hearts after growing up watching Carolina Tarheels basketball or attending the University of North Carolina themselves.

Life in Chapel Hill revolves around the **University of North Carolina**, the highly respected flagship school of the UNC system and the oldest public university in the nation. Around 23,000 undergrad and graduate students attend Carolina, but not all of them leave. The area boasts one of the highest concentrations of Ph.D.'s in the United States, while students claim the large number of pubs and clubs has earned Chapel Hill the distinction of the highest per capita beer consumption.

The university campus overflows with natural beauty all year long; dogwoods and azaleas in spring, lush green lawns and rose gardens in summer, a canopy of color in fall, and a serene, stark look in winter.

With football games and homecoming reunions, autumn brings alumni back for campus tours and cries of "I'll never forget . . ." and "Whatever happened to . . .?" Tailgating parties pop up wherever people can park, and tickets can usually be found from folks selling extra ones in the areas around **Kenan Stadium**. (Don't count on the same for basketball, however.)

At the university, the sights to see include the **Old Well** at the center of campus, the **Bell Tower** near the stadium, the **Quad** between **South Building** and **Wilson Library**, and **Silent Sam** and the **Davie Poplar** in McCorkle Place. **The Arboretum** is a perfect place to lie on the grass and reminisce.

All roads in Chapel Hill lead to **Franklin Street**, the main drag, where townspeople, students, alumni, and visitors mingle. Storefront shops, restaurants, and watering holes line both sides, and it's easy to spend half a day or more just wandering.

Several eateries have called Franklin Street home for decades. **Sutton's** is an old-fashioned pharmacy lunch counter with great club sandwiches, super-thick shakes, and hundreds of photos of its regular customers. **The Rathskeller**, a downstairs alley joint with waiters who've worked there for 40-plus years, specializes in pizza, bowl-of-cheese lasagna, and sizzling steaks called "gamblers." One street over, on Rosemary, **Dips Country Kitchen** cooks up chicken-and-dumplings and vegetables daily. And on west Franklin Street, **Crook's Corner** serves its specialty dish: shrimp and grits with bacon, scallions, and mushrooms.

In warmer months, the **Flower Ladies** sit on Franklin Street selling their small bouquets of locally grown, freshly picked flowers. For $5 or $6, they're yours complete with a coffee-can vase.

Chapel Hill is also home to **Morehead Planetarium**, the South's premier planetarium, with its 310-seat circular theater and dome screen simulating star-filled skies. Programs for kids and adults run regularly.

# TRIVIA

In Chapel Hill, the Morehead-Patterson Bell Tower sounds the time every quarter-hour. The chime, which can be heard throughout town, is made with dozens of bells weighing 300 to 3,500 pounds each.

Outside, in front of the building, a huge sundial and hundreds of rose bushes invite visitors to sit and relax on nearby benches.

When it's time to call it a night, Chapel Hill offers several grand lodging choices. The **Carolina Inn** is a historic 184-room hotel on campus; and the **Siena Hotel**, farther down Franklin Street from the university, features Italian marble, leather, and art.

Minutes outside Chapel Hill near Pittsboro, an English country community called **Fearrington Village** features gracious homes, quaint shops, and an award-winning restaurant and inn.

**Getting There from Charlotte**: Take I-85 North to Greensboro and I-40 East to Chapel Hill.

# Day Trip: Asheville

### Distance from Charlotte: 2 hours, 120 miles

Nestled in the Blue Ridge Mountains, Asheville overflows with natural beauty, arts, culture, grand resorts and history. Most Charlotteans head to the mountains in October to see fall foliage at its peak, but each season has its own allure.

In spring, wildflowers cover the countryside and the Biltmore Estate hosts its annual Festival of Flowers. Summer offers an escape from the heat with higher altitudes, cooler temperatures, and a place to hike waterfalls or go white-water rafting.

Fall blazes with color, and is the perfect time for a picnic on the Blue Ridge Parkway and horseback riding through the countryside. Ski slopes, holiday celebrations, and the crackling fireplaces of country inns draw Asheville's winter visitors.

*The North Carolina Arboretum in Asheville*

The North Carolina Arboretum

Asheville's main attraction is the 1895 **Biltmore Estate**, the largest private home in America, situated on 8,000 acres along the Blue Ridge Parkway. George Vanderbilt commissioned his summer home—that's right, this wasn't his main residence—after a château in the Loire Valley of France. It took stonecutters and artisans six years to build the 250-room mansion, which Vanderbilt then filled with treasures from his world travels. Visitors see artwork, antique furniture, Oriental rugs, and elaborate table settings, along with several of the 32 guest rooms, sitting areas, indoor gym, bowling alley, swimming pool, winter garden, and billiards room.

Frederick Law Olmsted, designer of New York's Central Park, created the 75 acres of landscaped garden, grounds, and park areas around the estate. Formal gardens and manicured grounds are a sharp contrast to the surrounding mountains and forests, and more than 50,000 tulips are showcased each spring. Nearby, in the former dairy barn, is the Biltmore Estate winery where guests can tour the cellars, see production areas, and unwind in the bricked courtyard.

You can't stay at the Biltmore Estate, but the **Grove Park Inn** is an impressive stone hotel that has hosted many celebrities, presidents, and other noted figures. Ask for room 441, where *The Great Gatsby* author F. Scott Fitzgerald did much of his writing.

Other attractions in Asheville include the **Thomas Wolfe Memorial**, the famous novelist's boyhood home and the setting for *Look Homeward, Angel*. It's at 52 North Market Street in downtown Asheville.

For shopping, try **Biltmore Village**, a restored, turn-of-the-century community of shops, restaurants, and galleries adjacent to the Biltmore

**TRIVIA**

The Biltmore Estate in Asheville took six years and 1,000 men to build before it opened its doors on Christmas Eve in 1895. The largest private home in America, the estate features a 390-foot facade, more than 11 million bricks, 250 rooms, 65 fireplaces, 43 bathrooms, 34 bedrooms, and three kitchens.

The massive stone spiral staircase rises four floors and has 102 steps. Through its center hangs an iron chandelier weighing 1,700 pounds and containing 72 electric bulbs.

The Vanderbilts could entertain as many as 64 guests at their dinner table in their 72-foot-by-42-foot banquet hall. Meals were usually seven courses and required as many as 15 utensils per person.

George Vanderbilt also commissioned his summer home to have indoor hot and cold running water, elevators, indoor heating, a fire alarm system, refrigeration, electric light bulbs, and 10 telephones—all unheard-of luxuries at the turn of the century.

Estate. Downtown Asheville's **Historic District** includes 100 retail shops and 40 restaurants, as well as guided walking tours. **Bele Chere**, held in Asheville each July, is North Carolina's largest street festival.

In east Asheville, the **Folk Art Center** houses the Southern Highland Craft Guild and work by the guild's 700 members. Reach it at milepost 382 of the Blue Ridge Parkway, just north of the U.S. 70 entrance to the city.

The **Blue Ridge Parkway** winds 469 miles along the highest ridges of Shenandoah National Park in Virginia to the Great Smoky Mountains National Park in North Carolina and Tennessee. The parkway intersects Asheville at several highways: U.S. 25, 70, and 74, and NC 191. Spectacular views await whether you head north or south.

*The Gardens at the Biltmore Estate, p. 219*

© The Biltmore Estate, Asheville, NC

Nature-lovers enjoy the **North Carolina Arboretum**, which displays gardens and plants representative of the Southern Appalachian region. The new facility offers educational programs, trail walks, more than 3,000 types of plants, and gardens in a quilt pattern.

Nature-lovers also head for nearby **Chimney Rock Park** to take an elevator 26 stories up inside the mountain and step out onto an ancient piece of granite that towers 1,200 feet over Hickory Nut Gorge. Hiking trails through the park feature subterranean passes, catwalks from rock to rock, and a stop at an old moonshiner's cave. The Skyline Trail offers a 45-minute scenic hike to the top of **Hickory Nut Falls**, a 400-foot-high waterfall featured in the recent version of *The Last of the Mohicans*.

**Getting There from Charlotte**: Take I-85 South to Kings Mountain and U.S. 74 West to Asheville. From North Charlotte and the Lake Norman area, an alternate route is I-77 North to Statesville and I-40 East to Asheville.

## Day Trip: Winston-Salem

**Distance from Charlotte: 1 hour, 20 minutes; 80 miles**
Winston-Salem, which combines with Greensboro and High Point to make up the Triad area, is an interesting day trip full of history, culture, and fun for kids.

**Old Salem**, in the heart of downtown, is a restored Moravian village considered one of the most authentic historic restorations in the United States. Costumed interpreters re-create late 18th- and early 19th-century life by chopping wood, baking bread, washing their linen, and then pressing the wash with a six-pound iron heated in front of the fire.

Winston-Salem's skyline looms nearby, but Old Salem's 90 restored and reconstructed buildings make it easy to step back in time. A dozen houses and seven gardens are open to the public for demonstrations of cooking, baking, sewing, spinning, dyeing, silversmithing, and blacksmithing as they were done in North Carolina's backcountry. Tours are self-guided, but docents are stationed around the town to answer visitors' questions.

So who were the Moravians? Old Salem was started by an ancient Protestant sect whose members established missions around the world in the mid-1700s. Salem was founded in 1766 as the second permanent Moravian settlement in the nation.

The church governed every aspect of community life in Salem, and men, women, and children of all races led daily lives focused on skilled work and frequent worship. Salem remained a church town until the mid-1800s, when it merged with sister city Winston.

The Old Salem you see today was created in 1950 to preserve and interpret the historic area. About 300,000 people a year visit Old Salem, walking its cobblestone streets, shopping in the historic district's gift shops, dining in its two restaurants, and strolling through its gardens.

Visitors can stay overnight at Old Salem in the 1844 **Augustus T. Zevely Inn**. If you're here only for the day, don't miss the popular 1800 **Winkler Bakery**, where docents bake in a brick beehive oven. No ticket is required in this building; anyone can enter, but you won't leave without buying freshly baked bread; cheese petites; thin, crispy Moravian cookies; or gooey sugar cakes.

Travel down Cherry Street to reach **Wake Forest University**, a private liberal arts school with a lovely tree-filled campus highlighted by **Wait Chapel** and its adjacent **Quad**. Fall football games draw alumni and visitors to **Groves Stadium**, closer to town.

Art-lovers shouldn't miss Winston-Salem's **Reynolda House**, an American art museum carved out of the 64-room bungalow of tobacco magnate R.J. Reynolds. An elegant green-and-white home with gardens and fountains, the museum exhibits such artists as Grant Wood, Georgia O'Keeffe, Frederic Remington, Jacob Lawrence, and Mary Cassatt.

More than 80 years ago, when Reynolds and his wife commissioned the estate, Reynolda House was a country home on a working farm with a post office, church, and other buildings. In 1932, scandal erupted when the couple's youngest son, Z. Smith Reynolds, married torch singer Libby Holman. Smith was found shot dead, and Holman and a gentleman friend were indicted by a grand jury. The Reynolds family later asked that charges be dropped.

The remnants of the working farm that surround Reynolda House make up the adjacent **Reynolda Village**. **The Village Tavern** serves a great brunch or lunch, and some of the city's best boutiques and gift shops are located here.

A second excursion for arts patrons is a few blocks away at the **Southeastern Center for Contemporary Arts** (SECCA), located in the English-style manor house of late industrialist James G. Hanes. See works from around the world, or participate in a range of programs focusing on exhibits and performing arts. Contemporary crafts are on display in the center's shop.

When the kids get restless, take them to the science center and environmental park known as **SciWorks.** Open daily, the center includes a planetarium, a 15-acre park filled with animals native to the state, and interactive activities and exhibits on everything from dinosaur fossils to fizzing chemical experiments.

**Getting There from Charlotte**: Take I-77 North to Statesville and I-40 East to Winston-Salem.

# Day Trip: Hiddenite

### Distance from Charlotte: 1 hour, about 60 miles

You won't find this tiny Alexander County town of 250 in many guidebooks, but Hiddenite is like a treasure chest of nature hidden away from the hustle and bustle of the world. The hamlet sits on NC 90 between Taylorsville and Statesville. Quiet, two-lane roads wind through country farmland still free from billboards, traffic jams, and industry.

Once a crowning jewel of the Carolinas, Hiddenite's claim to fame began when farmers found strange "green bolts" while plowing their fields. Inventor Thomas Edison heard about it and sent scientist and professor William E. Hidden and a gemologist to investigate. Edison hoped for platinum he could use in light-bulb filaments, but instead, the scientists found stunning gem-quality emeralds.

More than 63 different types of gemstones and minerals were documented, and it was the only place on earth where emeralds and sapphires were found within three feet of one another. Hidden also found a neon green gemstone never before recorded, and the gem and village were later named in his honor.

Prospectors seeking fortunes created an emerald rush in Hiddenite, and commercial mines thrived for the next 50 years. The rich soil was also thought to have healing properties, and people came by train to the Davis Sulphur Springs Hotel. Using the sulfur springs as a health spa, the hotel featured 150 beds, a bowling alley, swimming pool, tennis court, skating rink, and four-piece orchestra. Built in 1901, the hotel burned in 1925.

Colorful characters were drawn to Hiddenite, and in one case the legacy remains. "Diamond Jim" Lucas was a wealthy world traveler and flashy dresser known for his white suits, spats, diamond rings, jeweled scarf pins, and diamond-head walking sticks. Lucas's 22-room Victorian home now houses **The Hiddenite Center & Lucas Mansion Museum**. The museum has three floors: the first is a restored Victorian home from the days of Diamond Jim, the second features changing galleries, and the top houses antique dolls and toys.

Hiddenite was known for its wide variety and quality of stones, but it lacked the quantity to sustain commercial mining. Today, rock hounds head to **Emerald Hollow Mine and Hiddenite Gems**, the only mine still open to the public. Visitors can dig for gems in above-ground holes (there are no caves), or buy buckets of dirt that either come from the area or have had purchased gems added to them. You never know what you might find.

For a small town, Hiddenite also has a surprisingly active arts community, including community theater, a historical society, a series of art workshops, a quilt guild, and an arts affiliation with Appalachian State University. A weeklong community festival is held in late September.

Visitors stay at the **Hidden Crystal Country Inn**, a lovely, 14-room restored home with tulip gardens, a swimming pool, gazebo, fine-dining restaurant, and an atmosphere of comfortable elegance. Waterfalls, walking trails, bog gardens, and a nature preserve are nearby. The Hidden Crystal has been featured in *Inn Country USA*, *The Los Angeles Times*, *Our State* magazine, and many other regional publications.

**Getting There from Charlotte**: Take I-77 North to Statesville and NC 90 West to Hiddenite.

# APPENDIX: CITY·SMART BASICS

## EMERGENCY PHONE NUMBERS
Police/Fire/Ambulance, 911

## MAJOR HOSPITALS AND EMERGENCY MEDICAL CENTERS
### Central Charlotte
Carolinas Medical Center
1000 Blythe Blvd.
Charlotte
704/335-2000

Mercy Hospital
2001 Vail Ave.
Charlotte
704/379-5000

Presbyterian Hospital
200 Hawthorne Lane
Charlotte
704/384-4000

### South Charlotte
Mercy Hospital South
10628 Park Rd.
Pineville
704/543-2000

Presbyterian Hospital Matthews
1500 Matthews Township Parkway
Matthews
704/384-6500

### North Charlotte
University Hospital
8800 N. Tryon St.
Charlotte
704/548-6000

### Concord
NorthEast Medical Center
920 Church St. North
Concord
704/334-3613

### Gastonia
Gaston Memorial Hospital
2525 Court Dr.
Gastonia
704/834-2000

### Monroe
Union Regional Medical Center
600 Hospital Dr.
Monroe
704/283-3100

### Mooresville
Lake Norman Regional Medical
Center
610 E. Center Ave.
Mooresville
704/663-1113

### Rock Hill
Piedmont Medical Center
222 S. Herlong
Rock Hill, S.C.
803/329-1234

### Emergency Medical Care
Ask First
704/783-1275

Carolinas Poison Center
800/848-6946

Charlotte-Mecklenburg
Health Department
704/336-6500

Emergency Mental Health
Services
704/358-2800

Poison Control
Information Center
704/355-4000

Pro-Med Minor
Emergency Centers
800/467-5070

## VISITOR INFORMATION
The Charlotte Chamber
704/378-1300

INFO! Charlotte
(Walk-in traffic)
330 S. Tryon St.
704/331-2753/2720

Lake Wylie Chamber of
Commerce
803/831-2827

North Mecklenburg
Chamber & Visitors Center
704/892-1922

## CAR RENTAL
AAA Rent-a-Van
704/372-7605

Avis
800/831-2847

Budget
800/527-0700

Enterprise
800/736-8222

Thrifty
800/367-2277

Triangle Rent A Car
704/359-0541

**Weather Info**
Info Net, 704/845-INFO.
NBC-6 (WCNC) local
weather forecast
704/522-5566, ext. 3601.

## NEWSPAPERS
*The Charlotte Observer*
www.charlotte.com
704/358-5000

*The Business Journal*
www.amcity.com/charlotte
704/347-2340

*The Leader*
704/331-4842

*Creative Loafing*
www.creativeloafing.com
704/522-8334

## MAGAZINES
*Business North Carolina*
704/523-6987

*Charlotte*
704/335-7181

*Charlotte 's Best*
704/537-0593

*CITI*
704/372-0367

*Today's Charlotte Woman*
charwoman@earthlink.net
704/364-0225

*TRIP - Charlotte 's Visitor
Resource*
westraxpub@earthlink.net
704/376-7800

## GAY AND LESBIAN PUBLICATIONS
*C.L.N. Carolina Lesbian News
Community Yellow Pages
Q Notes*

## TELEVISION STATIONS
WAXN – Channel 64
(Independent)

WBTV– Channel 3 (CBS)
WCCB – Channel 18 (Fox)
WCNC – Channel 6 (NBC)
WFVT – Channel 55 (WB)
WJZY – Channel 46 (UPN)
WNSC – Channel 30 (PBS)
WSOC – Channel 4 (ABC)
WTVI – Channel 42 (PBS)
WUNG – Channel 58 (PBS)

## RADIO STATIONS
WEND 106.5 FM/alternative
WFAE 90.7 FM/National Public
   Radio
WLNK 107.9 FM/adult
   contemporary
WNKS 95.1 FM/Top 40
WPEG 98 FM/urban
   contemporary
WRFX 99.7 FM/classic rock
WSOC 103 FM/country
WXRC 95.7 FM/rock

## BABYSITTING/CHILD CARE
Charlotte Care Services Inc.
300 East Blvd., Charlotte
704/335-0501

Charlotte Select Sitting Service
7209 E. Harris Blvd., #151,
Charlotte
704/566-1117

Child Care Resources Inc.
700 Kenilworth Ave., Charlotte
704/376-6697 or 704/348-2181

Grandmothers Sitting Service
300 East Blvd., Charlotte
704/332-5386

## DISABLED ACCESS INFORMATION
**Programs for Accessible Living**
Charlotte Regional Resource Center for the Deaf & Hard of Hearing
704/367-0508

Metrolina Association
for the Blind
704/372-3870

N.C. Division of Services
for the Blind
704/342-6185

**Special Transportation Needs**
Charlotte Transit Information,
TDD-Hearing Impaired
704/336-5051

Charlotte Transit Special
Transportation
704/336-2637

Charlotte Transit Special
Transportation, TDD-Hearing
Impaired
704/336-6155

## MULTICULTURAL RESOURCES
**African American**
Charlotte-Mecklenburg NAACP
704/333-6457

Charlotte Urban League
704/376-9834

National Coalition of 100 Black
Women of Greater Charlotte
704/391-2600

100 Black Men of Greater
Charlotte
704/375-7300

**Gay and Lesbian**
The Gay and Lesbian
Switchboard
704/535-6277

Gay & Lesbian Youth Hotline
704/537-4948

Time Out Youth
704/537-5050

Metrolina AIDS Project
704/333-1435

Metropolitan Community Church
704/563-5810

New Life Metropolitan
Community Church
704/334-0350

## BOOKSTORES
**Barnes & Noble**
5837 Independence Blvd.
704/535-9810

3327 Pineville-Matthews Rd.
704/341-9365

4720 Sharon Road
704/554-7906

10701 Centrum Park
Pineville
704/541-1425

**Bedford Falls Toy Shop
& Bookstore (children's)**
625 S. Sharon Amity Rd.
704/365-2340

**Black Forest Books
& Toys (children's)**
115 Cherokee Rd.
704/332-4838

**Bookmark of Charlotte**
100 N. Tyron St. Suite 265
704/377-2565

**Borders Books & Music**
3900 Colony Rd.
704/364-4571

**Brentano's**
Carolina Place Mall
11025 Carolina Place Pkwy.
704/541-7474

**EarFull of Books**
601 S. Kings Dr.
704/343-0090

7868 Rea Rd.
704/341-0794

**Gray's College Bookstore**
9430 University City  Blvd.
704/548-8100

**Little Professor Book Center**
4139 Park Rd.
704/525-9239

**MediaPlay**
4716 South Blvd.
704/525-2416

8600 University City Blvd.
704/595-9956

10011 E. Independence Blvd.
Matthews, NC
704/847-4103

**Newsstand International**
5622-128 E. Independence Blvd.
704/531-0199

**Waldenbooks**
Eastland Mall
5643 Central Ave.
704/568-5782

Carolina Place Mall
11025 Carolina Place Pkwy.
Pineville, NC
704/544-2810

# INDEX

accommodations, 30–56; Uptown Charlotte, 31–35; North Charlotte, 35–41; South Charlotte, 41–44; Central Charlotte, 44–49; East Charlotte, 49; West Charlotte, 49–54
Asheville, 215, 218–220
auto racing, 176–177, 180

babysitting/child care, 226
ballooning, 180–181
Bank of America, 7, 14, 89, 93
baseball, 177, 181
basketball, 177–178, 181–182
Belmont Abbey College, 96–97, 110
biking, 26, 182–183
Blowing Rock, 213–216
boating, 178
bookstores and newsstands, 171, 227
bowling, 183
bus service, 29
business and economy, 14–15

calendar of events, 11–13
Calvary Church, 96–97, 101
Camp Greene, 111
campgrounds, 55–56
car rental, 225
Carillon Building, 89, 132
Carolina Panthers, 7, 178–179
Chapel Hill, 215, 216–218
Charlotte City Ballet, 200–201
Charlotte/Douglas International Airport, 6, 26–28
Charlotte Hornets, 6, 7, 16, 95, 130, 132, 177
Charlotte Knights, 177
Charlotte Motor Speedway, 88, 95–98, 176, 177
Charlotte Observer, 6, 89, 90
Charlotte Philharmonic Orchestra, 199
Charlotte Regional Farmer's Market, 96–97, 110–111, 172
Charlotte Repertory Orchestra, 199
Charlotte Repertory Theatre, 193, 196
Charlotte Symphony, 197, 198, 199–200
Charlotte Transit, 22, 23
Charlotte Transportation Center, 22
Charlotte Trolley, 23, 94, 102, 104–105, 120, 136
Charlotte Youth Ballet, 122, 201

churches, 113
Civil War, 6, 7
concert venues, 211–212
consignment shops, 164–165

Davidson College, 96–97, 98
day hikes, 184
day trips, 213–223; Blowing Rock, 213–216; Chapel Hill, 216–218; Asheville, 218–220; Winston-Salem, 220–222; Hiddenite, 222–223
department stores, 172–174
Dilworth, 3, 160–163
disabled access information, 226
disc/Frisbee golf, 184
Duke Energy, 14, 89

emergency medical centers, 224
emergency phone numbers, 224
Ericsson Stadium, 7, 89, 90, 136, 212

Federal Reserve Bank, 89, 90–91
First Presbyterian Church, 89, 91
Founder's Hall, 89, 91, 159–160
Fourth Ward, 89, 92

gallery crawls, 133
getting around, 19–29
gold, 4, 5, 6, 16, 134
golf, 179, 185–187

Hiddenite, 215, 222–223
Historic Brattonsville, 96–97, 101, 124
Historic Rosedale, 103, 104–105, 114
history, 4–8
hockey, 179
horse racing, 187
horseback riding, 187
hospitals, 224
housing, 15–16

Independence Square ("The Square"), 20, 89, 92, 132

James C. Dowd House, 103, 104–105
Johnson C. Smith University, 6, 103–106

kids' stuff, 116–128
Knights Stadium, 96–97, 102

Lake Norman, 3, 96–97, 98
Lake Wylie, 96–97, 112
Latta Arcade, 89, 92–93
Latta Plantation, 96–97, 98, 100, 119, 124, 187

markets and groceries, 171–172
media, 225
movies, 210–211
multicultural resources, 226–227
museums, 129–141; art, 130–131; science and history, 131–134; specialty, 134–137; art galleries, 137–141
Myers Park, 3, 104–105, 106–107, 166–168

Native Americans, 4–5
nightlife, 203–212
North Davidson (NoDa), 3, 104–105, 107, 169–170

Old Mecklenburg County Courthouse, 89, 93
Old Settler's Cemetery, 89, 93–94

Paramount's Carowinds theme park, 92, 96–97, 101, 112–113, 123
parking, 25, 26
parks, gardens, and recreation areas, 142–155
performing arts, 193–202
Plaza-Midwood, 3, 168–169
population, 8
professional sports, 176–180
public art, 132
public transportation, 21, 22, 23

Queen Charlotte, 2, 3, 5, 12, 26, 132
Queen's Landing/Catawba Queen Lake Cruises, 96–97, 99–100
Queens College, 12, 102, 104–105, 107

radio stations, 226
Reed Gold Mine, 96–97, 108, 110, 124
restaurants, 57–87; by cuisine type, 58–59; Uptown Charlotte, 59–63; North Charlotte, 63–65; South Charlotte, 65–72; Central Charlotte, 72–85; East Charlotte, 85–87; West Charlotte, 87
roads, 20–21, 25
rock climbing, 187–88
running, 188

schools, 14, 16–17
Scot–Irish, 4, 6, 109
shopping, 156–175; South Park Area, 156–159; Uptown, 159–160; Dilworth, 160–162; South End, 162–164; Myers Park, 164–168; Plaza-Midwood 168–169; NoDa, 169–170; South Charlotte, 170–171; bookstores and newsstands, 171; markets, gourmet groceries, and health food stores, 171–172; department stores, 172–173; shopping malls, 173–174; factory outlets, 175
skating, 188, 189–190
skiing, 190–191
soccer, 179, 191
softball, 179–180
South Charlotte, v, vi–vii, 3–4, 170–171
South End, 3, 163–165
SouthPark, 3, 156–159
sports and recreation, 176–192
St. Mary's Chapel, 104–105, 107
St. Peter's Catholic Church, 89, 94–95
streetcars, 6, 7
swimming, 192

television stations, 225–226
tickets, 202
timeline, 6–7
tours, 113–115
traffic, 19–20
train service, 28–29
Transamerica Square Building, 89, 95
trees, 153, 154
Tryon Street, 4

U.S. Mint, 5, 6, 134
University of North Carolina at Charlotte, 6, 96–97, 100, 132, 140
Uptown Circuit, 21, 23
Uptown, v, vi–vii, 1–3, 5, 6, 20–21, 90, 159–160, 162, 173

VanLandingham Estate, 46–47, 49, 52
Vietnam War Memorial, 104–105, 108
visitor information, 225

weather, 8–9, 10–11, 225
West Charlotte, v, vi–vii, 4
Winston-Salem, 215, 220–222

yard sales, 163

## ABOUT THE AUTHOR

Leigh Pressley is a Charlotte-based free-lance writer whose work has appeared in publications such as *Southern Living, Our State: Down Home in North Carolina*, the *Charlotte Observer*, and *Creative Loafing*. After graduating from the University of North Carolina at Chapel Hill, Leigh spent five years interviewing movie stars, traveling with rock bands, flying in hot air balloons, scuba diving, and driving NASCAR race cars as an entertainment and feature reporter with the *Wilmington Star-News* and the *Greensboro News & Record* in North Carolina. She grew up outside of Charlotte, and now lives with her husband, Scott Clinard, in the Dilworth area of the city.

Elwin Stilwell

# You'll Feel like a Local When You Travel with Guides from John Muir Publications

## CiTY·SMaRT™ GUIDEBOOKS

Pick one for your favorite city: *Albuquerque, Anchorage, Austin, Calgary, Charlotte, Chicago, Cincinnati, Cleveland, Denver, Indianapolis, Kansas City, Memphis, Milwaukee, Minneapolis/St. Paul, Nashville, Pittsburgh, Portland, Richmond, Salt Lake City, San Antonio, St. Louis, Tampa/St. Petersburg, Tucson*

Guides for kids 6 to 10 years old about what to do, where to go, and how to have fun in: *Atlanta, Austin, Boston, Chicago, Cleveland, Denver, Indianapolis, Kansas City, Miami, Milwaukee, Minneapolis/St. Paul, Nashville, Portland, San Francisco, Seattle, Washington D.C.*

## TRAVEL✦SMART®

Trip planners with select recommendations to: *Alaska, American Southwest, Carolinas, Colorado, Deep South, Eastern Canada, Florida Gulf Coast, Hawaii, Illinois/Indiana, Kentucky/Tennessee, Maryland/Delaware, Michigan, Minnesota/Wisconsin, Montana/Wyoming/Idaho, New England, New Mexico, New York State, Northern California, Ohio, Pacific Northwest, Pennsylvania/New Jersey, South Florida and the Keys, Southern California, Texas, Utah, Virginias, Western Canada*

## *Rick Steves'* GUIDES

See *Europe Through the Back Door* and take along guides to: *France, Belgium & the Netherlands; Germany, Austria & Switzerland; Great Britain & Ireland; Italy; Russia & the Baltics; Scandinavia; Spain & Portugal; London; Paris; or the Best of Europe*

## ADVENTURES IN NATURE

Plan your next adventure in: *Alaska, Belize, Caribbean, Costa Rica, Guatemala, Honduras, Mexico*

**JMP travel guides are available at your favorite bookstores. For a FREE catalog or to place a mail order, call: 800-888-7504.**

**John Muir Publications P.O. Box 613 ◆ Santa Fe, NM 87504**

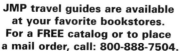
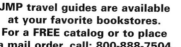